ROUTLEDGE LIBRARY EDITIONS:
URBAN AND REGIONAL ECONOMICS

Volume 10

REGIONAL IMPACTS OF
RESOURCE DEVELOPMENTS

REGIONAL IMPACTS OF RESOURCE DEVELOPMENTS

Edited by
CHRISTOPHER C. KISSLING,
MICHAEL TAYLOR, NIGEL THRIFT
AND COLIN ADRIAN

LONDON AND NEW YORK

First published in 1984 by Croom Helm

This edition first published in 2018
by Routledge
2 Park Square, Milton Park, Abingdon, Oxon OX14 4RN

and by Routledge
711 Third Avenue, New York, NY 10017

Routledge is an imprint of the Taylor & Francis Group, an informa business

British Library Cataloguing in Publication Data
A catalogue record for this book is available from the British Library

ISBN: 978-1-138-09590-8 (Set)
ISBN: 978-1-315-10306-8 (Set) (ebk)
ISBN: 978-1-138-10215-6 (Volume 10) (hbk)
ISBN: 978-1-138-10249-1 (Volume 10) (pbk)
ISBN: 978-1-315-10321-1 (Volume 10) (ebk)

Publisher's Note
The publisher has gone to great lengths to ensure the quality of this reprint but points out that some imperfections in the original copies may be apparent.

Disclaimer
The publisher has made every effort to trace copyright holders and would welcome correspondence from those they have been unable to trace.

Regional Impacts of Resource Developments

Edited by
Christopher C. Kissling,
Michael Taylor, Nigel Thrift
and Colin Adrian

CROOM HELM AUSTRALIA

© 1984 C.C. Kissling, M.J. Taylor, N.J. Thrift and C.J. Adrian
Croom Helm Australia Pty Ltd, 1st. floor, 139 King St, Sydney, NSW 2000
Croom Helm Ltd, Provident House, Burrell Row, Beckenham, Kent, England

National Library of Australia Cataloguing-in-Publication data

Regional impacts of resource developments

   Bibliography
ISBN 0 949614 08 4
1. Natural resources — Economic aspects — Australia
   - Addresses, essays, lectures. 2. Regional economics
   - Addresses, essays, lectures. 3. Australia -
   Economic conditions — 1976 — Addresses, essays
   lectures. I. Kissling, C.C. (Christopher Charles),
   1940-   . II. Regional Science Association.
   Australian and New Zealand Section.

333.7'13'0994

Printed and bound in Australia by Southwood Press. Sydney.

CONTENTS

Foreword

ECONOMIC AND SOCIAL IMPACTS IN AUSTRALIA

1. MANUFACTURING AND TERTIARY INDUSTRY IMPACTS
   B.L. Johns   1
2. ENVIRONMENTAL ASPECTS OF REGIONAL RESOURCE
   DEVELOPMENTS: A COMMONWEALTH PERSPECTIVE
   E.M. Anderson   17
3. THE ROLE OF IMMIGRATION IN RESOURCE DEVELOPMENT
   REGIONS
   E. Brookbanks   27
4. THE REGIONAL EMPLOYMENT AND POPULATION IMPACTS OF
   RESOURCE DEVELOPMENTS
   J.A. Gillett and A.D. Robertson   53
5. SOME PLANNING PROBLEMS IN THE PROVISION OF
   EDUCATION FACILITIES IN QUEENSLAND RESOURCE
   DEVELOPMENT AREAS: AN INITIAL OVERVIEW
   G.J. Butler and L.G. Harris   69

THE OVERSEAS EXPERIENCE OF RESOURCE DEVELOPMENTS

6. MINERAL RESOURCE TRANSPORTATION AND FRONTIER
   INFRASTRUCTURE PROVISION IN CANADA
   I. Wallace   103
7. OK TEDI; LESSONS HARDLY LEARNT
   R.T. Jackson   117

THE IMPACTS OF RESOURCE DEVELOPMENTS IN THE HUNTER VALLEY, NEW SOUTH WALES

8. RESOURCE DEVELOPMENT AND ENVIRONMENTAL PLANNING:
   THE HUNTER VALLEY EXPERIENCE
   D.G. Day and R.A. Day   137
9. THE ECONOMICS OF WATER USE IN THE HUNTER VALLEY:
   PRESSURES FOR REALLOCATION
   A.K. Dragun   153
10. ENVIRONMENTAL ASSESSMENT IN REGIONAL DEVELOPMENT
    WITH REFERENCE TO THE ATMOSPHERE ENVIRONMENT OF
    THE HUNTER VALLEY
    N.J. Daly and A.J. Jakeman   183
11. THE IMPACT OF THE COAL-BASED DEVELOPMENTS IN THE
    HUNTER VALLEY ON THE REGIONAL LABOUR MARKET
    F. Perkins   209

Notes on Contributors   267

References   269

This volume is published under the auspices of the **REGIONAL SCIENCE ASSOCIATION** – Australian and New Zealand Section which is dedicated to furthering the cause of regional research in Australia and New Zealand. Further details of the role of the Association can be obtained by writing to the Secretary, Dr R Batten, CSIRO Division of Building Research, P.O. Box 56, Highett, Victoria 3190, Australia.

Another publication arising from the conference on "Regional Impacts of Resource Developments", Papers of the 7th Australian/New Zealand Regional Science Conference 1982, can be obtained from the same address.

ACKNOWLEDGEMENTS

The **Regional Science Association** gratefully acknowledges the support for their 1982 Annual Conference, from which this volume is derived, from the following:

AMPOL LIMITED
ANSETT AIRLINES OF AUSTRALIA
ATLAS COPCO AUSTRALIA PTY LIMITED
BORAL LIMITED
BRAMBLES INDUSTRIES LIMITED
CRUSADER OIL NL
JAMES HARDIE INDUSTRIES LIMITED
MONIER LIMITED
QANTAS AIRWAYS LIMITED
SOUTHERN PACIFIC PETROLEUM NL
THE NEW ZEALAND HIGH COMMISSION (CANBERRA)
TNT MANAGEMENT PTY LIMITED

Carol McKenzie typed this manuscript and its many editorial corrections, an arduous task. We would like to thank her. We are also grateful for Jane Hirst's assistance with the preparation of the volume, especially by integrating and checking the bibliography.

FOREWORD

Although the resource boom of the early 1980s has now ended there seems little doubt that resource-related developments will continue to have widespread social, economic and enviromental effects in Australia. These effects will only be strengthened if and when the current world recession ends and the demand for Australian resources again picks up.

A relatively neglected dimension of resource developments in Australia has been their specific regional impacts. This volume is intended to highlight this regional dimension. It is in the nature of current research on this dimension, which is still very often tentative and exploratory, that this volume cannot stand as a definitive statement. Rather the volume provides summaries of the present state of our knowledge on the regional impacts of resource developments in Australia and points to the directions that further research must take.

The chapters that comprise the volume are divided into three sections. The first section considers the broad impacts. The section begins with two general introductory chapters by Johns and Anderson respectively. Johns' chapter provides a summary of the actual and expected impacts of resource developments on the manufacturing and tertiary sectors of the relevant regions of Australia. Anderson comments on the environmental aspects. A further two chapters consider the demographic impacts of resource developments. Brookbanks assesses the role of immigration while Gillett and Roberts look at the forecasts of employment and population growth associated with resource developments. In the fifth chapter which concludes the first section, Butler and Harris consider the social aspects of resource developments by concentrating on the case of Queensland.

The two chapters in the second section consider overseas experiences. Wallace looks at the problems associated with the provision of infrastructure for resource developments in Canada while Jackson discusses the dilemmas that the Ok Tedi mine has generated for Papua New Guinea.

The third section concentrates on a specific Australian regional example, namely the Hunter Valley in New South Wales, through the work of researchers in the Centre for Resource and Environmental Studies at the Australian National University. Day and Day consider the problems of environmental planning associated with rapid and concentrated resource developments. Dragun looks at the problems of water use in the Valley. Daly and Jakeman investigate the problems of modelling environmental impacts on regions, concentrating on the atmospheric effects. Finally, Perkins considers in some detail the labour market consequences of the coal-based developments in the Hunter.

ECONOMIC AND SOCIAL

IMPACTS IN AUSTRALIA

MANUFACTURING AND TERTIARY INDUSTRY IMPACTS

B.L. Johns*

INTRODUCTION

Now that Australia's latest resources boom has been attenuated by the
conjuncture of the world recession and the increase in domestic real
wage costs, it is easy to believe that it never happened. Was it simply
that firms, individuals and even governments, by striving to capture a
share of the anticipated benefits of the boom before they were realised,
ensured that little actual benefit could be gained? There is more than
a grain of truth in that view. Yet the resources boom was not entirely
a mirage and there is still good reason to believe that new resource
developments will play a major role in Australia's economic growth during
the remainder of this decade.

The extent of the upsurge in capital expenditure on resource
developments in 1981–82 is revealed in Table 1.1. In the last
financial year, new fixed capital expenditure by private enterprises in
the mining industry was more than double (in real terms) the
average annual expenditure in the three years to 1979–80. In the case
of the basic metal products industry, the level of such expenditure
was more than three and a half times the annual average expenditure
in that earlier period, thanks largely to the greatly increased capital
spending on aluminium smelters. There is no doubt that additional investment expenditure directly and indirectly associated with new
resource developments was the principal factor which led to an
average annual growth of 3.7 per cent in real non–farm GDP in the years
1980–81 and 1981–82. This was the highest rate of economic growth
achieved in Australia since the early 1970s.

The immediate outlook for capital spending on resource–based
projects does not appear as favourable. Nevertheless, while total
private fixed capital expenditure is expected to decline by more than
four per cent in real terms in the current financial year, [1,2] that in

* The views and opinions expressed are those of the author and
should not be attributed to the Bureau of Industry Economics or
the Commonwealth Government. I am grateful to Noel Benjamin for
his assistance in compiling statistical data for this chapter.

Table 1.1:   New Fixed Capital Expenditure by Private
             Enterprises at Constant 1979/80 Prices[a] $ million

Year	Basic Metal Products	Total Manufac- turing	Total Manufac- turing Excl. Basic Metal Products	Mining	Other Selected Indus- tries[b]	Total
1974–75	607	2587	1980	1183	3864	7634
1975–76	460	2153	1693	943	4575	7671
1976–77	349	2255	1906	632	4793	7679
1977–78	303	2478	2175	947	4927	8530
1978–79	360	2654	2294	1245	5723	9622
1979–80	532	2538	2006	1081	5702	9321
1980–81	1049	3351	2302	1693	6525	11569
1981–82	1464	3706	2242	2330	7402	13437
1982–83[c]	1146	3075	1929	2802	6970	12848

Notes:

(a) 1974–75 to 1981–82: deflated by the implicit deflators for
    private gross fixed capital expenditure (Australian
    National Accounts) 1982–83 only: deflated by the
    anticipated increase in the consumer price index (1982–83
    Budget Statements).

(b) Including Retail and Wholesale Trade, Transport and
    Storage, Electricity Gas and Water, Finance, Property and
    Business Services.

(c) Expected expenditure for the 12 months ending June 1983.

Source: New Fixed Capital Expenditure by Private Enterprises
        in Selected Industries, ABS Cat No. 5626.0.

the mining industry is expected to increase by a further 20 per cent compared with the high level of 1981–82. If an increase of this magnitude is achieved, it will partly reflect the fact that some mining investment projects commenced in earlier years have to be continued to completion, even though they might not have been started in the light of current economic conditions. Yet even if such projects fail to yield an operating profit in the short-run, the capital expenditure on them will for a time help to sustain the cash flow of the domestic manufacturing and service industries which supply the required inputs.

Based on the latest ABS estimates, it seems likely that in manufacturing industry fixed capital expenditure by private enterprises will fall in 1982–83 by about 17 per cent in real terms. One significant factor contributing to this decline is an anticipated drop in capital spending on aluminium smelters and alumina refineries resulting mainly from the cancellation or deferment of some proposed new projects. Thus, although the upward trend in mining industry investment has not yet been reversed there has clearly been a noticeable slowing down in the growth of capital expenditure on resource-based projects as a whole.

Most of the forecasts made only 12–18 months ago of additional investment and production from resource-based developments during the remainder of this decade, now appear rather optimistic. However, a downward revision of such recent forecasts does not necessarily imply a changed view aout the long-term determinants of Australia's position as an exporter of energy minerals and primary aluminium. Even if there were a prompt recovery in the world economy and a speedy restoration of Australia's international competitiveness the deferments of resource-based projects that have already been announced make it unlikely that the earlier forecasts of investment spending and export receipts can be achieved by the end of the 1980s.

This chapter does not present any new quantitative estimates of resource-based investment or production during the remainder of the 1980s. Such estimates are available elsewhere.[3] However, I have drawn on the evidence from these other sources in accepting the proposition that resource developments already completed, planned or contemplated will lead to a substantial increase in the real value of exports (or import-saving) during the remaining years of this decade. Further, the discussion in this chapter proceeds on the presumption that the resource-based activities likely to make the largest contributions to increases in investment and output (compared to the late 1970s) will be; aluminium and alumina, black coal (principally steaming coal), oil and gas, and uranium, probably in that order.[4] Clearly the regional impact of resource developments depends critically on the particular types of development that actually take place.

In this chapter I shall first describe briefly the geographical pattern of recent and expected resource developments in Australia. This is followed by a review of some of the recent empirical studies which have attempted to measure the economic impact of major resource develop-

3

ments upon the manufacturing and service industries and upon particular regions. The final part of the chapter examines the nature of the regional structural adjustment problems that may be posed by resource developments in the 1980s and considers some possible policy responses.

THE GEOGRAPHICAL PATTERN OF RESOURCE DEVELOPMENTS

In the opening years of this decade, capital expenditure on resource developments has been heavily concentrated in three States; Western Australia, Queensland and New South Wales. Recently released data on private capital expenditure by State[5] show that from the beginning of 1980 through to the first quarter of 1982 about 75 per cent of mining industry investment was in these States. In the first three quarters of 1981–82, the proportion was even higher, with 82 per cent of mining investment taking place in these three States. Allowing for capital expenditure on aluminium smelters and alumina refineries, which are not included in the mining industry, does not significantly affect this pattern of geographical concentration. Although expenditure exceeding $300 million has been incurred in the early 1980s at Alcoa's smelters at Portland and Point Henry in Victoria this is exceeded by the expenditure on two new alumina refineries in Western Australia and by the expenditure on the Boyne Island aluminium smelter near Gladstone. There have also been large capital outlays on two aluminium smelters in New South Wales, at Kurri Kurri and Tomago, both near Newcastle.

Although the inclusion of aluminium and alumina projects does not markedly change the observed State distribution of capital expenditure on resource developments, there are in fact important differences between the regional economic impact of aluminium smelters and that of most mining ventures. The smelters are located on the coast, are much less remote from existing centres of population and some (such as those near Newcastle) are close to a major city.

In general, this is likely to mean that the capital expenditure on infrastructure is less in relation to expenditure on the plant itself than would be the case with a remote mining operation. For example, expenditure on railway tracks, locomotives, and rolling stock is likely to be relatively lower. Moreover, the proximity to existing centres of population may mean that the smelter and its workforce can take up unutilised capacity in power stations, roads, dwellings, hospitals, and schools. In its study of the impact of resource developments the Bureau of Industry Economics (BIE) found that investment in infrastructure would account for about 22 per cent of aggregate capital expenditure on resource developments in the 1980s compared with 31 per cent in the years 1977 to 1979 (Johns, 1982, p66). This is a reflection of the changing pattern and location of the newer resource developments, including the increased importance of aluminium smelters.

A further difference between the aluminium smelters and mining ventures lies in the relative demands that are placed on the geographic mobility of labour. Whereas the establishment of a new mining venture in

4

a remote locality will normally require a net migration of labour into the region equal to the size of the mine's workforce, the same may not be true of a new aluminium smelter, either in the construction or he production phase. Two possibilities can be noted. First, the establishment of the smelter may lead (directly or indirectly) to a decline in the level of regional unemployment. Second, once it has commenced operations the smelter may lead to the displacement of workers from other (import-competing) industries in the same region. Some of these workers are then available for employment in aluminium production, thus reducing the need to attract additional workers from outside the region. The obvious example of this second situation is in the Hunter Valley, where employment in the steel industry could be adversely affected by additional production and exports of aluminium (some of this emanating from the same region) since additional aluminium exports would tend to produce a rise in the real exchange rate.

What can be said about the likely geographical pattern of resource developments in the remainder of this decade? Given the lengthy planning horizons for major resource projects, the location of nearly all the feasible ventures is already known. It is less easy to determine which new ventures will actually be commenced before 1990 and it is particularly difficult to forecast the exact timing of investment outlays and operating expenditures for such new ventures.

As far as aluminium smelting is concerned much of the additional investment expenditure can be expected to take place at existing locations, namely at Portland (Victoria), Gladstone (Queensland) and Tomago (New South Wales). Possible new smelters at Bunbury in Western Australia and Bundaberg (Queensland) are unlikely to be commenced until the second half of the decade, at the earliest. Additional capital expenditure on alumina refineries will be mainly concentrated at existing locations in Western Australia and at Gladstone, while additions to bauxite mining capacity are also likely to be confined to Western Australia and Queensland.

Queensland and New South Wales will be the focus of most of the additional capital expenditure on steaming and coking coal developments and some of these developments will be located relatively close to existing centres of population, thus reducing the associated infrastructure costs. A large fraction of capital expenditure on oil and gas will continue to be spent on the North West Shelf project. According to the December 1981 survey of Major Manufacturing and Mining Investment Projects by the Department of Industry and Commerce the remaining capital expenditure on this project at that date was $4.9 billion. It is also interesting to note that in the first three quarters of 1981–82 private fixed capital expenditure in the Western Australian mining industry (including that on natural gas projects) accounted for over 42 per cent of total private fixed capital expenditure in the State. In the corresponding period of 1979–80, the mining industry only accounted for about 22 per cent of the State's private fixed capital expenditure.

5

The uranium project at Jabiluka in the Northern Territory is expected to involve a capital expenditure during the 1980s of about $500 million (at December 1981 prices) but another possible major resource development in the Territory, the lead, zinc and silver mine at McArthur River is not expected to proceed until the 1990s. Finally, in South Australia two major resource developments originating in relatively remote areas, the Cooper Basin oil and gas development and the prospective Olympic Dam (Roxby Downs) copper, uranium and gold venture can be expected to result in increased capital expenditure on resource developments in that State.

The focus of this brief commentary on likely resource developments in the remainder of this decade has been on those mineral and processing activities where the level of investment is expected to increase in real terms compared with the late 1970s. For this reason, I have not commented specifically on capital expenditure on iron ore mines and associated facilities in Western Australia, since it is anticipated that the annual average capital expenditure on new and existing mines will be less in real terms in the remaining years of the 1980s than it was in the last three years of the 1970s. Given the other prospective resource developments in Western Australia, it does not seem likely that this reduction in capital expenditure will give rise to a significant structural adjustment problem.

ANALYSING THE ECONOMIC IMPACT OF RESOUCE-BASED DEVELOPMENTS ON MANUFACTURING AND TERTIARY INDUSTRIES

Following this brief sketch of the probable geographical pattern of new resource developments I now turn to highlight some of the results obtained from empirical studies which have attempted to assess the impact of recent or prospective developments on manufacturing and tertiary industries and on particular regions. There are now a relatively large number of such studies and the treatment here is by no means comprehensive. Rather the aim is to emphasise some of the general conclusions that can be drawn from these studies and to comment briefly on the various techniques that have been employed.

The studies can be classified in various ways, according to the range of resource developments that are covered; according to the analytical techniques that have been employed to derive the results; and according to the region which is the subject of the impact study. Focussing first on the range of resource developments covered, a distinction can be drawn between those investigations which have concentrated on a single major resource-based development and those which have attempted to examine the effect on output and employment of all the major resource developments in a State, or in Australia as a whole.

Studies of the economic effects of individual resource developments have included, for example:

6

the Boyne Island aluminium smelter near Gladstone (Mandeville, 1980);

the Gladstone power station (Mandeville and Jensen, 1978);

the proposed Rundle shale oil project in Queensland (Mandeville and Jensen, 1979);

the expansion of the Gladstone alumina refinery (Mandeville and Jensen, 1979);

Alcan Queensland Pty Ltd's proposed aluminium smelter (Mandeville and Jensen, 1979);

the aluminium smelter at Portland (Carter, 1982);

the economic impact of the Western Australia alumina industry (Department of Resource Development Western Australia, 1980); and

the impact of the Weipa bauxite mine on the Queensland economy (Mandeville, 1979).

At the other extreme, studies of the likely output and employment effects of the aggregate additional capital expenditure and additional production from a large number of major resource developments in Australia have been completed by:

the Bureau of Industry Economics (BIE, 1981) (where the emphasis was on backward linkage effects on industries which directly or indirectly supplied goods and services to the mining industry); and

the Industries Assistance Commission (IAC,1981) (using the ORANI model to explore the regional employment consequences of an above average increase in exports of selected minerals).

Most of these studies have employed input-output analysis in one form or another. However, some different approaches have been followed in analysing the likely labour market effects of resource developments. For example, Mr Norman Fisher, Director of the Bureau of Labour Market Research in a paper presented last year (Fisher, 1982) was able to draw on historical data relating to the earlier resource boom in Western Australia in the 1960s to suggest that the market for skilled labour in Western Australia, Queensland and New South Wales could be expected to adjust to the additional demands arising from the 1980s resources boom without the necessity for major wage increases. Again, Robert Carter in a study of the labour market effects of the Portland Aluminium smelter (Carter, 1982) employed an interview survey of local firms and concluded that the required migration of skilled labour into the region could be achieved fairly readily, subject to proper forward planning of housing requirements.

7

Manufacturing & Tertiary Industry Impacts

In assessing the impact of resource developments upon manufacturing and service industries it is important to distinguish between the investment phase and the subsequent production phase of the development projects. The inputs required in these two phases are quite different and accordingly the supplying industries are not the same. Moreover, the BIE study showed that the cost of imported goods usually represents a larger fraction of the capital expenditure on a project than of the operating expenses. Table 1.2 based on the BIE study, shows how the expected increase in value added generated by additional resource-based investment and production in the 1980s was likely to be shared among the broad industry sectors and imports. Table 1.2 is concerned only with the backward linkages arising from resource developments and does not take account of income effects. Indirect as well as direct demand for inputs are shown. Thus, for example, Table 1.2 records not only the direct imports of plant, machinery and equipment for use in resource developments in the 1980s but also imports of components by domestic firms which will be manufacturing plant and machinery for the mining industry. While such direct imports were estimated by consideration of the actual or likely import requirements of a large number of individual resource developments, the indirect imports were derived by input-output analysis.

Table 1.2 shows that increased capital expenditure on resource developments in the 1980's will have a larger (absolute) impact on value added in manufacturing industry than on the construction industry. Once the resource projects have commenced production, the construction industry ceases to be an important supplier of inputs. The service industries (apart from construction) will gain a relatively large share of the increase in domestic value added resulting from resource developments, notably during the investment phase. Finally, as the production of minerals is stepped up, the mining industry itself takes a large share of the increase in value added (about 59 per cent) reflecting additional wages, salaries, and gross profits arising in mining enterprises.

The BIE study examined the likely effects on value added in each of 113 input-output industries and on employment in some 70 occupational categories. It did not explore specifically the possible regional output or employment consequences of resource developments in the 1980s. Nevertheless the general point can be made that as the aggregate level of investment expenditure in mineral and resource-processing activities begins to decline (perhaps in the mid or late 1980s) while the level of resource-based production continues to rise this will not only cause a shift in the pattern of industries supplying the necessary inputs but will also have consequences for the distribution of regional employment and output.

As mentioned earlier the IAC has recently used the ORANI model to assess the regional employment changes that might be caused by an above-average increase in exports from selected mineral-based industries, of the kind that is expected to take place in the 1980s. In order to derive regional results for each of the 58 Statistical Divisions, the

Table 1.2:   Relative Impact of Increases in Resource-based
             Investment and Production in the 1980s Upon
             Imports and Value Added in Domestic Industries
             (percentage shares)

	Impact of increases in resource-based Investment and Production		
	Investment	Production	Investment and Production
Australian production	76.2	92.4	87.7
Gross value of imports (c.i.f.)	23.8	7.6	12.3
	100.0	100.0	100.0
Industry shares of the total increase in domestic value added:			
Mining	3.3	58.6	44.8
Manufacturing	39.0	23.8	27.6
Construction	20.4	0.8	5.7
Transport and Storage	5.9	6.5	6.3
Other Services	31.5	10.3	15.6
All other domestic industries	100.0	100.0	100.0

Source: Adapted from data in Johns (1982)

ORANI approach is to divide the input–output industries into two groups, to sell their output exclusively within a particular region, while national industries located in any region are assumed to sell their output nation-wide. Suppose there is a change in the aggregate output of a manufacturing industry induced by additional exports of minerals, then, if it is a national industry, the same proportionate change in the industry's output and employment will take place in all regions in which it is located. However, percentage changes in total employment may differ quite markedly among the regions because of the different industry mixes of each region.

The IAC simulation of the employment changes induced by resource developments was based on a scenario in which exports from three industries, other metallic minerals, coal and crude petroleum and other basic metal products were projected to increase by 11.5 per cent, or 7.5 percentage points more than the average growth for all exports. To pinpoint more precisely the regions where employment growth would result directly from resource developments the Commission used information on the regional distribution of likely increases in exports of coal, uranium, aluminium and alumina.

A summary of the results of the simulations is given in Table 2.3. To quote the Commission paper they are not "to be interpreted as precise forecasts, but rather as indicators of the broad spatial effects of the economic change being analysed". Bearing this qualification in mind it can be seen that in only about six of the 58 Statistical Divisions is there a strong rise in employment growth as a result of the resource developments. Three of these Divisions are in Queensland, (Fitzroy, Mackay and North Western Divisions) two are in Western Australia (South West and South Eastern Divisions) and the remaining one is in the Northern Territory (excluding Darwin). To the extent that resource developments also cause regional employment losses, because of the adverse effects of additional inflationary pressures on some import–competing and exporting industries, those losses are generally small and widely diffused, according to the IAC simulations.

Losses in regional employment of 0.1 per cent are projected to occur in four of the 12 Statistical Divisions in Victoria, although there is a negligible change in employment in the State as a whole. The only Division with an employment loss exceeding 0.1 per cent is Illawarra in New South Wales. It should be emphasised that these regional employment changes are those solely attributable to the increase in mineral and base metal exports and do not take account of other changes that may be occurring simultaneously such as a world recession, or changes in protection.

SOME LIMITATIONS OF THE EMPIRICAL STUDIES

The previous section was designed to give a flavour of the results that have been obtained from recent research on the likely economic effects on individual industries and regions of Australia's

Table 1.3:   IAC Study of the Regional Employment Effects of the Mining Boom

Statistical[a] Division	Employment projections from above-average annual growth in mineral exports[b]
	per cent
NEW SOUTH WALES (12)[c]	
Hunter	0.3
Illawarra	−0.2
Total New South Wales	..
VICTORIA (12)	
Total Victoria	..
QUEENSLAND (11)	
Fitzroy	2.4
Mackay	1.0
Northern	0.2
Far North	0.3
North Western	3.3
Total Queensland	0.3
SOUTH AUSTRALIA (7)	
Yorke and Lower North	0.2
Total South Australia	..
WESTERN AUSTRALIA (9)	
South West	1.4
South Eastern	3.5
Central	0.5
Total Western Australia	0.3
TASMANIA (4)	
Total Tasmania	..
NORTHERN TERRITORY	
Balance of Northern Territory	4.1
Total Northern Territory	1.9

Notes: .. No change (at first decimal place)
(a) The above-average portion of annual mineral export growth for those mineral industries estimated to achieve export growth greater than the average growth for all exports.
(b) Only the Statistical Divisions where the employment change was projected to be 0.2 per cent or more (regardless of sign) are shown in this table.
(c) The total number of Statistical Divisions in each State or Territory are shown in parentheses.
Source: Industries Assistance Comission (1981), Approaches to General Reductions in Protection Discussion Paper No. 3, "The Regional Implications of Economic Change".

11

resource developments in the 1980s. Although some useful broad conclusions can be drawn from the research results, it would be remiss
not to mention that all the studies have some limitations. In the
present state of the art it is not possible to make an accurate forecast of the
regional output and employment consequences of future resource developments. This is not simply because of the inevitable uncertainty about
the magnitude and timing of the capital and operating expenditure on the
resources developments, but also for two other reasons. First, the techniques employed in many of the empirical studies do not enable the
researchers to capture all the effects (macroeconomic and microeconomic)
of a resources boom. Secondly, even when most of those effects can
be captured in the one study, the procedure for allocating the employment
and output changes to individual regions is based on rather restrictive
assumptions which ignore some of the adjustment problems likely to be
encountered in practice.

Let me elaborate. An upsurge in capital expenditure on resource-
related activities and the consequent growth of mineral exports is likely
to have the following effects on the economy:

an increase in demand for those domestic industries which supply
investment or intermediate goods to the mining industry, either directly
or indirectly;

an increase in the real exchange rate, defined as a rise in the price
of non-tradeable goods and services relative to the prices of internationally tradeable goods and services (the so-called Gregory effect);

an increase in national income, inducing additional demands for
locally produced goods and services as well as for imports; and

possibly, a change in relative factor prices depending on the factor
intensities of production for those goods and services which are now
in stronger demand because of the new resource developments.

Several studies of the employment consequences of new resource
developments have focussed only on the first of these effects to the
neglect of the others. This is true of most of the input–output studies
of individual resource projects and of the BIE study. Moreover, input-
output studies are based on a constant employment to output ratio in
each industry, so that it is not possible to take account of variations
in labour productivity over time or between regions. This can lead to
some exaggeration of the employment gains realisable from new resource
developments, particularly those with a long gestation period. Further input-
output analysis is designed to focus on the additional demand for labour
in an industry or region. Whether that potential demand will be translated
into a corresponding increase in actual employment depends of course
on the availability of suitable labour within the region or on the mobility
of labour between regions. Finally, it is apparent that the extent of the
employment gains from a resource development will depend on the extent

to which the required inputs are purchased locally rather than overseas. Historical information on average import leakages may prove to be a misleading guide to the marginal import leakage associated with a major resource development, where local industry may have difficulty in supplying certain equipment and materials in the requisite time frame.

The ORANI model has the advantage that it can take account of some of the other effects of resource developments listed above in addition to the backward linkage effect. However, the model is timeless, so it cannot take account of the dynamic adjustment path by which the economy as a whole and the individual regions adjust to the rise in mineral exports. It has been suggested recently (Eastwood and Veneables, 1982) in relation to the United Kingdom economy that a major resource development can precipitate a recession following the initial exchange rate appreciation caused by the new development. This argument is based on the view that exchange rate markets and asset markets adjust very quickly in anticipating the favourable effects of the resource developments, while goods and factor markets adjust more slowly. If this applies to Australia, as it may well do, it may indicate that the unfavourable effects on import—competing and exporting industries arising from an exchange rate appreciation could precede the favourable impact of the resource developments on supplying industries. It is this type of dynamic adjustment which cannot be allowed for in the ORANI model.

It should also be mentioned that the distinction between regional and national industries which is made in the ORANI simulations is a device to avoid the problem that data on interregional trade flows is inadequate. However, the simple dichotomy between these two types of industries is not without difficulties. Implicitly the model assumes that costs of production and distribution are the same in each plant of a national industry wherever located. This results in a situation where it is just as possible (in the model) for say, Western Australian producers to supply the additional input for a new resource development in Queensland as it is for producers of the same product already located in Queensland. In the light of these considerations one should be cautious in inferring from the ORANI results that resource developments in the 1980s will not pose significant regional structural adjustment problems.

STRUCTURAL ADJUSTMENT PROBLEMS ARISING FROM RESOURCE DEVELOPMENTS AND POSSIBLE POLICY RESPONSES

This final section of the chapter focusses on only one of the several important policy questions that surround resource developments in Australia — the policies that may be needed to facilitate regional structural adjustment in the light of the increased level of expenditure on resource-based activities.

The possible policy initiatives can be looked at from the point of view of the State or region in which the resource developments are taking place; the State or region which is losing output and employment

13

as a result of resource developments elsewhere; and the Commonwealth Government.

The region in which the resource development is taking place typically faces a situation where the expenditure and employment associated with the new venture is large in relation to existing incomes and employment in the region. Public expenditures will often be needed for infrastructure, serviced land will have to be available for additional housing and for industrial use, and the local government authorities may have an interest in ensuring that manpower can be attracted into the region without a sharp increase in wages. In addition, there will be a number of environmental matters to be resolved, although these fall outside the scope of the present discussion.

The extent to which the public authorities are responsible for financing the additional infrastructure will evidently be a matter for agreement between those authorities and the enterprise responsible for the resource project. Once this issue has been resolved, however, it is clearly efficient to co-ordinate the construction of the infrastructure with that of the resource developments.

While in one sense the size of the resource development in relation to existing regional activities may appear a difficulty, this tends to force a degree of co-ordination and facilitates structural adjustment. The long gestation period and the relatively small manpower requirements of major resource projects, makes it easier to achieve the necessary migration of labour into the region. In general, as indicated previously, manpower shortages do not appear to have been a major impediment to the successful establishment of major resource developments in recent years.

The problems of adjustment are different in the regions facing a loss in output and employment as a result of increased resource-based investment. First, there is a problem of identifying in advance which these regions will be. It is probable, as the IAC simulations have indicated, that the employment losses are widely diffused and relatively small in each region. This is to be expected since the resource developments will have favourable effects on the demand for many industries through income effects and backward linkage effects. It is only the industries which are adversely affected by the real exchange rate increase or by a change in relative factor prices and which do not obtain offsetting benefits from these other effects, which are likely to encounter a loss of output and employment. It may be observed also that it is tariff-protected but not quota-protected import-competing industries which may suffer output and employment losses if the resource developments cause an appreciation of the real exchange rate.

Second, it is clear that if any policy measures are needed to facilitate structural adjustment from regions facing a loss in employment, in the long-run they should be directed towards all such regions whatever the causes of the employment decline. In other words, it would

seem inappropriate to focus exclusively on the regional effects of
resource developments alone without taking account of the regional
effects of other long–run economic changes taking place at the same time.

Local authorities in vulnerable regions may however have some
policy options open to them which could mitigate the loss of regional
output and employment before (or after) it occurs. Among these options
are measures to diversify the industrial base by attracting footloose
industries which would complement existing industries, without being
dependent on them. It has also been suggested that one significant
obstacle to the movement of labour from vulnerable or declining regions
is the differential cost of housing. While local authorities have limited
opportunities for addressing this problem, action may be possible at the
Federal level.

NOTES

1. New fixed capital expenditure by private enterprises in selected industries as anticipated at July/August 1982. See ABS Catalogue No.
5626.0.

2. The anticipated increase in the consumer price index in 1982–83
(10.75 per cent) was used as a deflator – see Budget Statements
1982–83.

3. For example – Department of Industry and Commerce Major Manufacturing and Mining Investment Projects June 1982 and Johns (1982).
Some of the estimates in the latter paper may now be considered
relatively optimistic in the light of recently announced project
deferments.

4. It should be emphasised that if resource based activities were
ranked according to the level of investment expenditure or value
of production in the 1980s the order would differ from that shown.
The main focus of interest in this chapter is on the increases in
capital and current outlays arising from particular types of resources
development because it is only such increases which add to
existing demands on domestic manufacturing and tertiary industries.

5. Australian Bureau of Statistics Catalogue No. 5646.0.

2

ENVIRONMENTAL ASPECTS OF REGIONAL RESOURCE DEVELOPMENTS
A COMMONWEALTH PERSPECTIVE

E.M. Anderson

INTRODUCTION

In recent years considerable attention has been given to the "resources boom" in Australia. While a diversity of opinions have been expressed regarding the benefits to Australians of such a "boom" – indeed, it is now apparent that the word "boom" is an overstatement – there has certainly been a major expansion of mining and mineral processing in Australia during the past decade.

In many cases this expansion has raised problems affecting the physical and social environment in which we live. Air and water pollution, noise, aesthetic degradation, housing problems and land use conflicts are some of the ways in which the "quality of life" can be eroded by mining and industrial projects.

These potential problems are exacerbated because they are, to a very large degree, concentrated into a few major regions where resource development is taking place. Areas where major attention has been focused are the Hunter Valley of New South Wales, the Latrobe Valley in Victoria and the Gladstone region in Queensland.

The Commonwealth has recognised a responsibility to be environmentally sensitive in actions and decisions of its agencies. This responsibility is given force through the Environment Protection (Impact of Proposals) Act. The application of the Act to decisions on export licencing and foreign investment involves the Commonwealth in the environmental assessment of many major mining and industrial development proposals. The approval and regulation of such developments are primarily a State responsibility, exercised through State legislation. Collaboration between Commonwealth and State authorities is necessary so that both can fulfil their obligations without unnecessary duplication.

This chapter examines the nature and scope of Commonwealth environmental assessment, with particular reference to its application to regional issues. Some ways are identified by which Commonwealth/ State co-operation in assessing regional resource developments might be improved.

COMMONWEALTH ENVIRONMENTAL ASSESSMENT

The principal mechanism by which the Commonwealth becomes involved in the environmental aspects of resource developments is through the application of the Environment Protection (Impact of Proposals) Act. The Act requires that matters of environmental significance be examined and taken into account in relation to decisions and actions of the Commonwealth Government and its authorities.

The Act defines environment as including "all aspects of the surroundings of man whether affecting him as an individual or in his social groupings". Thus social impacts, as well as impacts on the physical and natural environment, need to be examined and taken into account in government decisions.

The Impact Act came into force at the end of 1974 and its Administrative Procedures were approved in the middle of the following year. Initially, emphasis was given to assessing specific construction proposals made by Commonwealth agencies, particularly projects such as government offices and facilities for telecommunications, transport and defence. As experience developed, the Act was applied to a broader range of Commonwealth actions and decisions. In particular, there has been a steady increase in proposals brought forward for assessment as a result of the need for approvals under Commonwealth foreign investment policy and export licencing powers.

Although there have been no major amendments to the Act since 1974, there have been two significant developments in the procedure for assessing proposals. First, arrangements have been made with all States to avoid overlap or duplication by Commonwealth and State environmental authorities. Under these arrangements, where responsibilities of both Commonwealth and State Governments are involved, common documentation and arrangements for public comment are agreed. Except in Queensland, environmental assessment is carried out jointly to efficiently utilise the resources of both Governments, to identify any problems at an early stage, and to develop solutions co-operatively.

The second development has involved a general widening of the scope of environmental assessment. Partly this has been a result of a broadening of the matters which the public consider important, as shown by comment on draft environmental impact statements, and partly because of a general increase in the size and complexity of development projects. In particular, examination of the social implications of projects has become increasingly important.

In recent years the Department has assessed a number of coal proposals in the Hunter Valley and the Bowen Basin in Queensland, coal-to-oil proposals in the Latrobe Valley of Victoria, aluminium smelter proposals in the Hunter Valley, bauxite mining in the Darling Ranges of Western Australia, uranium mining in the Alligator Rivers Region of the Northern Territory, and a variety of industrial proposals in the Gladstone region of Queensland. This experience has exposed the Department to issues affecting the physical and social environment in relation to mining and industrial proposals being developed in key regions throughout Australia.

REGIONAL ASSESSMENT PARAMETERS

In order to determine the likely effects of a proposed development on a community, the current status and trends of key parameters at the local and regional level must be understood. Existing lifestyles can then be assessed in terms of community attributes and any existing problems identified. As a first step, an information baseline is established on which future impacts attributable to the proposed development can be superimposed.

Important parameters for such baseline studies are population characteristics and trends, labour force and employment profiles, current and planned land use, settlement patterns, availability and cost of residential land and housing for rent or sale, availability of any surplus capacity of existing infrastructure services and facilities. The latter include power, water supply, sewerage, waste disposal, sport, recreation, education, health care, welfare, commercial, communications and transport facilities. Features of cultural, scientific or historical significance to the immediate community or general public are also important.

Workforce and Employment – the acquisition and retention of a stable and contented workforce is clearly essential to a successful project. Planning needs to take into account the dynamic character of the workforce. The long lead times commonly associated with major development projects allow time for significant changes to occur. Account needs to be taken of changing societal attitudes in workforces, such as the increasing tendency of young, single workers to choose individual rental accommodation in preference to communal living in camps and barracks.

The engagement of a suitable project workforce (especially in skilled categories) is dependent in part on existing regional, State and national levels of unemployment. Where particular skills are in short supply in the host region, a new developer may be competing for available resources against existing employers. Shortages of skilled labour, especially in remote locations, are likely to result in bidding up of wages, with implications for the local and regional economy. While most communities benefit from development through increased employment opportunities, groups such as women and school leavers are often dependent on the developer's willingness to institute training and apprenticeship schemes, and to employ women in traditionally male occupations.

Resource development proposals also provide opportunities for indirect or secondary employment. Indirect employment may include jobs in new or expanding industries providing industrial support to major developments. Additional employment opportunities can arise through the service and infrastructure requirements of increased populations. By estimating the population increases and their implications for secondary

19

employment opportunities (the multiplier effect) some indications can be gained of the likely impact on public finances, infrastructure and community service needs.

The effects of development of the existing business community may not always be beneficial. Local retail businesses for instance, may suffer as a result of competition from large national chain stores attracted to areas undergoing economic growth. The income generating capacity of competing sectors such as the rural industry, may also be adversely affected by resource development. During the environmental assessment of the Woodlawn base metals project, in New South Wales, for example, graziers from adjoining properties expressed concern over possible effects of mine dust on pasture quality and on essential groundwater supplies if the water table was lowered by mine pit excavation. In another instance, the possibly damaging effect that fluoride emissions from aluminium smelters may have on grape vines has received considerable public attention.

Workforce dispersion, particularly the need to draw workers from beyond the immediate area, has important implications for public transport facilities and roads. The availability of accommodation in regional population centres together with the locational preferences of incoming households are also important assessment factors.

Land and Housing – the availability, quality and cost of residential land and housing are matters that require careful consideration. Where housing stocks are limited, competition for available resources is likely to inflate prices. Advance planning to ensure the availability of housing to meet the needs of workers and their families may appear to solve the problem. However, the building industry may have difficulty in meeting scheduled targets if labour shortages occur through regional competition for skilled workers. New housing quality is another important factor particularly where, in estblished areas, it may be of a markedly lower, or higher standard than existing housing. Alternatives to conventional housing are often poorly planned, a fact which has contributed to their reputation for producing social stresses. For instance residents of caravan parks have experienced psychological strain through inadequate living standards and lack of privacy, which may have been avoided or at least reduced by better planning.

Infrastructure and Services – the provisions of adequate services and facilities to meet the industrial needs of new developments and the domestic needs of expanded populations generated by them, is of critical concern to project planners, local administrators and the existing community. Financial resource allocation decisions that are not carefully planned can have the effect of favouring development of one region over another, or one development proposal over another within a region. Policy decisions need to be taken against the background of a comprehensive assessment of the socio-economic environment.

20

Advance planning and investment in the provision of power and water supplies is also critical, particularly where new developments are major consumers, necessitating significant expansion of existing facilities and long construction lead times.

Adequate and timely provision of community support services and facilities is also essential. The ready availability of schools, social services, health care (hospital, medical, dental, paramedical, and specialised health services for the young, the aged and the handicapped), commercial services, and facilities for recreation and entertainment, all contribute to the ability of project developers to attract suitable workers.

Local Government – major development proposals have significant implications for local government authorities, who must deal with the financial and administrative pressures brought about by the needs of an expanded population. The environmental assessment process can help to alert local authorities to possible problems and identify areas where existing Commonwealth, State and local government policies and programs are inadequate. Often there is a case for special government assistance to facilitate regional adjustment to development. When local government experiences difficulty in coping with its expanded responsibilities and satisfying community expectations, public opinion may turn against new projects. This could lead to unwelcome delays and possible confrontations.

REGIONAL IMPLICATIONS

In the case of regions which are particularly favoured with resources there is a strong tendency for several projects to be brought forward at about the same time. Under these circumstances, assessing the impact of each project in isolation fails to take into account the likely cumulative effects that the projects will have on the region. There is a particular problem regarding cumulative social impacts, highlighted by overseas cases such as the development of the North Sea oil during the past decade, which caused major social and environmental problems in the long established stable communities on the North Sea coasts of Scotland and Norway.

In Australia, important cumulative regional effects are being experienced in the Hunter Valley, the Gladstone region and the Latrobe Valley. Problems associated with one of these regions, the Hunter Valley, have been examined in some detail. The Department's experience with impact assessment in the Hunter region suggests that the main problems include:

Environment Protection – major resource developments result in air and water pollution, noise and reduced aesthetic quality of the landscape. Mines, power stations and mineral processing plants are all potential sources of gaseous, liquid and solid pollution. The adverse effects of fluoride emissions from aluminium smelters posed

21

a significant problem in the Hunter region, particularly with respect to their impact on vineyards, orchards and pastoral activities.

Land Use Conflicts – there is significant competition in land use involving established agricultural uses (dairy farming, beef cattle, fruit growing and vineyards) and expanding mining and industrial activity. In the Upper Hunter in 1979, it was estimated that 60 per cent of the total land was under some form of mining tenure, while 85 per cent was under crops or pasture. A particular area of conflict is the alluvial land along the Hunter River, which is a prime agricultural and groundwater resource, but is underlain by valuable coal reserves.

Unemployment – while regional resource developments create a demand for labour, many employment opportunities require specialized skills which may be either unavailable within a region, or in short supply. At the same time, the region as a whole may be suffering from a high rate of unemployment, particularly among females and junior males, who do not have the skills to match the requirements of potential employers.

Accommodation – severe housing shortages combined with major population increases have occurred in the Hunter region. Competition for housing has led to inflation of prices and the building industry has had difficulty in meeting scheuduled targets because of labour shortages occuring as a result of regional competition for skilled workers.

Infrastructure – there is a need to provide adequate water, sewerage and road services to meet the needs of new industrial development and to satisfy the domestic requirements of the expanding population in the region. Advance planning and careful investment decisions covering the provision of essential services for both industrial and domestic use will be needed if intra-regional imbalances and environmental hazards are to be avoided.

Community Facilities – the provision of adequate community facilities to meet the needs of a rapidly expanding population is a source of concern to local government and the community at large. While community expectations are high, the availability of funding appears inadequate to the task, particularly in the light of rating bases being eroded by the resumption of large areas of land for public purposes such as power station development.

Companies involved in developing large scale natural resource proposals have recognised that the environmental effects of their projects can extend well beyond the boundaries of the project area. For example, in its 1981 environmental impact statement (EIS) on the proposed United Colliery at Warkworth in the Hunter Valley, United Collieries stated:

The United development is of moderate size when compared with other mining and industrial developments planned for the Hunter Region in the next decade. The colliery development will provide employment both directly and indirectly for both skilled and unskilled workers in a region that has suffered high unemployment rates in recent years. The wages of its workforce will provide a notable boost to regional income and will support the provision of improved urban facilities. The Colliery's participation in the Mt Thorley rail development will ensure an improved regional transportation system for the movement of coal. On the other hand the Colliery's expansion will also add to the demand for improved regional facilities such as housing and urban services, and rural roads.

Elsewhere, it has been made clear that an adequate identification and response to the regional and cumulative impacts of natural resource development is beyond the scope of individual companies and that co-ordinated and co-operative action by the public and private sectors is essential if potential problems are to be overcome. This was well summarized in the United Collieries EIS, where the proponent indicated that:

> An accurate assessment of the regional impact of the cumulative development of coal mines in the Hunter is a task beyond this report, since it entails a thorough knowledge of the timing of all mining developments, a detailed schedule of the provision of infrastructure and housing in all towns, and an understanding of the workings and implications of the regional income and employment multipliers identified for the coal industry and quoted in this report. It has also to be appreciated that the socio-economic environment of any region is dynamic and constantly changing. The Hunter Region is no exception; indeed, the very size of proposed coal developments suggests the region is quite likely to be volatile (in socio-economic terms) in the coming decade.

A more ominous note was sounded by the State Electricity Commission (SEC) of New South Wales in its 1981 EIS on the Mount Arthur North Coal project, near Muswellbrook in the Hunter Valley. Commenting on urban expansion and regional structure, the SEC stated that:

> Unless co-ordination and co-operation can be achieved between the development organisations, relevant agencies at all levels of government, and community groups, the inherent problems of development will be exacerbated.

COMMONWEALTH ENVIRONMENTAL IMPACT ASSESSMENT IN THE REGIONAL CONTEXT

Commonwealth environmental impact assessment, or EIA, undertaken under the provisions of the Environment Protection (Impact of Proposals) Act is subject to certain limitations, particularly when applied to the assessment of major mining and industrial proposals. In particular:

23

the Act is limited by the Constitution and is thus confined to matters which involve the Commonwealth;

the Act's coverage is limited to matters "affecting the environment to a significant extent". Thus it is not concerned with the many issues which are not environmentally important; and

the Act's objective is to ensure that environmental matters are examined and taken into account in the Commonwealth's decision making process. It provides no form of environmental veto over decision making.

Although the Act gives prominence to arrangements for public inquiries, these mechanisms have been used infrequently (although those inquiries that have been held[1] have had far reaching results). In the great majority of cases the Act has been applied to individual projects using the mechanism of environmental impact statements (EIS's). While it has been possible to apply the EIS mechanism flexibly to accommodate the particular features of individual projects, it does have significant limitations for assessing regional impacts, particularly when several major projects are related, and for developing arrangements to mitigate particularly adverse impacts.

Nevertheless, the EIS mechanism has provided a valuable tool for assessing major mining and industrial proposals. In developing the scope of individual assessments, and in considering the results, the Department is able to draw on the experience of other projects and other regions, and to take some account of cumulative effects. Some emphasis is given to issues of national environmental importance.

In reaching conclusions regarding the impact of particular resource development projects, the Department has explored the need for action at two levels:

issues falling within the responsibility of Commonwealth authorities; and

issues requiring co-ordinated action by a range of authorities (including the Commonwealth).

Taking asessments of major industrial proposals in the Hunter Valley as an example, the Department has stressed the need to establish mechanisms to co-ordinate monitoring of the social effects of development and to take action necessary to ameliorate adverse effects. The employment of community welfare officers has been suggested as one way of initiating such co-ordination. The Commonwealth Department of Social Security has been asked to advise on existing community infrastructure so that consideration can be given to the provision of new and expanded community services.

Responding to the need for co-ordinated action is more difficult. The general problem was indicated by comments made by the Department, in 1981, in relation to its assessment of the Tomago Aluminium Smelter project:

> The Department is concerned about the cumulative impacts of the several large projects proposed for the Hunter Valley and the current practice of assessing the environmental impact of each in isolation. The Department believes there is a need to establish some co-ordination mechanism through which individual proposals can be environmentally assessed in the context of overall development planning for the region.

The general problem was also identified in the report on "The Development of the Bauxite, Alumina and Aluminium Industries", tabled in Parliament on 25 November 1981, by the Senate Standing Committee on Natural Resources. The Committee noted that:

> A recurring problem with which environmental protection processes have as yet not come to terms is that of regional development. A number of areas of Australia, but most particularly the Hunter Valley of New South Wales, are experiencing the rapid development of a number of projects more or less simultaneously with environmental problems arising from the concentration and interaction of these projects. In this circumstances the existing project by project assessment does not provide a satisfactory method of evaluating the overall impact of development.

Having identified this problem, the Committee recommended inter alia, that:

> the Department of Home Affairs and Environment prepare a draft programme for the conduct of regional environmental impact inquiries and that such a draft be used as a basis for discussion in the Australian Environment Council with a view to developing joint Commonwealth/State procedures for the conduct of regional inquiries.[2]

The Committee report does not elaborate on the nature of "regional environmental impact inquiries". However it appears clear that they would include the essential features of environmental impact assessment, and also encompass considerations of the regional land use planning normally undertaken by State authorities. Indeed recent legislation in N.S.W. and South Australia has brought the two processes into close association. The question now is whether current legislation and administrative arrangements are adequate to deal with the regional problems which the public has identified in the environmental assessment of many major projects, and which have been drawn to broader attention by the Senate Committee report. In considering this question, the adequacy of existing arrangements might be tested for circumstances when:

major decisions on particular projects were required by both a State (or States) and the Commonwealth;

the critical impacts of the projects were expected to be environmental rather than of a traditional land use nature; and

the projects involved particular environmental impacts where some national collaboration could be beneficial in establishing guidelines for some particular environmental impacts of the industry involved (eg. uranium, coal liquefaction).

Earlier in this chapter, reference was made to the bilateral arrangements between the Commonwealth and the States for co-operation in the assessment of proposals involving the responsibilities of both governments. Experience gained in this bilateral co-operation suggests that where there are: both Commonwealth and State decisions required, several major proposals in a region, environmental impacts with important regional implications, important implications for other parts of Australia, or other implications of a national character, then there is a good case for the proposals to be examined by an appropriate Commonwealth-State inquiry. In appropriate circumstances, a joint inquiry would overcome important disadvantages associated with a series of individual project assessments, and could be conducted more expeditiously than any alternative process. The terms of reference and arrangements for any such joint inquiry would depend on the particular circumstances, and would require close consultation in advance by the relevant governments.

CONCLUSIONS

In general, existing legislation and administrative arrangements allow the environmental impacts of major projects to be identified by the Commonwealth and States acting either jointly or independently, and for appropriate measures to be taken to mitigate adverse impacts. However there are circumstances in which the regional implications are such that the existing mechanisms may not be adequate. In such circumstances, a regional impact assessment inquiry, conducted jointly by the Commonwealth and a particular State (or States), could be an effective and expeditious form of assessment. Such an inquiry would be consistent with the already existing satisfactory Commonwealth/State arrangements for co-operation in the environmental assessment of proposals.

NOTES

1. Ranger Uranium Environmental Inquiry and Fraser Island Environmental Inquiry

2. At the date of writing this chapter, the Government has not responded to the above recommendations

3

THE ROLE OF IMMIGRATION
IN RESOURCE DEVELOPMENT REGIONS

E. Brookbanks

INTRODUCTION

Resource development in Australia is highly sensitive to international economic pressures. The rapid surge in resource based investment in 1980 and 1981 was triggered by the second international oil price rise, and the resulting interest in potential alternative energy sources (Figure 3.1). The current world recession has led to a fall in demand for Australia's major energy resources. Nevertheless, the nation's reserves and mineral and energy resources, especially coal, gas, oil, shale oil, uranium, bauxite, nickel, zinc, copper are so extensive and internationally significant that the impact of the recession must be viewed simply as a delay in the timetable of long term development.

Many projects, especially aluminium refining and smelting, export coal, and synthetic fuels, have been deferred or cancelled. Overall, however, private non-dwelling construction and public capital works have stood up well against the general trend of decline in most economic indicators. This reflects the inertia of the building and construction process: investment decisions were made two or three years ago and lead times are long. Thus there is still considerable activity on a number of projects, especially in the resource development regions.

A major feature of the planned investments under the 1980 and 1981 surge was the significant difference in regional demand for labour. The major investments were concentrated in Central Queensland (including Gladstone), South West Western Australia, the Pilbara (and North West Shelf), Portland, Latrobe Valley, Cooper Basin and Roxby Downs. Only the Hunter could be considered as being close to or within the sphere of metropolitan economic activity. A further feature of the demand for labour was the bias towards Queensland and Western Australia.

The large scale and rapid pace envisaged for these developments would have a major impact on the regions because of their superimposition on relatively small economic bases. The supply of skilled labour was seen at the time as a most important constraint.

27

Figure 3.1: DIC Mining and Manufacturing Projects Planned and committed 1979–1982[1]

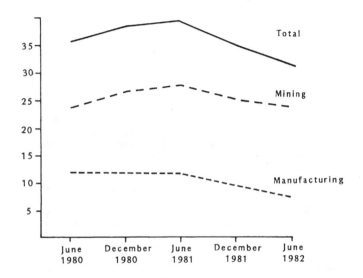

(1) Aggregate Estimated Remaining Cost of Projects Listed by Developers as at "Committed" and "Final Feasibility" Stages. $ values as at June quarter 1982 using Implicit Price Deflator for Total Private Gross Fixed Capital Expenditure from ABS Publication "Quarterly Estimates of National Income and Expenditure Australia June Quarter 1982" Cat. No. 5206, Table 42.

Source: Department of Industry and Commerce (1982)

To a large extent it was assumed that inter-regional mobility of skilled workers would be facilitated by wage rises, hopefully confined to categories in short supply. Apprentice-ship training and retraining programs would also be important. The immigration program was seen as having a complementary role to training in the supply of these skills. Migrants were seen as having the advantage of being quickly and easily attracted to those regions where skills would be needed. Migrants would also have a key role to play in providing specialist skills, especially where short term contracts were required.

This chapter examines the role that immigration can play in long term regional resource based development. For the purposes of this chapter the concept of immigration includes permanent and temporary entry. It acknowledges that:

the role is most significant in the supply of highly specialist workers, often under temporary resident status;

immigration programs must complement internal mobility and training programs; and

the role of immigration will change during the life of the project, as it moves from design through construction to operation.

THE ROLE OF IMMIGRATION IN REGIONAL ADJUSTMENT

Development of new resource based industries at the scale suggested by the investment plans of 1980 and 1981 would have a major impact on regional and structural change. Existing patterns of resource allocation would be radically altered through the transfer of population, skilled manpower and finance from those regions with declining and less efficient economic bases to those with potential for more rapid growth.

The process of regional and structural change is constrained by inertia in the system. This can take many forms. Population mobility is inhibited by housing commitments, family and community ties, childrens' schooling and so on. Public finance both for capital and recurrent expenditures tends to be locked into historical regional patterns.

The constraint applies particularly to skilled labour. Firms will attempt to hold on to skilled workers who have established a long-term employment link. A great deal of employment skills are learnt on the job and firms have invested in their skilled workforce, especially at the beginning of their employment contract and returns are received later. Such workers are often held by what Blandy and Richardson (1982) term wage-like adjustments. These are non-wage adjustments and include promotion rate, recruitment rate, quality and hours changes.

The Role of Immigration

Table 3.1 DIC mining and manufacturing projects planned and committed 1979–1982.

Region/Project	1980	1981	1982	1983	1984	1985	1986	1987	1988
CENTRAL QUEENSLAND									
Blair Athol, $500m, (C)[a], Ex[b]						1200c[c]	600p[c]		
Daunia, $400m, (F), Ex.			100c	620p					
German Creek, $400m, (C), Ex.	1570c	862p							
Goonyella, $50m, (C)	160c	80p							
Hail Creek, $700m, (F), Ex.					1200c	765p			
Nebo-Riverside, $312m, (F), Ex.				NAc	430p				
Oaky Creek, $300m, (C), Ex.	1000c	6000p							
Moura/Kianga, $60m, (C), Ex.					NAc	160p			
Peak Downs and Saraji, $52m, (C)	150c	65p							
South Blackwater, $285m, (F), ExD.				NAc	NAp				
Theodore, $300m, (F), Ex.				220c	600p				
Collinsville, $160m, (C), Ex.			NAc	NAp					
Newlands, $550m, (C), Ex.			NAc	400p					
HUNTER, N.S.W.									
John Darling/Stockton Borehole, $260m, (C), ExD.				60c	100p				
Hunter Valley No1., $112m, (C), Ex.		20c	333p						
Drayton, $150m, (C), Ex.					100c	403p			
Mt Thorley, $140m, (C), Ex.		200c	300p						
Ulan, $215m, (F), Ex.	300c	450p							
Warkworth No 1, $86m, (C), ExD.		Stage 1 NAc	164p						
Saxonvale, $86m, (C), ExD.		Stage 1 450c	250p						
Saxonvale, $205m, (F), ExD.							Stage 2 NAc	800	
Gloucester, $100m, (F), Ex.				100c	300p				
Hunter Valley No 2, $100m, (F)					200c	230p			
Mt Arthur South, $150m, (F), Ex.					150c	270p			
Glendell $135m, F, ExD.		300c	500p						
Glennies Creek, $50m, F, Ex.		Stage 1		100c	350p				
Mt Arthur North, $400m, F, ExD.					150c	1000p			

Notes:

(a) The letters in brackets here refer to the level of commitment of the project. The categories are as follows: (C) Committed; (F) Final Feasibility; (P) Preliminary Studies.

(b) This indicates the market orientation of the project, where known, i.e.; Ex = Export; D - Domestic.

(c) The estimated workforce generated by each project is denoted by c or p for construction and production workforce respectively.

Source: Publications of the State Governments, namely, "Queensland Development", 1980 and "Development Projects in New South Wales", January 1981. Supplementary information was obtained from the Commonwealth Department of Industry and Commerce Survey of Major Manufacturing and Mining Investment Projects, December 1980. The caveats applying to that survey also apply to this table.

The lack of significant regional wage differentials can act as a bar to inter-regional mobility; although special remote area allowances can be used to attract workers.

A feature of the resource developments is their time profile of employment. In the short run there is a rapid build up towards peak construction employment. This is followed by a gradual decline to a lower level of employment for long term operation of plant and equipment. Depending on the nature of the development, there would also be longer term employment generated by indirect multipliers. Such indirect employment would be more likely to be generated in other regions, especially metropolitan areas.

The scale of activity, and the regional distribution of projects is illustrated in Tables 3.1 and 3.2 for two sectors of resource development: bauxite, alumina and aluminium projects, and export coal. The feature of the programming of the projects is their coincidence over time. If all projects had gone ahead as planned, they would have been competing for the same specialist workers at the same time. Extreme lumps and peaks in demand for each type of skill would have been created.

This time profile has particular significance to immigration as well as employment opportunities for Australians. Each phase in the project development generates demands for special skills and work contracts:

Exploration and project feasibility studies require;

    a) highly specialised skills, (for example, geophysicists),
    b) skills often in shortage world-wide, and
    c) skills which are needed in the short-term (for example, two year contracts);

Design and construction require;

    a) specialist engineers,
    b) skills often in shortage world-wide, and
    c) skills which are needed in the short-term (for example, two year contracts), and
    d) overseas consultants in some cases;

Operating phases require;

    a) highly specialisd maintenance and safety-engineers,
    b) skills often in shortage world-wide, and
    c) a greater number of permanent employees, and
    d) some scope or training for locally recruited workers;

The Role of Immigration

Table 3.2   Regional distribution and timing of major bauxite, alumina refinery and aluminium smelter developments[a]

Region	1980	1981	1982	1983	1984	1985	1986	1987	1988	1989	1990
HUNTER VALLEY - N.S.W.											
Alcan Smelter expansion Kurri Kurri (C)(b) $200m			200(c)[c] 200(o)[c]								
Alumax Smelter - Lochinvar (C) $640m			2000(c) 900(o)								
Tomago Smelter (C) $620m			1500(c) 800(o)								
PORTLAND - VICTORIA											
Alcoa Smelter Stage 1 (C) $360m (d)		1200(c) 550(o)									
Stage 2-4 (P.S.) $700m					300(c) and 200(o) per stage						
GLADSTONE - CENTRAL QUEENSLAND											
Gladstone Aluminium Ltd (Comalco) Smelter:											
Stage 1 (C) $600m	1200(c)		1080(o)								
Stage 2 (P.S.) $450m						1000(c)		770(o)			
Alcan Smelter - Gladstone/ Bundaberg:											
Stage 1 (F.F.) $400m		1200(c)	650(o)								
Stage 2 (P.S.) $600m							1200(c)	1000(o)			
Qld. Alumina Refinery expansion (F.F.) $300m			850(c)	100(o)							
Comalco Alumina Refinery - Gladstone/Bowen (P.S.) $700m			No timing								
FAR NORTH QUEENSLAND											
Comalco bauxite mine expansion - Weipa (F.F.) $100m			n.a.(c)		n.a.(o)						
SOUTH-WEST WESTERN AUSTRALIA											
Reynolds Aluminium - Worsley mines and refinery: Stage 1 (C) $1,000m	3000(c)	750(o)									
Stage 2 (P.S.) $400m						n.a.(c)n.a.(o)					
Alcoa - Wagerup mine and refinery: Stage 1 (C) $300m	1200(c)	550(o),									
Stage 2 (F.F.) Stage 3 (P.S.)				1000(c) n.a.(o)							
Alcoa Smelter - Bunbury: Stage 1 (F.F.) $750m				1200(c)	550(o)						
Stage 2 (P.S.) $7m							100(c)n.a.(o)				
Shell Smelter - Collie/ Bunbury (P.S.) $620m				1500(c)	100(o)						
NORTHERN WESTERN AUSTRALIA											
Mitchell Plateau - mine and refinery (P.S.) $1,000m				n.a.(c) n.a.(o)							
Alcoa - Cape Bougainville mine and refinery (P)			Timing 1990 and beyond								

Notes:
(a) Sourced mainly from information available in the Commonwealth Department of Industry and Commerce Survey of Major Manufacturing and Mining Investment Projects (December 1980). The caveats applying to that survey also apply to this table.
(b) The letters in brackets here refer to the above Survey's categories as follows: (C) Committed; (F.F.) Final Feasibility; (P.S.) Preliminary Study; and (P) Possible.
(c) The (c) refers to the number of peak construction jobs generated and (o) refers to the number of operational jobs generated by the project.
(d) Excludes $130m transmission line from Melbourne to Portland.
    n.a. Information not available

Source: Department of National Development and Energy (1981)

Overall project management (for all phases of a project) requires;

    a) specialist management and project finance skills, and
    b) personnel on both short–term and long–term contracts.

Immigration has a key role to play in providing such highly specialist skills, on both temporary and long term contracts, for re-source development projects. It also has a role to play in providing a significant proportion of the more general skills and unskilled labour for the projects, because recently arrived migrants are potentially able to move quickly and readily between States and regions.

The role of migrants in resource development should not however be over–estimated. The contribution of migrants to the labour force in any given year is quite small. For the decade ended August 1982 migrants contributed an average increment of approximately 0.5 per cent per annum to the total labour force each year compared with a 2.0 per cent per annum growth in the total labour force.

There are also significant differences between types of migrant. Those migrating to meet labour shortages are highly mobile while others migrating to effect family reunion, for example, are less flexible. The distribution of migrants between States also shows a tendency for more to go to States such as New South Wales and Western Australia, and less to Victoria, South Australia and Tasmania than their shares of national population.

THE IMMIGRATION PROGRAM

The Australian Immigration policy is selective, developed on the basis of benefit to the total community. There is no discrimination on grounds of race, ethnic origin or sex. Migrants are accepted for family reunion, as refugees, or if they have skills or qualities needed in Australia.

The program is designed primarily to meet national long term objectives, based on social and humanitarian as well as economic objectives. Regional and short term needs are, however, taken into account in planning. Thus the intake each year represents a trade–off between a number of short term and long term economic, political and social factors.

Each year the Government decides on the size of the immigration program as part of a rolling triennium. The 1982/83 figure was set for between 115,000 and 120,000 people to be selected for migration to Australia but this number can be varied during the year to take account of short term developments.[1] This overall figure is made up of a number of individual categories. These are family, labour shortage and business, independent, refugee and special humanitarian and special eligibility. The program does not include New Zealanders who under current arrangements are free to come and go as they wish.

33

Table 3.3:   The Immigration Program - Settler Arrivals

3.3 (i):   Year of Arrival

1977/78	75732
1978/79	68749
1979/80	81271
1980/81	111190
1981/82	118700

3.3 (ii):   Components of Settler Arrivals

	1981/82		1980/81	
	No.	per cent	No.	per cent
Family Reunion	21436	18.1	19570	17.6
- Spouses and Dependents	12320	10.4	10311	9.3
- Special Family Reunion	6823	5.7	6715	6.0
- Finance(e)	1557	1.3	1486	1.3
- Other (special approval)	736	0.6	1058	1.0
General Eligibility	57562	48.5	45189	40.6
- Independent applicants	50377	42.4	40776	36.7
- Employment Nominees	7185	6.1	4413	4.0
Special Eligibility	1478	1.2	858	0.8
- Patrials	52	-	79	0.1
- Entrepreneurs	810	0.7	347	0.3
- Retirees	268	0.2	168	0.2
- Others	348	0.3	264	0.2
Refugees	20733	17.5	21847	19.7
New Zealand Citizens	12923	10.9	19053	17.1
O/S born children of Australian citizens	1177	1.0	1545	1.4
Other	1812	1.5	3128	2.8
Total new policy (K codes)	1579	1.3		
Total	118700	100.0	111190	100.0

3.3 (iii): Intended State/Territory of Residence

Intended State/ Territory of Residence	1981/82 No.	per cent	Population Proportion in each State
NSW	44010	37.1	35.1
VIC	28130	23.7	26.5
QLD	16716	14.1	15.7
SA	8008	6.7	8.8
WA	18331	15.4	8.7
TAS	1050	0.9	2.9
Intended State/ Territory of Residence	1981/82 No.	per cent	Population Proportion in each State
NT	1190	1.0	0.8
ACT	1265	1.1	1.5
TOTAL	118700	100.0	100.0

3.3 (iv): Age Structure

Age	1981/82 No.	Per cent
0-4	14696	12.4
5-9	12215	10.3
10-14	10553	8.9
Sub-total 0-4	37464	31.6
15-19	9254	7.8
20-24	14081	11.9
25-29	15982	13.5
30-34	14317	12.1
35-39	9418	7.9
40-44	5535	4.7
45-49	2969	2.5
50-54	2012	1.7
55-59	1692	1.4
60-64	1971	1.7
Sub-total 15-64	77231	65.1
65+	4005	3.4
Total	118700	100.0

3.3 (v): Settler Arrivals by Category and Level of Skill
1981/82

Level of skill	Family Reunion	General Eligibility	Refugees	Special Eligibility	Total
Professional & Technical	890	6708	204	1883	9685
Clerical Comm & Administ	1216	4303	257	1423	7199
Skilled	416	8393	200	1699	10708
Semi-skilled	2117	5540	4195	2074	13926
Unskilled	997	822	5035	592	7446
Not Stated	241	119	1012	93	1465
Sub-total					
Workers	5877	25885	10903	7764	50429
Dependents	15560	31643	11014	10054	68271
Total	21437	57528	21917	17818	118700

Table 3.3 (vi): Expected Migration Numbers by Category for
1982/83

Family Migration

A.	Spouses, Dependent children, fiances and other limited groups of immediate relatives	12,000
B.	Retired parents, working age parents and other limited groups of close relatives	13,000
C.	Non-dependent children, brothers and sisters	19,000

Labour Shortage and Business Migration   28,000[1]

Persons with occupations in shortage, employer
nominations and business migrants

Independent Migration   7,000[2]

Outstanding applicants with occupations not in
shortage (including arrivals issued visas under
old policy)

Refugee and Special Humanitarian Programs   17,000[3]

Refugees largely from Indo-china and Eastern
Europe, and SHP cases from a wide range of countries

Special Eligibility   4,000[4]

Exceptional sporting or creative talents, self-supporting retirees and Australians entering for first time

Total Program   100,000[5]

Trans-Tasman Free Flow Arrivals   14,000
(ie New Zealanders)

Total Arrivals   114,000

(1) This estimate has recently been revised downwards from 28,000 to between 24,000 and 28,000 due to changes to the Occupational Demand Schedule
(2) This has recently been revised downwards from 14,000 — a number of approved applicants will have withdrawn due to the subsequent deterioration in the Australian Labour market and new applications are also expected to decrease
(3) This has been revised from 24,000 due to smaller flows from Eastern Europe and the introduction of a case by case selection policy
(4) Revised from 5,000
(5) Revised from 115,000-120,000

The Role of Immigration

Details of the immigration program, its change over time, break up by categories, occupations and skills, age structure and destination by States, are set out in Table 3.3. The intake figure represents a ceiling and not a target. When prospects for the economy are reasonably bright the annual figure can be used as an upper limit for migration. When economic prospects are clouded some downward adjustment of the program or its composition could be necessary. Thus the actual numbers of migrants entering Australia may be significantly less than the figure set at the beginning of the financial year.

Of the annual intake of migrants, only about 50,000 will join the workforce on arrival. The remainder are dependants, not seeking to join the workforce at the time of arrival, although the children will obviously join the workforce at some later date.

An innovative feature of the new migrant selection system is the provision of points for people intending to settle in designated growth areas. Up to six points may be awarded towards a pass score of 60 in economic/employment assessment. Areas are identified by State and Territory Governments. At this stage only Northern Territory (whole Territory) and Western Australia (all non-metropolitan areas) have been nominated. Other States are still considering. It is likely that the factor will only be relevant to borderline family migration applicants. The points would not be needed by labour shortage applicants with skills in demand in resource development regions.

The Government's entry policies recognise that in addition to migrant settlers, there are many other categories of people who wish to enter Australia for various reasons, and for varying lengths of time. These include everything from highly specialised workers required to set up technologically advanced plant and equipment, highly specialised programmers introducing new software packages, students and trainees and working holiday makers from many countries.

Approximately 60,000 temporary resident visas were issued in 1981/82. Of these only 7,000 were issued to dependants. Thus, the impact on the labour market of new workers entering the labour force in any given year is the same as or possibly more than the permanent entry intake. The cumulative effect is, however, far different. Migrants make a long term cumulative impact, temporary residents do not.

International demands for temporary resident entry are increasing rapidly with the moves towards highly mobile international labour forces, especially for the multinational companies. Resource development projects are generating special demands for temporary residents. For example a deep sea drilling firm may employ a worker for two years in the North Sea, two years in the Gulf of Mexico, and then two years on the North West Shelf.

Other demands come from students seeking to broaden their education; and young people wanting to holiday and work overseas

38

before settling down. This kind of movement could well increase dramatically with our neighbours in the Pacific Basin as a consequence of the trends towards greater economic and social co-operation in the region.

Program Adjustment

In general the immigration program tries to adjust the level of intake and skills in line with labour market needs. Controls to fine tune this adjustment are only available, however, in the labour shortage and parts of the family migration categories.

In the labour shortage category, the main control mechanism is the Occupational Demand Schedule (ODS)(Harris, Struik and Brookbanks, 1982). The schedule is restricted to the main skilled occupations in over 200 broad groups. This covers about 25 per cent of the work-force. Occupations are listed by State and assessed to reflect "average" levels of current demand. It is not possible to disaggregate by regions; nor to identify workers in highly specialised areas, as is common on high technology resource development projects.

The schedule is presently produced by the Department of Employ-ment and Industrial Relations (DEIR) at six monthly intervals. Because of the time lags in the preparation of the schedule, and between approval and arrival, labour shortage migrants can find that the job shortages no longer exist in that location by the time they arrive in Australia. To alleviate this situation, it is intended that DEIR provide information on any major shifts in the labour market which occur between ODS revision, to supplement the ODS. This additional inform-ation will also assist in counselling migrants about the changing job opportunities, especially between regions, before their departure to Australia. In an effort to reduce the time lag itself, the Department of Immigration and Ethnic Affairs (DIEA) has recently issued an instruc-tion that the period for which a migration approval remains valid is now six months instead of twelve months in appropriate parts of the labour demand and family reunion categories.

It is rather more difficult to fine tune skills to labour market needs in the family migration and refugee categories. It is recognised that the most severe labour market problems arise from the intake of unskilled and semi-skilled workers. It is in these areas that the greatest competition is felt with Australian workers. Significantly, these are also the workers who concentrate in the manufacturing and build-ing and construction industries. Migrants in these groups are mainly in the family migration and refugee categories. Even so, policy is applied to bring these areas as far as possible into line with labour market needs. Thus approval under many of the family reunion categories, will only be obtained with arranged employment. The labour market, and immigration program adjustment is discussed more fully in Harris, Struik and Brookbanks (1982). There is, however, something of a paradox in that even during a recession, with high levels of unemployment, employers

Figure 3.2: Changing Structure of the Major Sources of Skilled
Tradesmen 1970/71 to 1980/82

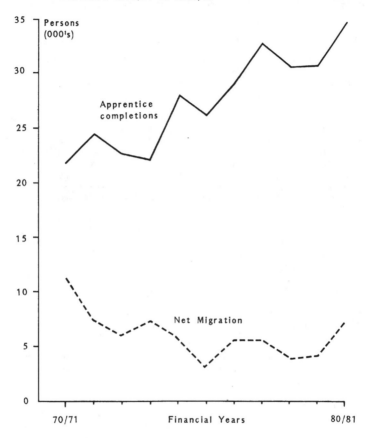

Source: (1) Department of Employment and Industrial Relations

(2) Department of Immigration and Ethnic Affairs –
Consolidated Statistics No 12, 1981 – Skilled Trades

in some regions and industries find it impossible to recruit skilled workers. A special category of labour shortage implemented to meet these problems has been the Employer Nomination Scheme (ENS). This scheme was introduced to meet the special needs of employers. Australian employers unable to satisfy their particular labour requirements locally, can obtain workers through the ENS. However, employment nominations will only be accepted when the nominating employer has demonstrated an inability to recruit or train a suitable employee in Australia, and has a satisfactory record of training.

While the Government permits migration of workers in this way, it places high priority on the training of Australians. The recruitment of overseas workers should not be seen as a substitute for local training, but rather complementary to it. Figure 3.2 shows how the intake of tradesmen in the immigration program has been at a much lower level than apprenticeships. The movements have been in line with overall demand, and are essentially complementary. Unfortunately, the experience of the ENS has been that in many cases, Australian employers have not tried very hard to recruit locally or train workers. In a deteriorating labour market, this cannot be tolerated and recruitment through the ENS will in future only be ratified in the most genuine cases.

Many of the skills required in resource development projects are for short periods only. Under temporary residence policy, the sponsoring employer is required to adequately test the local labour market first. Australian residents are awarded first priority, and thus entry of overseas personnel is permitted only when they possess specialist skills or expertise not readily available in Australia.

Government policy is that the temporary entry adjustment mechanism should not be overused and abused. Australia should not be continually reliant upon the importation of short term labour. Where appropriate, sponsors may be required to introduce a training program to ensure that Australian residents are given the opportunity to acquire specialist skills possessed by the overseas personnel. A requirement is that employment and remuneration of temporary entrants must not be inferior to those enjoyed by Australian personnel in comparable circumstances.

Program adjustment is made difficult because of the long lags in the migration process. There are significant delays in the production of the ODS. The time taken to process applications and for migrants to conclude their various domestic arrangements can add up to around a year between applying and actually arriving in Australia. Pressing the brake to the migrant intake in response to short term economic problems can give a counter-cyclical result. In other words, migrants processed and approved during a time of economic growth may begin to arrive during a downturn, and vice versa.

Table 3.4: Temporary Resident Visas Issued 1981/82

Category	
Company staff	6913
Working holiday makers	8935
Education and research staff	2147
Entertainers and sports people	5482
Professional workers	7758
Technical workers	4654
Other	6045
Dependents	7389
Not available	110
Total	60323

Table 3.5(i): Persons Aged 15 and Over – Who Changed Usual Residence by Birthplace, Year of Arrival, and Type of Move for the Year Ended 31 May 1981

	Within State capital	Other intra- state	Inter- state	Total	Total movers (000s)	Mobility rate
Born in Australia	46.1	43.0	10.8	100.0	1372.2	16.9
Born overseas – arrived post 1976	73.6	14.1	12.1	100.0	88.4	40.9
– 1967–76	72.1	20.3	7.6	100.0	157.2	18.7
– pre 1967	59.4	28.9	11.8	100.0	190.6	12.1
Total overseas born	66.9	22.8	10.3	100.0	436.2	16.6
Total movers	51.1	38.2	10.7	100.0	1808.5	16.8

Source: Internal Migration Australia. Twelve months ended 31 May 1981. ABS Cat. No. 3408.0.

MIGRANTS IN RESOURCE DEVELOPMENT PROJECTS

Migrants working on resource development projects are recruited either: (1) directly from overseas by the project for their specialist skills, with permanent or temporary resident status; or (2) from within Australia to be employed with the general project workforce. The timing of many resource development projects is critical. It is important to be able to get workers with the right skills into development regions quickly and with minimum disruption. It is often argued that migrants, by definition, are more mobile than Australians, and thus have a key role to play. But does this extend beyond the most recently arrived, and is it true for all categories of migrant?

Migrant Mobility

The argument that recently arrived migrants are more mobile than Australian born workers is based on the assumption that they have few ties or commitments to any location, they tend to be younger, they have fewer dependants (either children or old age relatives), and their skills can be pre-selected. It is also argued that migrants are prepared to accept harder working conditions than Australians.

Analysis of mobility rates (defined as the number of persons who changed their place of residence during the previous 12 months per 100 of the population, according to place of residence at the survey date) in the Internal ABS Migration Survey (Table 3.5 i – iii) suggests that:

overall, there is little difference in mobility between Australian born and overseas born (16.9 per cent and 16.6 per cent respectively);

however, for recently arrived migrants, the mobility rate is far higher. Post 1976 arrivals have a rate of 40.9 per cent. This drops to 18.7 per cent for the 1967–76 arrivals, and 12.1 per cent for the pre–1967 arrivals; and

intercensal estimates (1971 to 1976) of mobility indicate that the rates vary between country of birth. UK and Eire born migrants are more – Yugoslav born generally more – and Italians generally less – mobile than Australian born. However, this reflects the different age structures and period of residence of these migrants.

Much of the 'mobility' of migrants however is simply a move within the same State or Territory (90 per cent); or within a capital city (51 per cent). The seemingly high mobility of the recently arrived migrant is often merely a move within the same urban area. The proportion of moves that are within a capital city is higher for migrants than Australian born and increases substantially for recently arrived migrants.

The Role of Immigration

The potential mobility of migrants, especially to move to remote areas, can vary significantly between migrant categories. The variations reflect differences in selection criteria, family and community networks, methods of obtaining jobs both before entering Australia and after arrival, and skills and English language ability.

The "Labour Shortage" and "Business Migration" categories consists of occupations in demand, employment nominees and business migration. The bulk of arrivals are people with occupations in demand, as shown in the ODS as being in shortage or minor shortage. It is expected that these people would be highly flexible in their choice of initial settlement location due to the lack of close family ties and because they have skills which are easily transferable between countries.

The mobility of "General Eligibility Migrants" (a category under previous policy that included both labour shortage and some family reunion migrants) was examined in a DIEA longitudinal survey in 1980. The survey showed that 25 per cent of all moves interstate were for employment related reasons. However in the first six months in Australia 69 per cent of all interstate moves were for these reasons. More migrants moved interstate in the first six months than in the next nine months, and respondents in the professional and technical and skilled classifications tended to be more mobile.

"Family reunion" migrants would be expected to be less flexible in their choice of location due to strong family and community ties. An assurance of support by the sponsors for a specified period is required where the migrant is unlikely to be able to support himself initially. Having relatives in Australia thus effectively determines the initial place of residence as having to be close to that of the sponsor. Subsequent moves would tend to be inhibited by the desire to stay close to the family and community.

Sponsors often pre-arrange jobs or help with obtaining jobs either on arrival in Australia or subsequently if the migrant becomes unemployed. The sponsor must arrange employment where the migrant's occupation is in oversupply in Australia. These migrants are thus unlikely to move large distances, especially to remote or rapidly growing resource development regions for employment reasons.

This provision is supported by some of the findings from the DIEA 1980 Survey of General Eligibility Migrants. Location of friends and relatives was found to be the biggest factor in determining where migrants initially settle, thus restricting on arrival mobility and limiting migrant response to regional occupational demand. Decisions on employment and housing are influenced by friends and relatives. The support of friends and relatives can act as a disincentive to learn English, further reducing flexibility in location and type of employment.

Table 3.5(ii):   Persons Employed for Less Than 12 Months in a
Job who Change their Usual Place of Residence
when Obtaining that Job by Birthplace and
Type of Move (for year ended December 1979)

	Born in Australia	Overseas born	Total
Within capital city	29.8	54.7	35.1
Other intrastate	54.8	30.8	49.7
Interstate	15.4	14.6	15.2
Total percentage	100.0	100.0	100.0
Per cent of total moves	78.6	21.4	100.0

Source: Labour Mobility Australia.   February 1980.   ABS Cat.
No. 6209.0.

Table 3.5(iii):   Movers and Stayers Classified by Country of
Birth, 1971–76

	Born in Australia	UK and Ireland	Italy	Greece	Yugo-slavia	Other Europe	Other	Total
Did not move	60.2	55.1	66.0	56.1	49.7	49.7	47.1	59.4
Moved within LGA	11.3	12.3	12.5	15.7	18.6	11.5	14.2	11.6
Other intrastate	23.5	26.3	19.9	26.0	26.8	23.6	31.5	23.9
Interstate	5.0	6.2	1.5	2.2	4.9	5.2	7.2	5.1
Total percentage	100.0	100.0	100.0	100.0	100.0	100.0	100.0	100.0
Per cent moving	39.8	44.9	34.0	43.9	50.3	40.3	52.9	40.6

Source: Census of Population and Housing (1976).

Table 3.6:   Migrants in Selected LGAs

	Est. residential population 1981	per cent increase 1976-81	Total overseas born per cent	Overseas in 1980 per cent 1980/81 movers
NSW Maitland	41 250	10.1	7.5	10.7
Singleton	28 650	18.5	12.5	6.2
Rest of State	1 956 200	7.7	11.4	2.7
NSW (total)	5 237 068	5.6	20.3	13.6
VIC Morwell	26 280	10.3	20.8	9.6
Traralgon (C)	18 630	16.0	15.7	8.9
Traralgon (S)	3 430	110.0	15.8	5.3
Moe (C)	17 250	7.3	23.1	12.9
Rest of State	1 145 000	5.4	11.9	5.1
VIC (total)	3 948 555	3.6	22.8	11.5
QLD Gladstone	23 960	21.0	14.1	12.6
Broadsound	7 180	109.3	11.8	5.8
Rest of State	1 258 865	15.3	10.7	7.9
QLD (total)	2 345 335	12.1	14.4	9.4
SA Unincorporated	13 950	-0.7	21.5	10.2
Rest of State	366 600	4.7	12.4	5.2
SA	1 319 327	3.5	23.9	9.3
WA Port Hedland	13 610	28.6	28.3	9.4
Roebourne	15 160	54.6	25.4	8.3
West Pilbara	8 850	29.8	29.7	15.5
East Pilbara	9 970	36.8	32.7	15.2
Mandurah	13 700	53.3	19.3	7.0
Waroona	2 500	23.2	19.8	3.5
Collie	9 200	13.9	17.1	9.4
Murray	6 630	24.4	21.9	8.9
Rest of State	381 100	12.7	17.1	7.5
WA (total)	1 299 094	10.2	27.4	14.1
NT Jabiru	1 022	-(a)	19.9	5.6
Tennant Creek	3 148	31.1	15.5	7.6
Rest of State	67 300	20.0	12.3	3.0
NT (total)	124 500	24.1	18.1	8.8

Note: (a) Nil population in 1976.

The other major migrant category, "Refugees", tend to concentrate in the capital cities. The 1981 Population Census indicates that between 88 per cent and 98 per cent of Indochinese refugees (defined as Vietnamese, Laotian and Kampuchean) in each State live in the capital cities (compared to 60 per cent to 70 per cent of the State population in most capital cities). A higher percentage live in Sydney or Melbourne (73 per cent, compared to about 41 per cent of the total population in these cities). This in part reflects the high proportion (about 87 per cent) of refugees who live in a migrant centre on arrival in Australia. These centres are all located in capital cities.

Internal migration of refugees appears to be predominantly towards capital cities and especially to Sydney and Melbourne. In a DIEA study of refugees in 1979/80, comments from residents, friends and welfare organisations indicated movement of refugees from Perth and Adelaide to Sydney and Melbourne. DIEA studies of Community Refugee Settlement Scheme refugees, who are often placed in communities outside the capital cities, indicate that many subsequently move from smaller towns to the capital cities – even from larger urban centres such as Albury-Wodonga.

Studies of refugees indicate that gaining employment is very important to those that perceive job opportunities to be better in large cities. Closeness to the ethnic community and friends and relatives is also important and seen as lacking outside the capital cities.

New Zealanders also tend to be concentrated in the capital cities; in particular Sydney and Brisbane (including the Gold Coast). In Western Australia, however, the concentration of New Zealanders in the Pilbara region is high compared to Perth and the rest of the State indicating that some movement to large resource areas occurs.

Migrants in Resource Development Regions

Despite claims that recently arrived migrants are potentially highly mobile, they nevertheless tend to concentrate more in the capital cities than the population as a whole. In all States except Queensland and the Northern Territory, more than 80 per cent of migrants locate in the capital cities. Migrants, however, make up a significant proportion of the population and workforce in resource development regions.

A number of major resource development regions, especially those experiencing recent rapid growth have been examined in terms of their migrant populations (Table 3.6). Projects in these regions include oil and gas, coal, uranium, iron ore, gold and aluminium smelting and refining.[2]

A number of significant features emerge from the analysis. First, most of the LGAs showed rapid population growth through internal migration in the period 1976–81. Second, the proportion of migrants (defined as overseas born) varied considerably between LGAs. It was

47

highest in the LGAs in North West Western Australia, and lowest in the LGAs of the Hunter Valley in NSW. Third, a high proportion of the most recent arrivals into the LGAs in 1980/81 had been overseas in 1980, i.e. were recently arrived migrants. However, as more information becomes available from the 1981 Census a more detailed look at migrants in these areas can be undertaken.

No published statistics are available on where temporary residents go to work in Australia. There is some indication however that significant numbers, especially of technically skilled workers, go to resource development areas. In New South Wales and Victoria numbers are probably small. It is estimated that about 80 temporary entrants are working in the oil and gas industry in the Gippsland area. In South Australia many temporary residents are outside Adelaide working on the Moomba to Stoney Point pipeline and in mineral exploration. Similarly in Queensland most temporary residents go to outlying areas to work for coal, gas and oil developments. In the Northern Territory a number of temporary entrants brought out by firms go to Jabiru and Tennant Creek. In Western Australia a large proportion go to the North West Shelf as well as into the desert for oil and mineral exploration.

The employment of migrants in the general workforce can be illustrated by the experience of the Pilbara and North West Shelf Region. It is estimated that approximately 40 per cent of the Pilbara region workforce is overseas born: compared to 27 per cent Australian born. At Hammersley Iron in 1978, 36 per cent of employees were overseas born. While both Hammersley Iron and Mount Newman projects employ people from up to 50 different countries, the majority are UK or New Zealand born due to the requirement of the Mining Act for employees to understand English for safety reasons. The workforce tends to be young. Hammersley Iron employed 62 per cent males and 65 per cent of females between the ages of 23 and 37.

Many construction companies and sub-contractors doing site work employ migrants. The proportion of overseas born in the workforce in the Pilbara region has now probably decreased due to the completion of much of the construction work.

In the Pilbara Region labour turnover rates are often high and one company, for example, turned its workforce over 4 times in 10 years. This increases the need to advertise outside the region. Recruitment of unskilled labour, however, tends to be local or from Perth, but for skilled labour recruitment is generally Australia-wide with some overseas. In 1978, Hammersley Iron recruited 57 per cent of its tradesmen outside Western Australia.

The CSIRO "Remote Community Surveys" study in 1971-76 at Mt Isa, Newman, Dampier, Hedland and Nhulunbuy noted that the preferred areas for recruiting skilled workers were capital cities and larger urban areas, and elsewhere for less skilled workers. Overseas born recruitment was high; sometimes from the country of origin, more often after arrival in Western Australia. Many people move for economic reasons especially those who move to new or unattractive inland areas. As the labour market tightens up, firms in this region will recruit less from overses directly. This has already started occurring with more skilled people being recruited within Australia where possible.

Migrants as specialist workers

Although migrants form a high proportion of the general workforce on resource development projects, their major role is more specialised and selective. Many companies bring in highly skilled workers, under both permanent and temporary entry guidelines, to fill specialist needs. For example, such workers have played a key role in the North West Shelf Project.

The Project, located 1300 km north of Perth has been one of the major resource development projects in the past few years. It began in 1979 and consists of offshore production platforms on the North Rankin gas field from which a 135 km submarine pipeline will carry gas and hydrocarbon liquids to shore. Gas will be treated for domestic use by the State Energy Commission and for export as liquid natural gas (LNG). Total cost of the project is around $7 billion. Employment is around 1500 for construction and 800 for production.

The North West Shelf Project has been technologically challenging, and required highly specialised skills in offshore drilling and production not generally found in Australia. Skills in similar offshore oil and gas projects would be more readily found in locations such as Brunei in SE Asia, UK (North Sea), USA and Canada.

The company has tried to recruit key workers in Australia. Workers recruited locally are far cheaper and easier for the company. Recruitment has only been undertaken from overseas where specialist technology is not available in Australia. Many key positions are filled by Australians.

During the construction phase, the company filled around 10 per cent of its workforce from overseas. Many of these workers were brought in under temporary entry visas for their skills in offshore platform construction and drilling. At the same time a small number of senior management were recruited to work on longer term (four to six years) contracts through to completion of construction and commencement of pipeline gas production.

At current levels of overseas recruitment, the company would expect to bring in around three to five per cent each year of its production workforce of 800 under both permanent and temporary residency visas. A shift towards permanent residency would reflect the needs of the longer term operation of the plant. Longer term operational skills recuited from overseas would include fire and safety engineers and platform maintenance supervisors. These are highly specialist positions

49

for which recruitment within Australia is not easy because of lack of similar projects on which workers could gain experience. During the operational phase, however, increasing numbers of Australian workers could be expected to gain specialist training and gradually take over responsibility in these areas.

Most of the specialist staff recruited for this project would be of UK, Dutch, Canadian or American nationality. A special case of overseas recruitment would be the employment of consultants. These could be either seconded for periods of up to two years from associate overseas companies, or consultants brought in for short periods (e.g. three to six months) to install and test specialist equipment.

CONCLUSIONS

The scale of investment in resource development has slackened from its peak in 1980 and 1981, in the face of world recession. Even so, because of long term commitments and lead times in construction, a good deal of resources activity is still taking place. A high proportion is located in non-metropolitan regions.

Immigration has a significant role to play in the provisions of labour for the resource development projects. The role must however be seen in its correct perspective. The major part of the resource development workforce will be recruited from the existing Australian labour force. Training and retraining of Australians will be the major means of filling shortfalls in available skills. Recruitment will obviously include many workers born overseas. It should be noted that migrants are not a homogenous group. Their social and economic characteristics, especially skills and mobility, vary considerably between categories and ethnic groups.

Probably the most important role for immigration is in the direct recruitment from overseas of specialist skilled workers, but only when it has been clearly demonstrated that suitably qualified Australians cannot be found. Often such specialist workers are only required for short periods and will work in Australia under a temporary entry visa.

The resource development projects link Australia to increasingly complex trading relationships with other countries, especially in the Pacific Basin Region. Demand may well increase for entry policy to become more flexible to accommodate the wide range of movements into and out of the country needed to finance, construct, operate and manage the projects. This could lead to "immigration", or the control of entry movement into Australia, playing a stronger role in resource development projects. The kind of immigration that results may well be radically different, however, from traditional Australian concepts of what is a migrant.

NOTES

1. This figure has recently been reduced to between 96,000 and 10,000.

2. The resource developments reviewed in terms of their migrant populations included:

   New South Wales – Port Stephens and Maitland;

   Victoria – The Latrobe Valley LGAs of Morwell, Traralgon (City and Shire) and Moe;

   Queensland – Gladstone and Broadsound (Bowen Basin);

   South Australia – unincorporated (Cooper Basin and Leigh Creek);

   Western Australia – East and West Pilbara, Roebourne and Port Hedland in the North West, Collie, Murray, Waroona and Mandurah in the South East; and

   Northern Territory – Jabiru, Tennant Creek.

4

THE REGIONAL EMPLOYMENT AND POPULATION IMPACTS
OF RESOURCE DEVELOPMENTS

J.A. Gillett and A.D. Robertson

INTRODUCTION

This chapter outlines the need for, and approaches to, preparation of
forecasts of regional employment and demographic impacts of large scale
resource developments in Australia. The chapter draws on work undertaken by Kinhill Pty Ltd in the preparation of environmental impact
studies on a number of projects which represent a cross section of
the regional effects of resource development in urban and remote
locations.

   The chapter describes the need for and expectations that have
arisen with regard to information about the forecast of social and
economic effects of proposed development projects. The dimensions
of the impact of projects are described and the need for information
particularly at the local and regional levels is demonstrated. The
methods used and results of three studies are summarised and the
merits of this individual project assessment approach are discussed
in the conclusions to the chapter.

THE NEED FOR ASSESSMENT OF THE EMPLOYMENT AND DEMOGRAPHIC
EFFECTS OF DEVELOPMENT PROJECTS

Population growth arising from development projects generally gives rise
to a number of effects on existing and new communities. These effects
vary depending on the size and characteristics of the growth stimulus
and on the capacity of the existing community and infrastructure to
absorb growth. Because of this variety and the serious nature of some
effects, it has now become accepted that project impact assessment
should include a comprehensive and soundly based forecast and
assessment of social and economic effects with particular emphasis
on population-related and employment effects.

   A number of regions in Australia have experienced significant
population growth and urban expansion as a result of development
projects. In some areas lack of planning of population impacts has
led to social problems and an unsatisfactory standard of amenity in
the affected towns.

Regional Employment and Population Impacts

Since the world's largest alumina refinery was constructed in the small central Queensland coastal town of Gladstone, the name of Gladstone has become synonymous with the problems caused by ill-planned growth associated with resource development. Initial backlogs in service provision were compounded in later years by the sub-sequent development of other major industries in and near the town. While some actions taken recently should assist in overcoming the difficulties which Gladstone has experienced, there are a number of lessons which can be drawn for other development areas of Australia:

infrastructure backlogs must be understood and rectified before additional demands are added;

likely population-related demands must be anticipated in scale and timing, and the possibility of concurrent projects needs to be considered; and

financial responsibilities for meeting the demands need to be defined and agreed upon prior to the start of development.

The first of these points requires that detailed baseline studies are undertaken so that a comprehensive profile of the region's exist-ing demography and physical services prior to the project is complete. Accurate baseline studies are essential for projecting the scale of the project effects.

The second of the above points gives rise to the need for population projections in the affected region. Population, character-istics are the primary determinants of key elements of costly social infrastructure such as housing, serviced land, community facilities and trunk services, many of which have a significant lead time to allow funding to be arranged for and for construction. The increasing importance of the question of who should pay for the direct and indirect infra-structure requirements is focussing considerable public and political attention on these population projections and the related forecasts of community requirements.

Changes in employment patterns are in turn the primary determinant of population change in most areas of Australia and for this reason project impact assessments must first focus on this variable. However, in an under-employed economy, when projects are introduced into regions of existing population, due account needs to be taken of the number and skills of unemployed or under-employed people already resident in the region.

This combination of population and employment issues has emerged as a key area for improvement of forecasting techniques in order to provide a sound basis for social and economic policies in development regions. In addition, these forecasts are required to form the basis of negotiations between project proponents and governments as to the appropriate financial contribution by proponents to community infrastructure.

54

REGION OF INTEREST

The distribution of impacts is of concern, and each project assessment usually makes a convenient definition of the region of interest in two or three levels.

Local area This is usually a local government area (LGA) or small group of LGAs (such as Portland, Town and Shire for the Alcoa smelter project). Impacts of concern at this level are particularly employment, housing, land, infrastructure, community facilities and the funding of these.

Region This is usually defined to coincide with a pre-existing statistical or study area comprising part of a state (such as the Iron Triangle Area of South Australia for the Olympic Dam Project). The effect of the project on the immediate hinterland, regional employment multiplier effects and indirect impacts on neighbouring towns and other possible projects are of interest at this level.

State and National effects At this level more macro-economic effects are of interest, including value added, balance of payments, inter-industry trade flows, income, output and overall employment multiplier effects.

It is the findings of the authors that the prediction of local and regional effects is of most immediate practical utility because at these levels the impacts are relatively greater. At the local and regional level, employment and population projections are therefore of paramount importance and the rest of this chapter is directed to discussing some approaches to these.

CHARACTERISATION OF TYPES OF PROJECT IMPACT SITUATION

The methods followed to prepare forecasts of employment and population impacts of projects have varied for a number of reasons and a few examples illustrate the need to vary the approach according to the nature of the project and the region.

At one end of the scale of assessment is the remote area project as characterised by the Olympic Dam Project in South Australia (Roxby Management Services and Kinhill Stearns Roger, 1982). In this case the project employment stimulus is to be introduced into a semi-desert region with the nearest settlement being at Andamooka (population about 400) some 30 km to the east. In this case a completely new town is to be built. The effects on the existing pastoral economy will be minimal and virtually all of the project and services jobs will have to be filled by in-migrants to the new town. An important issue therefore is the projected size and characteristics of this town's population. The project is large enough to have regional and state/national implications and it was advantageous that two separate studies were available to provide a context for these (Iron Triangle

Regional Employment and Population Impacts

Study, 1982 and Cook and Trengrove, 1982).

Another situation, perhaps more common than the above, is "the large project near existing small town" situation. This was the situation at Gladstone in the 1960s and also at Portland in Victoria with the advent of the Alcoa Aluminium Smelter. In the Portland case, direct employment at the smelter was forecast to rise to some 1000 people within three years of the project starting (Alcoa of Australia Ltd and Kinhill Planners, 1980). This was forecast to have significant local effects on the town and adjacent shires with a then current total employment of around 6000 (population around 15,000) prior to the smelter beginning operations. With a weak and seasonal economic base, the town was likely to benefit substantially from the smelter but its infrastructure was clearly unable to absorb the change without provision over and above that possible from existing sources.

Another example of a project with a forecast large impact on the local area and region is the proposed 4000MW Driffield Power Project in the Latrobe Valley. Although the region has a relatively large population (urbanised population of 65,000, with some 100,000 people in the immediate region), the project itself is so large as to have a major influence upon the region over a period of several decades (State Electricity Commission of Victoria and Kinhill Pty Ltd, 1981). While the scale of this project is so large as to make it atypical (estimated cost $3500 million, 1980 prices, excluding interest and overheads), the methods of population and employment impact assessment are considered to be relevant for many smaller projects.

A third category of project impact is characterised by a relatively small project in a well established urban area. Examples with which the authors are familiar are the BCLV pilot coal to oil conversion plant in the Latrobe Valley and the major ($400 million) Stage II expansion of the ICI Australia petrochemical plant at Botany in Sydney. In both of these cases the employment issues are important from a local political and social viewpoint, but the projects do not have the same relative impact on population (and hence on population related infrastructure) as the first two examples. The BCLV project is rather uncommon in that it has a short planned life as a research facility. In addition its employment impacts have been forecast to be relatively small compared with the contemporaneous and nearby Loy Yang and possible future Driffield power projects. As planned, the ICI plant was to provide welcome employment in an area of Sydney which had historically lost manufacturing employment, but on a metropolitan scale it was not forecast to influence population patterns and hence the question of social infrastructure was not relevant.

It is clear that the first two situations require the most attention to population and employment effects because of the direct implications for urban management and funding in a local area.

56

METHODOLOGY FOR EMPLOYMENT PROJECTIONS

Since all of the examples quoted above have been the subject of detailed reports, all of which have been made public, it is not necessary to repeat the details of the assessments in this chapter. Rather, the aim is to summarise the different approaches used in the assessment of projects with important local region effects and to compare some of the more important findings.

It should be noted that all methods depend on an accurate assessment of direct project construction and operations employment. It is often very difficult for a proponent to estimate direct employment, especially construction employment. Since this is a basic input to all projections of employment impacts, considerable effort is needed to prepare the best possible estimates of direct employment. The distribution and quantity of indirect and induced employment is usually addressed by using economic models as is illustrated in the examples described below.

The Olympic Dam Project

In the case of the Olympic Dam project, three scales of interest were defined, namely, local, Northern Region and South Australia representing the local, substate and statewide scales respectively. The state economic effects of the $1.4 billion Olympic Dam copper and uranium project in South Australia were estimated using a twenty-five sector Input-Output (I-O) model of the South Australia economy constructed by the Centre of Policy Studies (CoPS) (Cook and Trengrove, 1982). The regional effects were estimated using the result of the Iron Triangle Study (ITS, 1982).

The CoPS model

The CoPS model estimated the project effects on output, prices and employment within South Australia using three different scenarios, each embodying different assumptions about the ability of the South Australian economy to respond to the project's requirements. These were labelled 'optimistic', 'pessimistic' and 'probable'. Because this approach attempts to represent a more dynamic, interactive method of estimating the project economic effects, its assumptions are presented in more detail below.

The Optimistic scenario
For this set of circumstances the standard assumptions of the static I-O model are adopted, which assumes that all inputs in production are required in fixed proportion to output and that all factor and commodity supplies are available at established prices which do not rise in response to increased demand. A limitation of the optimistic case is that, in practice, some supply bottlenecks may occur. Consequently some demand may be switched away from locally produced commodities toward those imported from outside the region. By

57

Regional Employment and Population Impacts

Table 4.1:   Type II Employment Multiplier, Olympic Dam

Region	Construction Phase	Production Phase
South Australia:		
— Optimistic	9.5	3.43
— Probable	7.0	2.67
— Pessimistic	4.76	2.35
— Iron triangle study	5.5	3.5
Northern region:		
— Port Augusta	0.2	0.15
— Whyalla	0.3	0.1
— Olympic Dam	1.15	1.3
— Northern region	1.8	1.7

Source: cook and Trengrove (1982) and ITS (1982).

Table 4.2:   Distribution of Olympic Dam Employment Effects
within South Australia(a)

Region	Construction Phase	Production Phase
South Australia:		
— Optimistic	18,600	8,300
— Probable	13,800	6,500
— Pessimistic	9,300	5,700
— ITS	10,800	8,500
Northern region:		
— Port Augusta	390	365
— Whyalla	590	245
— Olympic Dam	295	730
— Other	295	360
Sub total northern region	1,570	1,700

Note: (a) Assuming average construction employment of 1,960
workers per annum and average production workforce of
2,248 workers per annum.

Source: Cook and Trengrove (1982).

not allowing for this possibility, the optimistic case probably overstates the effect of the Olympic Dam project on the Australian economy.

The pessimistic scenaro Under these circumstances attempts are made to include the price effects of the supply and demand situation caused by the project's construction and production expenditure. Assumptions are made about the ability of South Australian producers to supply various goods and services to the project. It is assumed that competition for the available scarce factors of production drives up the prices of such South Australian goods and services, leading to the substitution of imported goods from other States. This case is likely to understate the effects of the project, because it assumes that locally produced and externally produced commodities are perfectly interchangeable, and that even the slightest pressure on prices (through supply bottlenecks) in South Australia would result in a large increase in imports.

The probable scenario This set of circumstances is similar to the pessimistic set in attempting to take into account the capacity of the South Australian economy to supply the project's requirements, but differs in assuming only a moderate degree of substitutability between imported and South Australian produced commodities. These factors allow for some freedom of price movement as the South Australian economy adjusts to the new supply and demand balance likely to flow from the project's requirements.

The probable scenario was held to be a more accurate reflection of the project's effects on the South Australian economy. An important assumption of this model was that relative real wages in South Australia will not increase at a faster rate then the rest of the nation. If real wages were to increase at a greater rate, then the number of jobs generated for South Australians by the Project would be reduced. The reason lies in the cost-increasing effect on those sectors which have prices largely determined by conditions outside South Australia. These sectors would be unable to fully recover cost increases, and consequently would experience contracting output and employment. The effect of the project on material costs is likely to be very small, but the effect of any increase in nominal wages would be much more substantial.

The Iron Triangle Study (ITS)

The ITS used the Generation of Regional Input-Output (GRIT) system of tables to simulate the output and employment effects of the Olympic Dam Project on the Northern Region and on the South Australian economy as a whole. The GRIT model adopts the usual assumptions of the standard input-output model (similar to the optimistic case described above). The ITS used data from interviews with industry

Table 4.3:   Employment Multipliers Assumed for Portland Smelter

Multiplier	Portland area	Victoria including Portland area	Australia including Victoria
Construction phase			
Type I	1.15	1.67	1.88
Type II	b	2.66	3.61
Operational phase			
Type I	1.15[a]	1.33	1.34
Type II	1.80[c]	3.13	3.78

Notes:

(a) Reduced from Gladstone's 1.19 to 1.15
(b) Not used in regional assessment
(c) Reduced from Gladstone's 1.92 to 1.80.

Source: Mandeville and Jensen, 1978, except as noted above.

groups in the Iron Triangle region to improve the accuracy of the model. Adjustments were made to allow for the temporary construction workforce spending only a proportion of its wages within the region, consequently reducing the consumption induced effects which are an important component of the total employment effects.

Results

Table 4.1 outlines the employment multipliers produced fom the CoPS report and those from the Iron Triangle Study. The CoPS study estimated multipliers for the whole state only. The ITS Type II employment multipliers derived from the GRIT I–O tables for the whole of South Australia of 5.5 for the construction phase and 3.5 for the production phase are similar to the lower and upper range of the CoPS Type II employment multipliers of 4.76–9.5 for the construction phase and 2.35–3.43 for the production phase. Table 4.2 outlines the CoPS estimate of the project effects on the South Australian economy together with the results of the Iron Triangle Study estimates of the economic effects for the Northern Region and the major urban centres in this region.

These two approaches to the assessment of the effects of the Olympic Dam project are interesting because they allow the comparison of the relatively sophisticated CoPS approach (incorporating varying assumptions regarding the adaptability of the South Australian economy), with the simpler and more widely used GRIT I–O approach. It is interesting that the ITS result lies between the 'pessimistic' and 'probable' CoPS results for employment multiplier. Thus with some confidence, the ITS results for multipliers in the Northern Region of South Australia can be used. For the projection of population and the related design of the Olympic Dam township, an employment multiplier of 1.3 in the production phase was used.

The Portland Aluminium Smelter

In the case of the proposed Alcoa Aluminium smelter at Portland, Victoria, the Type I and II employment multipliers were derived from Mandeville and Jensen's (1979) work on the Gladstone smelter in the absence of available regional I–O tables. These multipliers are listed in Table 4.3. The Gladstone smelter Type I and II employment multipliers were adjusted to take account of the low relative development of the Portland economy compared with Gladstone. In addition, the Type I employment multiplier was used rather than the Type II multiplier to estimate the construction phase employment effects on the grounds that the construction phase would be too short to allow the full multiplier effects to occur.

An estimate of the employment effects of the smelter on the Portland region was derived using the total employment (direct, indirect and induced) likely to be generated by the project and an estimate of the number of jobs that would be filled from the existing regional

Table 4.4:   Forecast of Employment in Portland Town and Shire
with Effect of Smelter

Component of employment	Year		
	1980	1985	1990
Portland labour force without smelter:			
• employed	6000	6000	6000
• unemployed	600	600	600
• potential workforce	300	300	300
Potential workforce available (if participation rates increased to Australian average and if unemployment falls to Australian average)			
Direct construction workforce	260	300	300
Direct operating workforce	–	611	1177
Indirect employment construction phase	26	45	–
Indirect employment operating phase	–	92	177
Induced employment operating phase	–	–	549
Total new employment	286	1048	1903
Employees already resident			
• construction	130	150	–
• other	–	305	500
• total	130	455	500
Net new employees from outside region			
• construction	130	150	–
• other	26	443	1403
• total	156	593	1403

labour market. The ability of the local labour market to supply workers to the smelter was based on assumptions regarding current numbers of suitably skilled workers, unemployment levels and participation rates. Table 4.4 outlines the assumed breakdown into resident and non-resident employees. The table assumes that the local labour market would have been able to supply a maximum of approximately 500 workers to the smelter. The remainder were assumed to migrate to the region. The assumption that some of the jobs would be filled by existing residents was reflected in the population projections for the town.

The Driffield Power Project

The regional economic and demographic effects of the Driffield Power Project were assessed for the four LGAs which comprise the central Latrobe Valley area. The existing GRIT I-O table for Gippsland based on 1976/77 data was revised in the light of limited superior data for the Latrobe Valley, mainly from a 1978 survey of manufacturing firms in the region, and the table was altered to reflect the Gippsland Energy Resources Area (essentially the area of Central and South Gippsland). The regional output, income and employment multipliers are outlined in Table 4.5.

An economic base multiplier of 1.9 was estimated for the power generation and coal mining industrial sectors from the existing economic structure of the region. This figure was used on conjunction with the I-O employment multiplier to define an employment multiplier range of between 1.7-1.9. The average employment multiplier of 1.8 was used to estimate the total employment effects of the project in the Latrobe Valley. These results are listed in Table 4.6.

Unlike Portland, the Latrobe Valley was not assessed to have a large number of unemployed to the extent that the full employment multiplier was assumed to flow through to population growth.

The higher regional multiplier of 1.8 assumed for Olympic Dam or Portland, reflects the existing regional industrial development and capacity for local industry to benefit from the project. This contrasts with the comparatively low involvement of the local regional economies in the case of the Portland and Olympic Dam projects in supplying the projects requiremets for goods and services.

METHODOLOGY FOR POPULATION PROJECTIONS

The methods for projecting populations in the project areas were all based on the projections of direct and multiplier employment. Different approaches were used in the three examples reflecting the different circumstances.

63

Table 4.5:   Regional Output, Income and Employment Multipliers,
              Latrobe Valley

Multiplier type		Construction phase	Operations phase
Output	– Type I	1.16	1.13
	– Type II	1.22	1.24
Income	– Type I	1.07	1.11
	– Type II	1.22	1.27
Employment	– Type I	1.32	1.30
	– Type II	1.68	1.73

Source: State Electricity Commission of Victoria   and   Kinhill
        (1981).

Table 4.6:   Direct and Regional Multiplier Employment Estimates
              for Proposed Driffield Project

Employment	1991	1994[a]	1996	2000
Direct construction	2000	2800	1800	300
Direct operations	500	1650	2550	2050
Total direct	2500	4450	4350	3350
Indirect and induced[b]	2000	3560	3480	2680
Total employment in Latrobe Valley	4500	8010	7830	6030

Notes:

(a)   1994 is peak year for construction employment.
(b)   Multiplier assumed to be 1.8.

Olympic Dam

Population was projected for the new township by applying a mixture of experience from other remote mining town and housing and recruitment policies to be implemented by the proponent. The proponent has previous experience of building and operating remote area towns and this formed the basis of a policy to maximise the recruitment of married employees and to encourage permanent settlement in the new town. Caravan park accommodation and a single men's construction village are proposed for a proportion of the workforce.

The population was projected by applying previous mining town experience (mainly from Kambalda) to the assessed numbers of the proponent workforce, the contractor workforce and the non-project workforce. In each category the numbers of married heads of households, dependant workers and single status workers were estimated. In turn, necessary accommodation types and occupancy rates were estimated, and an overall population estimate derived. For production year four and a total town workforce estimated to be 3130, a population of 7900 was estimated (an overall population multiplier of 2.52 for each employed worker in the town).

For the construction years a similar approach was adopted and the number accommodated in the construction village was forecast to rise to around 2500 people during the peak construction years, falling away to zero when the production level stabilises.

Portland

The historic patterns of population movement in the Portland area were analysed to assess the prospects of growth in the absence of a growth stimulus (i.e. without the smelter). Both the Town and Shire of Portland have a history of out-migration, the Shire showing an actual decline. Detailed population projections for the Town and Shire were available from a comprehensive forecast of populations in all Victorian LGAs up to 1996. These projections were consistent with State Co-ordination Council projections for Victoria. In the case of Portland, no special allowance was made for the smelter because it had not been announced at the time. These projections were therefore representative of a no smelter situation and the outcome was expected to be a virtually static population in the Town and Shire combined. This projection reflected expectation of a static labour force. In 1979 unemployment was significantly higher in Portland (9.7 per cent of the workforce) than in Melbourne (5.8 per cent) and non-metropolitan Victoria (7.5 per cent).

The registered unemployment was primarily among people working in (male) unskilled and (female) commercial occupations. The picture was of serious unemployment in the Portland area. The impact of the smelter would be beneficial to many of these people but an important question was how many jobs could be filled by local people and how

65

Table 4.7: Forecast of Population in Portland Town and Shire with Effect of Smelter

Component of Population	Year		
	1980	1985	1990
Portland population without smelter	15250	15250	15250
New population associated with construction[b]	236	273	→
New population associated with operations indirect and induced effects[c]	62	1055	3340
Total population increment due to smelter	298	1328	3340
Forecast population of Portland with smelter	15548	16578	18590

Notes:

(a) From Table 5.4 rounded.
(b) Assuming participation rate of 55 per cent and allowing for up to half of the jobs to be filled by people presently resident.
(c) Assuming participation rate of 42 per cent and allowing for up to half of the jobs to be filled by people presently resident.

many would require skills not available locally. An analysis of occupations required at the smelter and skills available to the unemployed
led to the estimated resident and non—resident employment projections
shown in Table 4.4 and these were extended into population projections assuming up to half of the jobs could be filled by residents and
using employment participation rates as shown in Table 4.7.

Driffield Power Project

As for Portland, the methodology adopted in relation to the Driffield
Power Project first involved estimation of the expected growth rate of
the Latrobe Valley region in the absence of the project. The region
has a history of growth but this could be shown to correlate strongly
with periods of SEC employment growth. In the absence of new basic
employment from coal based projects, the region was likely to stagnate
after the current growth impetus of the Loy Yang and other projects
had faded. As for Portland, the 1979 statewide projections were based
on such a scenario and these showed population growth tapering off
by the end of the 1980s.

Unemployment in the region was analysed and was found to be
less problematic than in Victoria as a whole and in the Metropolitan
area, especially in adult male employment. The last regional figures
available from the Commonwealth Employment Service (CES) showed a
ratio of registered unemployed to vacancies of 2.1 for adults in the
Morwell employment district compared with 17.3 in Melbourne and 15.9
in Victoria. On this basis it was assumed that there was no significant
pool of unemployment which would affect population projections and
all new jobs were assumed to require a net increase in the region's
workforce.

Analysis of employment participation indicated that the Latrobe
Valley had been approaching Victorian trends. A changing age profile
of the population was forecast to result in a steady increase in the
proportion of the total population employed from around 39.5 per cent
in 1976 to 43.2 per cent by the end of the century. Converting these
figures to multipliers, the following were used:

Employment multiplier	1.7–1.9
Population multiplier	2.3–2.5
Range of overall multiplier	4.3–4.8

An overall 'people' multiplier of 4.6 was used to multiply the
basic jobs created by the project to convert the direct construction
and population workforce into population estimates.

An additional component of the input assessment for this project
was the need to consider simultaneous resource development projects
in the region. Some projects were planned or committed such as the
Loy Yang project, the BCLV pilot plant and the APM Maryvale pulp mill
expansion. Other power projects were notionally assumed to commence

67

before completion of Driffield. However in the absence of public data on non-power generation coal projects, no allowance could be made for these.

The Driffield Project assessment therefore virtually required a regional assessment incorporating an overall regional population. The Driffield proportion of the growth was calculated to show the relative direct impact on the Driffield workforce and related population.

Of great importance was the location of the population impacts. Spatial analysis of historic location patterns of SEC workers was undertaken and a future pattern was derived assuming similar locational choices as in the past with respect to distance from work and attraction to the main towns. Although these locational projections could only be approximate, further division of population between the towns in Morwell Shire was undertaken. In each area, the approximate proportion allocated to the Driffield Project was estimated.

APPPLICATION OF THE FORECASTS

There is an obvious need from an urban management and equity point of view to inform the community and governments of the population impacts of major projects and the examples quoted here have fulfilled that purpose. In the case of Olympic Dam a detailed Indenture Agreement was negotiated between the proponents and the State Government and embodied in an Act of Parliament. That agreement contained detailed provisions and the relative responsibilities of the parties for provision of urban infrastructure based on the forecasts of population and employment. At Portland, assessment of social impact gave rise to a negotiated agreement on Council rates, and to the decision by Alcoa to make direct provision of housing for its workers.

In the Latrobe Valley, for the first time a planned major power project has been placed in the context of the region. A healthy employment and population growth was forecast for the region as a result of the project, and data was provided to allow the debate on who should pay for community infrastructure to be carried on in the public enquiry process to which the project is being subjected.

This latter case revealed the need for a regional framework for population and employment projections in situations where a number of major projects may proceed simultaneously. There are several regions in Australia where such a need exists and the collection and dissemination of regional employment data should be encouraged. In this respect the lack of regional unemployment data since the demise of Commonwealth Employment Service publication of registration by region is a particular concern. It would be beneficial for future regional impact analysis if this data could again be collected and published.

5

SOME PLANNING PROBLEMS IN THE PROVISION OF EDUCATION FACILITIES IN QUEENSLAND RESOURCE DEVELOPMENT AREAS: AN INITIAL OVERVIEW

G.J. Butler and L.G. Harris

INTRODUCTION

> "The discovery of gold was the dominant factor in the dramatic formation of Queensland towns — characterized in the main by their sprawling ugliness and the brash optimism of their inhabitants ... Banks, stores, shanties and other buildings of wood and iron, had sprung, as if by magic, from the ground ... Charters Towers ... had risen spectacularly ... With a population of over twenty thousand, it remained second only to the capital and a monument to the nineteenth century cult of progress ... It became such a mining, business and social centre for north Queensland that it was referred to far and wide as "The World" — indicative, perhaps of the degree of parochialism engendered in Queensland society towards the end of the last century". [But the author adds] "In Queensland, as in the south, the exultation of the boom years was, in most cases, followed by a period of stagnation".

These words by Fitzgerald (1982, p.20) deserve to be reflected upon for a moment. The parallels with present resource development, though somewhat different in degree and kind, are nevertheless just as relevant.

EDUCATIONAL CONSEQUENCES OF RAPID DEVELOPMENT

As was the case in the nineteenth century, resource development — though in the main far less labour intensive today — still causes rapid population growth and associated social and economic disruptions in the areas directly affected.[1] Mining and related resource towns have until recent times suffered to varying degrees from a lack of adequate social infrastructure such as educational, recreational and other community facilities. However, sheer population growth is not the sole contributing factor. Two demographic characteristics which exacerbate the problem are extremely high rates of population turnover and the relative inbalance of age structure. For example, the population structure of mining towns is usually over-represented in the five to nine and 20 to 40 age groups.

In a major survey of mining communities, Brealey and Newton (1980) found adverse comment on education in most towns.[2] In fact, they found that, "...a major factor often cited as affecting the lengh of residence of families in mining townships is the conern held for the children's future" (Brealey and Newton, 1980, p.). Of major concern was the lack of adequate school facilities, particularly for secondary education, as well as the lack of opportunities for school leavers.

High rates of workforce turnover significantly influence the performance of mining companies.[3] For example, staff training costs increase, and staff morale and therefore productivity can fall. On the other hand, mining companies also point out that too low a turnover of employees in these isolated and atypical communities can also have consequences. What is often not recognised is that a high turnover of workers and the resulting movement of children through schools can put a considerable strain on these schools to maintain their quality of education provision. Though not as tangible as a loss of company profits, the costs to the community generally and to the children and schools concerned, in particular, from problems attributable to high student turnover are just as real. The only major Australian studies on the consequences of student turnover, by Bourke and Naylor (1971) and Mackay and Spicer (1975), found that the short-term adverse effects on both the student and the education system can be quite substantial. Therefore, when providing education facilities in resource-based communities, recognition should not only be taken of net enrolment changes but also of turnover within the student population.

There are a number of spatial and demographic characteristics of resource communities that need to be fully appreciatd when planning for education services. First, areas about to be influenced by resource development are usually characterised either by a complete absence of education facilities (new mining towns) or have inadequate facilities to cope with the proposed development (expansion of an existing mining town or an agricultural town). If, in contrast, there is a significant influx of school children into a certain section of a metropolitan area due to a large residential development, then it is highly probable that these children can be relatively easily assimilated into a number of existing government schools. However, if the same influx of population occurs in a remote area then it is most likely that there will be no school at all, or at best, one that is too small to cope with growth. Therefore, accuracy in enrolment forecasting for resource development areas is imperative. More generally, while enrolment growth in absolute terms for mining areas is not comparable to

70

that in the metropolitan area, the impact on resource allocation within the education department is relatively greater. One reason for this is that unlike the metropolitan situation where the impact is more diffuse, in the mining centres the impact is concentrated in one or two schools.

A second important, and related, factor associated with mining towns is that their school populations are almost "instant", and fore-casting the precise time for arrival of these populations is in some instances difficult. This is so because the size of the workforce, and resulting enrolments depend on the timing and staging of the par-ticular project, which in turn is dependent upon such factors as market forces, internal company finances, company market commitments and development priorities. A change in these factors will inevitably result in a change in the educational needs of the mining town. In view of the lead time required to have school facilities incorporated in the works programming, it is essential that the planning process be able to anticipate changes in the development priorities of mining companies and to respond quickly.

Third, population growth in mining towns is exceptionally rapid in the initial years of development, particularly as the project moves from the construction to the operational phase.[4] Unlike urban areas where new schools are usually built when enrolments in existing schools reach a certain point, resource areas have to be provided with some form of school accommodation once a "reasonable" number of students reside in a particular area.[5] Compared to most large urban areas, schools in resource areas usually have an opening enrolment which is somewhat lower, but which grows very rapidly over the first few years. This intense pressure is usually felt first in the pre-school and primary school area with secondary school needs manifesting themselves only in the latter stages of development. Primary school chidren are usually not expected to travel long distances to attend school. consequently, nearly all remote communities of varying popula-tion sizes have their own primary school. Secondary schools are a more expensive proposition per student, due to the necessary pro-vision of certain facilities like science blocks and libraries, and a larger population base is desirable.[6] Consequently, secondary school facilities are usually provided on a more 'regional' basis.

GOVERNMENT RESPONSE TO THE PROBLEM

In recent years considerable attention has been focussed on mini-mising some of the adverse economic and social effects of rapid population growth, turnover, and the peculiar demographic structures, associated with resource development. In particular, the educational consequences of resource development discussed above, are import-ant constraints when planning for the adequate provision of schools. The Government, resource developers and the community generally now agree that comprehensive planning is essential in order to at least alleviate, if not remove, some of the more pressing problems that

71

usually arise in communities affected by new mining developments.

Governments now require an Impact Assessment Study (IAS) whenever any major development is undertaken. Part of this study is an assessment of the likely workforce size and structure, and the concomitant demographic profile for the population in the area concerned. From this the demand for various community facilities and residential facilities such as education, health, welfare services, road and sewerage can be ascertained.

The provision of educational facilities in Queensland involves two State government departments, namely the Department of Education and the Works Department. The Department of Education identifies the need for educational facilities in the State and assigns priorities for construction. This list is approved and modified as necessary. The Works Department is responsible for the construction and provision of school buildings. The role played by the Department of Education's Planning Branch in the provision of educational facilities is to estimate the magnitude and composition over time of school enrolments and the resulting manpower and accommodation needs. Despite the apparent simplicity of this task, the actual planning process itself is extremely complex and fraught with both organisational problems and major data deficiencies.

OUTLINE

The aim of this chapter is three-fold. First, it describes some of the more important aspects of Planning Branch's involvement in the process of supplying appropriate education facilities in resource development areas. In the course of this discussion, data deficiencies and organisational problems encountered in the planning process will be highlighted. Second, it documents current and planned research being undertaken by Planning Branch to overcome some of the major data deficiencies facing planners in this area. The findings of a study of the size, composition and consequences of student turnover in Queensland mining towns are discussed. As well some initial results from a major planned research project into the population and workforce profiles of resource areas are summarised. Third, possible improvements to the education planning process are then considered.

This chapter does not comment on Fitzgerald's historical observation about boom years, being usually followed by a period of stagnation. Nor does it discuss the current downturn in mining and associated development activity, and future prospects in the industry. However, this is not to say that planning in this area should follow the downturn. On the contrary, now is the time to introduce some long overdue planning initiatives so that when mining activity does pick up again and pressure mounts for the provision of facilities, the appropriate Government departments will have more confidence in their planning procedures.

PLANNING BRANCH'S ROLE IN THE PROVISION OF EDUCATIONAL FACILITIES FOR RESOURCE PROJECTS

The Planning Branch of the Queensland Department of Education is responsible for a large number of Departmental planning activities and plays an important role in providing basic information for Departmental decision-making. The activities undertaken by the Branch may be grouped into five major categories: statistics, investigations, plan formulation, plan implementation and monitoring, and policy and analysis. Planning for the provision of educational facilities for resource projects is a specific responsibility of the Demography and Manpower Section of Planning Branch.

In practice, the forecast of the magnitude and composition over time of school enrolments and resulting accommodation needs, is often an extremely involved and time consuming procedure.

This section describes some of the more important aspects of our involvement and the organisational procedures required. Perhaps the most appropriate introduction to describing our involvement is to discuss the basic information needs of the Department in planning for resource areas.

INFORMATION NEEDS OF THE DEPARTMENT

The provision of education facilities is both population sensitive and locationally specific. The type of information required by this Department for planning purposes must reflect these two characteristics.

Firstly, to enable adequate assessment of student yields (e.g. school children per married worker) associated with a project, a demographic profile of the proposed workforce is required. Specifically, detailed information on, or an informed estimate of, the following is essential for such an assessment: the single to married ratio, the number of dependants, average family size and the age structure of the workforce. It is also necessary to identify the 'staging' of increments to the workforce, as well as to delineate between the anticipated component of the workforce that will need to be imported into the local area and the component of the workforce that will be derived from the local area. The latter information is required in order to avoid double-counting of components of the workforce and hence anticipated student enrolments, and is of particular importance when mining activity is grafted onto an existing economic base.

Secondly, the locationally specific nature of educational provision necessitates that some indication be given of the intended geographic location of the housing of the workforce, both within and relative to, existing towns and/or cities. Further, if a project includes several development sites, and/or some related developments, then it is important to know the profile of the workforce and the population likely to be associated with each site and each development. In

addition, information concerning access routes and transport availability is required, in order to assess the feasibility of busing students
to existing schools, as opposed to establishing new facilities.

These and other information needs are set down in guidelines
produced by Planning Branch as requirements of the Department of
Education for inclusion in impact assessment studies undertaken by
or for resource development companies. These are discussed now.

Staging and timing of project

A prime information requirement once the project is actually announced
as going ahead is the timing of the various stages i.e. construction,
construction–operation and operation. It is sometimes very difficult
because of the variability of market forces to be precise in this regard.
Consequently, consultation between the Department and the developers
about timing of project stages is an ongoing process. For example, in
a new mining town students are sometimes housed in temporary
accommodation at the actual mine site during the construction phase,
while permanent accommodation is built in the proposed town in time
for the commencement of mining operations. Since the operational phase
coincides with a rapid growth in enrolments, it is therefore essential
that suitable accommodation be available at the appropriate time.

Workforce and population profile

As mentioned previously resource areas have certain demographic
features which make education planning for them a vastly different and
in some respects more demanding task than that for urban areas. It
is essential of course to distinguish between the construction workforce and the operation workforce. The following profile needs to be
established for the construction and operations workforce.

A comprehensive statement of demographic characteristics of the
expected workforce is essential. This should include the ratio of
single and married workers, married workers with children and average
family size and age profile of workforce, plus associated assumptions.

Any estimated overlap within the workforce as a result of two–income
families is required. The proportion of two–income families will vary between
towns, according to the size and diversity of the area's economic base.

A time profile of the build–up of the workforce preferably by
quarterly periods, including its location are also required. Additional
workforce data of importance in educational planning are the source
of the workforce, the size of the existing workforce and its capacity
to supply the skills directly required for the project, and the turnover
rate of the workforce.

In addition to mining and associated skills demanded during the
construction and operation phases, the increased population will lead

to a rise in demand for general goods and services within the town. This indirect effect should increase employment in the service sector of the workforce. The increase in job opportunities for this sector is usually more marked during the operational phase than during the construction phase.

Finally, estimates of the number and timing of Government personnel involved with other aspects of the project (apart from education) are necessary. These would, for example, include additional Railways and Queensland Water Resources Commission personnel.

Accommodation

Another requirement is a statement of the manner in which the company proposes to accommodate its workforce, both construction and operational, the timing and location of such housing, and how the company see this as fitting into the existing town structure, where applicable. The form of accommodation available in a town can sometimes influence the type of family coming to the area and thus affect the number of schools required. Although this will be reflected of course in the composition of the workforce expected by the company, it is, nevertheless, a valuable additional piece of information which will enable a more reliable student yield to be derived.

More specifically, information on various types of accommodation is desirable. A profile of proposed sub-division projects, if applicable, specifying the following detail is required: a plan of proposed subdivision; rate of housing construction either on a quarterly basis or by contract number and completion date; occupancy basis, for example, home ownership or rental; construction authority, for example, the company, Queensland Housing Commission, local entrepreneurs, etc. The department also requires information on the possible size and location of hostels, caravan parks, existing housing and borading houses. Details such as numbers to be housed, occupancy basis, location, timing, construction authority and management basis are needed for the above.

Transportation routes

Also essential to the planning process is some description of the existing and proposed access roads and transportation modes. Such a statement should include the distance from the mine site or project to the residential location of the workforce, the distance between any construction camps and the nearest major centre and/or other construction camps, the date when any access roads between population centres will become usable, the condition and type of roads and anticipated travel time, and finally the transport proposed by the company.

These transport-related factors can have an important bearing on the provision of education facilities. For example, if there is not

75

suitable access between the project site and a nearby major centre then school facilities would most likely be provided at the site. How—ever, if the company proposes to upgrade the road link between the project site and the larger centre, than some children who would have otherwise attended school at the project, may now commute to this nearby town.

SOME MAJOR DATA PROBLEMS AND THEIR IMPLICATIONS

The information requirements specified above represent the 'total' in—formation needed by the Department of Education to adequately assess the impact of a development project on the demand for education facilities. It is acknowledged that these information requirements are detailed and extensive, and that it could be considered that they represent an almost ideal situation. However, if detailed and comprehen—sive planning is to be undertaken for the provision of educational facilities, then the input information has to be similarly detailed and comprehensive. If this is not the case, the planning undertaken may reflect the shortcomings of the data. While it is important that the information be provided, it is realised that a company's plans are dependent, to a certain extent, on prevailing market conditions. Further, the company, and for that matter other departments, may be reluctant to "show their hand", even to a government department. Hence the company is often unable to provide the information in as detailed, accurate and timely a form as is required.[7]

Most 'official' information relating to proposed developments is in the main provided to the relevant government departments by the companies concerned, in the form of the Impact Assessment Study (IAS), which is a necessary requirement under the State Development and Public Works Organisation Act, 1971–1981. However, data provided in the IAS are often vague and descriptive rather than quantative, and are sometimes based on dated studies. As well it is not uncommon for assumptions referring to similar data bases to vary amongst consultants. For example, the assumed percentage of the construction workforce that is married with families has varied from 25 per cent to 80 per cent in assessment studies undertaken recently. Little, if any, justification is given for the particular value chosen. This often unexplained variation makes the task of accurate—ly assessing the demand for education facilities extremely difficult indeed. For instance, a workforce of, say, 100 with a 25 per cent married component can be expected based on Planning Branch esti—mates to yield around 24 primary and secondary school aged children (see Table 5.7). However, if 80 per cent of this workforce is married then the likely number of primary and secondary children will be around 75. This is a variation of about 50 students, which in practical terms equates to two or three teachers and perhaps the same number of classrooms.

The cost of constructing a primary school in most resource development areas is conservatively estimated to be 1.5 times that for

Table 5.1: Comparison of Estimated Primary School Construction
Costs for Brisbane and Mining Towns

Construction component	Enrolment size			
	360 (Brisbane)	360[a] (Mining)	720 (Brisbane)	1 400[b] (Brisbane)
Teaching blocks	426 000	639 000	852 000	1 905 000
Other building	487 000	730 500	701 000	–
Site works etc	357 000	535 500	387 000	–
Total[c]	1 270 000	1 905 000	1 940 000	1 905 000

Notes:

(a) This is allowing a cost index of 1.5.

(b) This is the extra number of students that can be accommodated in existing Brisbane schools for the same cost as
accommodating 360 students in new schools in a mining
town.

(c) Excludes site acquisition.

77

the Brisbane area. Table 5.1 compares the estimated primary school construction costs in Brisbane and mining towns for similar and differing enrolment sizes. A primary school to accommodate 360 pupils costs approximately $1.3 million in Brisbane but $1.9 million in mining areas. Because not all construction component costs increase proportionately with the enrolment size, it is possible to build a new school in Brisbane to house 720 pupils for almost the same cost it takes to house 360 pupils in a new school in a mining centre. Further, it is also possible, at the extreme, to accommodate an extra 1,400 students in existing Brisbane schools for the same cost as accommodating 360 students in a new school in a mining area. Consequently, the marginal cost of providing school facilities in resource development areas is extremely high.

Another aspect of the data content of some IAS's is that workforce and population estimates are often incorrect soon after the report is produced. This is often unavoidable. However it does emphasize the need for Planning Branch to make use of additional data sources other than the assessment study. It has been found that the best method of obtaining more reliable data is to maintain constant contact with the mining company. However, this can become a very time consuming exercise.

As well, the reliability of employment and population estimates produced by some of the IAS's depends on the validity of the modelling techniques used. The GRIT (Generation of Regional Input-Output Tables) model developed originally at the University of Queensland by Jensen, Mandeville and Karunaratne (1978, 1979), has been used as a basis for estimating employment and population data for most of the proposed resource projects in Central Queensland. This technique has proved to be fairly reliable when appropriately applied to large regions, such as the whole of Central Queensland or at the State level. However, the employment multiplier estimates, in particular, need to be interpreted very cautiously when the model is applied at the town or shire level. In some cases the companies using the results of this technique do not fully appreciate the assumptions upon which it is based.

ORGANISATIONAL PROCEDURES IN THE PLANNING PROCESS

Over the last few years the number of major resource development projects planned has increased substantially. Whereas previously, projects and associated provision of educational facilities were few in number and planned well in advance, the dramatic increase in activity in the mining industry has placed pressure on the organisational process.

As a rule the Department of Education becomes formally aware of the details of a proposed development through advice from the Co-ordinator General's Department. This advice generally takes the form of an overview of the project and is accompanied by a request for the Department's information needs. The Co-ordinator General's main function under the appropriate Act is to compile an acceptable infrastructure (physical and social) for the project. In particular, the Co-ordinator General has the responsibility for overseeing and drawing-up a 'contractual' agreement between the company and the Shire concerning the provision by the company of the necessary physical urban infrastructure, such as roads, sewerage, water supply and some recreational facilities. The data needed for this assessment of infrastructure needs are relatively straight forward, in that they are based mainly on well understood and accepted engineering requirements. In addition, because of the existence of a contractual agreement there is thus a desire by all parties to ensure that this data base is accurate.

On the other hand, the information provided in the IAS relevant to planning for the provision of social infrastructure such as education, health, community and welfare services etc., is on the whole usually of a considerably poorer quality than that for the physical infrastructure assessment. There would seem to be two reasons for this. Firstly, because of the lack of any contractual agreement between the company and the relevant Government Departments concerning the provision of social infrastructure, there is no immediate financial inducement for the former to be precise in its assessment of the likely, say, number, composition and time of arrival of school children. Secondly, the information required is, in any case, more difficult to provide. As mentioned before, it is essential that education planners have information on the type of dependence associated with the workforce, the precise build-up of the workforce over time and the frequency and nature of population mobility. However, these types of data are peripheral to the company's construction programme and are not part of the negotiated agreement. Consequently, it is understandable that no consistent and detailed analyses of the workforce and associated population structure of mining towns has been undertaken by the various companies, and that any information that is provided is sometimes inaccurate and somewhat haphazardly organised.[8]

Partly because no formal organisational structure exists between the Education Department and the companies for the exchange of relevant data, and partly because of some companies' inability or unwillingness to provide appropriate data, then the workforce and associated population estimates from the IAS intended as a basis for education provision are usually treated by Planning Branch with caution.[9] From experience it has been necessary for Planning Branch to undertake its own calculations of population and school children associated with a development's workforce. Details regarding timing and staging have also been a factor of great concern. Should the Education Department proceed with the provision of school facilities solely on the basis of information provided by the Company then in some instances facilities would be inadequate to meet the demand, while in others facilities would be underutilised. Because of extremely severe budget constraints the department cannot afford to build facilities to open in year x if they are not required until year x + 1, or afford to build facilities for a school population of 400, if there is an initial population of only 300. To take a hypothetical example based on actual data, in October 1981 one particular company involved in a resource project forecast the number of families in the town to be 100 by December 1982. However, by July 1982 this forecast was revised downwards by 50 per cent to 52 families as the likely result for December 1982.

RESEARCH ON STUDENT TURNOVER AND POPULATION STRUCTURE IN RESOURCE AREAS

This section outlines the current and planned research being under-taken to alleviate some of the more important data deficiencies facing social infrastructure planners in resource areas. The results from a study of the magnitude and nature of student mobility in Queensland mining towns are discussed. In addition, the results of research into population and enrolment structure of mining towns undertaken to date, are reported.

Survey of student turnover

Throughout 1982 the Planning Branch of the Queensland Department of Education has been engaged in compiling information about student movement into and within Queensland. The project began in February 1982 when the Branch conducted a major survey of the sources of present students in all Queensland schools. The survey sought infor-mation on the location of the school they last attended in 1981. The Survey of Sources of Students in Queensland Schools (SSS) was undertaken in response to the need to identify those areas of the State that are receiving large numbers of interstate and overseas students as well as to assess the size and composition of student turnover. As well as co-operating fully in the implementation of the SSS, a significant number of principals from Government schools pro-vided additional information they considered might be of use in the study. A number suggested that monitoring student turnover in their schools for the whole year would provide a more complete picture of student movement; selected schools have therefore provided Planning Branch with monthly details of arrivals and departures so far this year, and will continue to do so throughout 1982.

An extensive analysis of the size, composition and destination of student movement into and within Queensland based on the currently available results of the SSS and on the further information provided by some principals in the first six months of 1982 has been recently completed in the Planning Branch. As well, Planning Branch has surveyed teachers in a number of recently established mining towns so as to ascertain their views regarding the effects of mobility on student performance. The results from these surveys for areas influenc-ed by resource development are discussed at length in a later section.[10]

Survey of workforce and population structure

In order to obtain an insight into workforce, population and enrolment structure of mining towns, several case studies of developments located at towns displaying differing structures were planned. The research undertaken to date and planned has four parts: an historical analysis; a "here-and-now" analysis of several towns in various stages of development, i.e. longitudinal study; and a collection of family background information through the relevant schools.

The first part, the historical analysis, requires the collection and analysis of available data from companies, and other souces where necessary. The type of information required includes workforce and population data over, say, the last five years, as well as an indication of company policy at the time towards such things as source and housing of workforce. It was intended that this information would then be related to available population census data and school enrolments over the same period, in an attempt to construct a more complete profile of the population.

The second part of the survey was designed to ascertain whether towns in various stages of development would have different population and workforce parameters, and if so, to identify these parameters. Three different types of mining communities were selected, namely: expansion of mining operations in an established mining town – Moranbah; an existing small agricultural town onto which mining has been grafted – Clermont; and an isolated 'new' mining town – Glenden.

The third part of this project comprises a programme that will monitor future workforce and population movements in the same three towns. This monitoring has been started by one company, but as yet no results are available.

Fourthly, it is planned to survey the parents of children enrolled in schools located in resource areas. Besides gathering information on family structure, it is also intended to elicit reasons for moving to the town as well as identifying parents' reaction to high levels of mobility. Some information has been collected from school admission forms and a questionnaire has been designed to collect other information required.

Survey forms were designed to gather information from the relevant companies, in order to make the collection of such information as simple and non-time consuming as possible.

Problems have been experienced in acquiring data from the companies and this has resulted in a delay to the research programme and a change in direction. Specifically, it has become apparent that certain historical information, namely details of contracted workforce, indirect and/or service workforce, origin of workforce and dependents of workers imported into the region, is not available from existing company records. Thus, more emphasis will be placed on the gathering of this information through the monitoring programme and the survey of parents of school children in resource areas.

To provide a basis for comparison, demographic factors and/or parameters used by companies in their projections and also those contained in impact assessment studies, have been identified.

RESEARCH FINDINGS ON STUDENT TURNOVER IN RESOURCE AREAS

This section discusses the main results to emerge from the "Survey of Sources of Students" (SSS) plus the more detailed but confined analysis of turnover in selected government schools. Our comments on the size and nature of student turnover will focus on government schools only.

Student turnover:
initial observations on magnitude and structure

Table 5.2 indicates the various origins, and their relative importance, of pupils enrolled in Year levels two to seven at 26 February 1982 for Government schools in a sample of resource development and other towns. The schools are arranged in order of decreasing student turnover from left to right. Although these results need to be interpreted somewhat cautiously, due to the timing of the survey, they nevertheless provide a very useful starting point for an analysis of student turnover in Queensland schools.[11]

When considering population turnover it also needs to be borne in mind that one is dealing with a "dynamic" phenomenon. "High rates of population turnover distinguish the new mining towns from old mining towns, from long established remote settlements and also from most towns without a mining function ... the new mining communities had two or three times the turnover experienced by the old remote communities ... they also experienced turnover at a considerably higher level than ... non-mining towns" (Brealey and Newton, 1980, p.6). The general state of the economy will influence the level of mobility of the population. In addition the characteristics (age, sex, origin etc.) of the migrants moving to a town will vary with such things as the recruiting policy of the mining company concerned and the facilities provided.

Firstly, from Table 5.2 it can be seen that those schools in areas most recently influenced by resource development have the higher rates of student turnover (that is, the smaller proportion of students who did not change schools). Middlemount, Emerald, Black-water North, Yarraman, Nanango and Blackwater primary schools all have turnover rates more than the State average of 10.3 per cent (100 − 89.7). The more established mining areas like Moranbah and Dysart, where there have not been any recent large scale expansions of mining, have turnover rates less than the State average, with non-resource based areas such as Mareeba and Ayr having markedly low

Table 5.2 Location of pupils at end of school year 1981 who at 26 February 1982 were enrolled in year levels 2 to 7 in government schools in selected resource development and non-resource development areas

Mobility category %	Middlemount	Emerald	Blackwater North	Yarraman	Nanango	Blackwater	Dysart	Esk*	Gatton*	Gladstone West	Moranbah	Mareeba	Ayr*	Moura	State total
Did not change schools (a)	79.9	80.4	80.5	84.5	85.1	86.8	91.8	92.3	92.7	92.9	93.6	95.6	95.8	97.2	89.7
Changed schools (b) in same education region	10.9	10.2	12.8	0.7	1.5	4.3	4.7	1.6	1.8	2.3	2.1	0.6	1.6	1.7	5.4
Changed (c) education regions	4.6	5.2	5.6	14.8	10.5	5.0	2.1	5.4	3.7	1.0	2.0	2.1	1.6	0.7	2.4
Moved from (d) interstate	2.9	4.2	1.0	0	2.4	1.2	1.4	0.7	1.4	3.1	1.6	1.2	1.0	0	1.9
Moved from (e) overseas	1.7	0	0.1	0	0.5	2.7	0	0	0.4	0.7	0.7	0.5	0	0.4	0.6
TOTAL	100.0	100.0	100.0	100.0	100.0	100.0	100.0	100.0	100.0	100.0	100.0	100.0	100.0	100.0	100.0

Notes:

(a) These pupils did not change schools between December 1981 and February 26, 1982.

(b) These pupils changed schools in the same education region.

(c) These pupils moved from a school in one region to a school in another region.

(d) These pupils moved from interstate to a Government school.

(e) These pupils moved from overseas to a Government school.

* These are non-resource deveopment areas.

Source: Survey of Sources of Students in Queensland Schools, 26 February 1982.

rates of student movement.

Gladstone, not surprisingly, has a lower turnover rate than those towns most recently affected by development. This has arisen because the construction phase of most projects in the area is nearing completion, and a transition to the operations phase is occuring which is less labour intensive.

Perhaps what is of greater interest, and in which there is greater certainty, is the relative importance of the origins of moves made by migrants to these areas. When the sources of the new pupils in primary schools located in the towns most recently affected by development are identified, it is evident that most of the migration in-flow is from other mining towns and urban centres in the region or from other regions in the State, rather than from interstate or overseas. Middlemount, Emerald and Blackwater North primary schools received over half of their new pupils from other schools within the region,[12] presumably other mining or urban centres in the region, whereas Yarraman and Nanango which are more isolated from existing mining centres received most of their pupils from outside their immediate regions. In proportion to their total turnover Emerald and Gladstone received a significant number of pupils from interstate. In the case of Gladstone this is partly explained by the fact that it has the type of development which requires very highly skilled labour that is more likely to be attracted from interstate. As well for a family considering an interstate move there is a higher probability that a large provincial city like Gladstone will be selected at least as a point of initial settlement. Also, a considerable proportion of pupils leaving Gladstone primary schools move to the mining towns in central Queensland. The relatively high proportion of interstate migrants to Emerald is less easy to explain. Also about half of those pupils moving from other regions of the state to the region concerned, come from the Brisbane Education regions.

Student turnover:
some detailed analyses of its size and composition

Table 5.3 records the results available at the time of writing from a detailed survey of student turnover being undertaken by Planning Branch. Information on the source of arrivals at and the destination of departures from selected primary and secondary schools is being collected on a monthly basis for all of 1982. As mentioned previously, the "dynamic" aspects of population turnover needs to be appreciated when interpreting these results.

When selecting the schools shown in Table 5.3, it was necessary for them to be located in mining towns at various stages of their productive life, that is the construction and operational phase of a project. It was also recognised whether schools were in completely new towns or in exiting towns influenced by mining development. Information was recorded on the arrivals and departures of Year two to seven and nine to 12 students for the period January to June 1982.

84

Table 5.3   Arrivals and departures of year levels 2 to 7 and 9 to 12 by source and destination in selected schools in mining and other resource developments for the period January to June 1982[a]

Type of student movement / School		Moved within same education region		Moved from or to another education region	Moved from or to another State	Moved from or to another country	Total all movers	Total school enrolments	New enrolments as per cent of total enrolments	Total movement (arrivals & departures) as per cent of total school enrolments	Total all movers for Jan-Feb only	Movements for Jan-Feb as a per cent of those for Jan-June
		Other mining towns	Rest									
		1	2	3	4	5	6	7	8	9	10	11
Dysart Primary	A	32(27.4)[b]	18(15.4)	41(35.0)	24(20.1)	2(2.1)	117	720	16.3	23.1	69	58.9
	D	33(67.3)	6(12.2)	7(14.3)	3(6.2)	0	49				11	22.4
Emerald Primary	A	14(13.7)	5(4.9)	46(45.1)	29(28.4)	8(7.9)	102	362	28.2	46.9	58	56.9
	D	32(47.1)	9(13.2)	21(30.8)	5(7.4)	1(1.5)	68				17	25.0
Moranbah Primary	A	21(18.9)	15(13.5)	55(49.5)	15(13.5)	5(4.6)	111	870	12.8	17.7	47	42.3
	D	24(55.8)	7(16.3)	10(23.3)	2(4.6)	0	43				7	16.3
Total	A	67(20.3)	38(11.5)	142(43.0)	68(20.6)	15(4.6)	330	1 952	16.9	25.1	174	52.7
	D	89(55.6)	22(13.8)	38(23.8)	10(6.3)	1(0.5)	160				35	21.9
Dysart Secondary	A	42(40.8)	18(17.5)	26(25.2)	15(14.6)	2(1.9)	103	216	47.7	64.8	65	63.1
	D	18(48.6)	10(27.0)	5(13.5)	4(10.8)	0	37				7	18.9
Emerald Secondary	A	16(27.1)	16(27.1)	18(30.5)	5(8.5)	4(6.8)	59	441	13.4	19.5	38	64.4
	D	6(22.2)	16(59.3)	3(11.1)	1(3.7)	1(3.7)	27				2	7.4
Moranbah Secondary	A	8(14.3)	15(26.8)	20(35.7)	11(19.6)	2(3.6)	56	245	22.9	30.6	35	62.5
	D	8(42.1)	4(21.1)	5(26.3)	2(10.5)	0	19				0	0
Total	A	66(30.3)	49(22.5)	64(29.4)	31(14.2)	8(3.6)	218	902	24.2	33.4	138	63.3
	D	32(38.6)	30(36.1)	13(15.7)	7(8.4)	1(1.2)	83				9	10.8
Gladstone West Primary	A	12(13.5)	22(24.7)	29(21.3)	31(34.8)	5(5.7)	89	779	11.4	20.2	51	57.3
	D	10(14.7)	15(22.1)	24(35.8)	10(14.7)	8(11.8)	68				12	17.6
Nanango Primary	A	2(1.7)	13(11.3)	79(68.7)	19(16.5)	2(1.8)	115	335	34.3	45.7	53	46.1
	D	-	-	-	-	-	38				4	10.5
Yarraman Primary	A	0(0)	3(8.6)	22(62.9)	6(17.1)	4(11.4)	35	150	26.9	37.7	15	42.8
	D	-	-	-	-	-	14				4	28.6
Total	A	2(1.3)	16(10.7)	101(67.3)	25(16.7)	6(4.0)	150	465	32.2	43.4	68	45.3
	D	-	-	-	-	-	52				8	15.4

Notes:

a) The movement patterns of year levels 2 to 7 in Primary and 9 to 12 in Secondary were considered. This removes some of the distortion that year level 1 and 8 have in the primary and secondary areas respectively. As well it permits a more valid and easier comparison with results from the survey of sources. Though the total number of movements will be reduced, the relativities between arrivals and departures, as well as between the various types of student movement are not distorted.

b) The figures in brackets express each component of student turnover as a percentage of total arrivals and departures respectively.

Source: Survey of Student Turnover in Selected Queensland Government Schools.

Provision of Education Facilities

New enrolments for this period as a percentage of total enrolments (of course excluding Years one and eight for the primary and secondary schools respectively) were also recorded.

Firstly, primary schools located in areas most recently influenced by resource development have higher rates of student turnover (Emerald – 28.2 per cent; Nanango – 34.3 per cent; Yarraman – 26.9 per cent) compared to the more established mining towns (Moranbah – 12.8 per cent and Dysart 16.3 per cent) where there have not been any recent large scale expansions. Gladstone West Primary, not surprisingly, has a lower turnover rate than schools in those towns most recently affected by development. This is partly explained by a nearing to completion of the construction phase of most projects in the area, and a transition to the operatons phase which is less labour intensive. Secondary schools, particularly, in the more established towns of Dysart and Moranbah have higher rates of student turnover than even in some primary schools. In fact, Dysart Secondary has the highest turnover rate (47.7 per cent) of all the schools in Table 5.3.

Secondly, in relation to the sources of new students in both primary and secondary schools, it is evident that most of the migration in-flow is from other mining towns and urban centres in the region or from other regions in the State, rather than from interstate or overseas (Table 5.2).

All the schools except Gladstone West Primary, and to a lesser extent Emerald Primary, receive at least 70 per cent of their new students from either other schools in the region or from schools in other education regions. Primary schools in Dysart and Moranbah receive 27.4 and 18.9 per cent respectively of their new students from other mining centres in the region, and 15.4 and 13.4 per cent respectively from large urban centres in the same region like Gladstone, Mackay and Rockhampton. The schools in the more recently developed areas of Nanango and Yarramen receive few students from other schools within their regions, reflecting simply the lack of other mining activities in their respective regions. However, these towns receive the highest and second highest levels of inter-regional student movement. Moranbah, Dysart and Emerald, receive 49.5, 35.0 and 45.1 per cent respectively of their new enrolments from other education regions, while the value of the corresponding migration component for Gladstone is only 21.3 per cent.

The relatively small importance of inter-regional migration for Gladstone is reflected partly in the fact that it has the highest (34.8 per cent) number of new school children who have moved interstate. Emerald Primary has the second highest level of interstate school children. In the case of Gladstone this is partly explained by the fact that the highly skilled labour needed that for this type of development is more likely to be attracted from interstate. Also, for a family considering an interstate move, there is a higher probability that a larger provincial city like Gladstone will be selected at least as a point

Table 5.4:   Arrivals$^{(A)}$ and Departures$^{(D)}$ of Year Levels 2 to 7
by Source and Destination for Selected Mining Town
Primary Schools as a Whole for the January–February
and January–June Periods

Type of Student Movement		Moved within same educa- tion region ------------ other rest mining towns		Moved from or to another education region	Moved from or to another state	Moved from or to another country	Total all movers
Selected schools Jan–Feb only	A	40 (16.5)	27 (11.2)	115 (47.5)	50 (20.7)	10 (4.1)	242
	D	–	–	–	–	–	–
Selected schools Jan–June	A	69 (14.4)	54 (11.3)	243 (50.6)	93 (19.4)	21 (4.3)	480
	D	–	–	–	–	–	–

Note:

Primary schools included here are Dysart, Moranbah, Nanango and
Yarraman.

Source: Survey of Student Turnover in selected Queensland
government schools.

Table 5.5: Arrivals[A] and Departures[D] of Year Levels 9 to
12 by Source and Destination for Selected Mining
Town Secondary Schools as a Whole for the January–
February and January–June Periods

Type of Student Movement		Moved within same education region ------------ other rest mining towns		Moved from or to another education region	Moved from or to another state	Moved from or to another country	Total all movers
Selected schools Jan–Feb only	A	46 (33.3)	29 (21.0)	42 (30.4)	16 (11.6)	5 (3.7)	138
	D	–	–	–	–	–	–
Selected schools Jan–June	A	66 (30.3)	49 (22.5)	64 (29.4)	31 (14.2)	8 (3.6)	218
	D	–	–	–	–	–	–

Note:

The above results are based on student movements for Dysart,
Emerald and Moranbah Secondary schools.

Source: Survey of Student Turnover in selected Queensland
government schools.

of initial settlement not least because, being larger, it is more economically diversified. It is significant that a considerable proportion
of pupils leaving Gladstone primary schools move to mining towns in
central Queensland. The relative proportion of interstate migrants to
Emerald, however, is less easy to explain.

Thirdly, in the case of departures the mobility patterns of school
children are more complex. Nanango and Yarraman are excluded from
this analysis owing to lack of data, and total primary (except for Gladstone) and secondary departures are aggregated. Of those children who
left primary schools in the three mining centres, 55.6 per cent went
to other mining centres in Central Queensland, while 13.8 per cent
departed mainly to large urban centres elsewhere in the region. Nearly
24 per cent of students moved to other education regions. In contrast, for secondary students there was an almost equal split between
students leaving for other mining towns and those moving elsewhere
in the region. The fact that twice as many secondary compared to
primary students leave for large urban centres is a function of the
more comprehensive range of secondary education options available
in these centres.

Fourthly, Emerald and Gladstone lose relatively more school
children to other education regions, than do the other purely mining
areas. Gladstone also has the highest proportion of departures who
move interstate, and secondary students leaving Moranbah and Dysart
have a greater tendency to move to another State than do primary
students leaving those towns.

Fifthly, there is seasonal variation in the arrival and departure
of students. This seasonality can be measured as movements for the
January–February period as a percentage of those for the January–June
period for both arrivals and departures. Seasonal variation in student
turnover appears to be partly explained by two factors – whether a
student is of primary or secondary school age, and the stage of
development of the area. Over 63 per cent of new secondary students
resident in schools in established mining areas by the end of June
1982 arrived before the end of February, whereas the corresponding
values in primary schools in established and new mining towns are
53 per cent and 45 per cent respectively. This reflects the tendency
for secondary students to move less as the year progresses, and that
turnover will probably continue at a reasonable level in new towns
throughout the year.

Relativities between the various categories of student movement
also need to be examined for any seasonal variation. Tables 5.4 and
5.5 record the relative importance of these movement categories for
primary and secondary schools respectively. For primary schools there
was a marginal decrease in the relative importance of student movements from other mining towns as the year progressed, 16.5 to 14.4, and
an almost corresponding increase in arrivals from other education
regions in the State. There was also a marginal drop in the importance

Table 5.6:   Proportion of New Enrolments Arriving at the
School by 26 February Who Still Remain by the End
of Each Month

School	Cumulative Percentage				
	End of February	End of March	End of April	End of May	End of June
Dysart Primary	97.9	92.6	89.5	89.5	88.4
Emerald Primary	94.8	86.0	78.1	72.0	69.3
Moranbah Primary	98.8	96.9	96.9	95.7	93.9
Dysart Secondary	98.6	94.9	92.8	92.8	90.6
Emerald Secondary	99.1	98.1	96.2	93.3	92.3
Moranbah Secondary	100.0	98.6	98.6	97.8	97.2
Gladstone West Primary	98.7	96.2	95.0	90.0	89.4
Nanango Primary	94.8	88.7	81.5	80.4	75.3
Yarraman Primary	90.0	90.0	90.0	70.0	70.0

Source: Survey of Student Turnover in selected Queensland
government schools.

of interstate movement. However, despite these small variations, the source of new primary arrivals has not shown any major seasonal changes. Secondary students moved less from other mining towns, 33.3 per cent to 30.3 per cent, but more from interstate. However, as in primary schools there were no major seasonal changes in the relative importance of the various student movement categories.

Sixthly, Table 5.6 looks at student turnover in a slightly different manner. It records the proportion of new enrolments arriving at school by the end of February who still remain by the end of each sub-sequent month. This highlights again the high turnover rates of primary schools in new development areas, with Emerald, Yarraman and Nanango having lost between 25 and 30 per cent of their January-February enrolments by the end of June.

Some consequences of high levels of student turnover

"Steven has attended eighteen different schools in the past ten years. His home has been a caravan...Steven's schooling is a record of changing levels and curricula. Many times he found that subjects he had been taught in one school were not even touched on in another, or that he had no knowledge of a subject being taught in the new school...The state school systems are like railway gauges. They are all different and everyone thinks theirs is best" (Parker, 1978).

These comments certainly dramatise the effect that continual relocation of families can have on a student's educational progress. However, also of concern is the influence that a highly mobile popu-lation will have on the education system itself, mainly through the provision of extra capital and labour. This is an aspect of student turnover that is often overlooked, though in fact it is integrally related to the influence on the child.

As referred to in the introduction, research which has been undertaken in Australia to date has shown that even though there may be only minimal long-term effects (beneficial or harmful) resulting from a high level of student turnover, the short-term adverse effects on both the student and the education system can be quite substan-tial (Bourke and Naylor, 1971; Mackay and Spicer, 1975). More recently findings have emerged from a Western Australian study of student mobility, which indicate that most teachers saw highly mobile children as performing below their peers (Bell, 1982).

Planning Branch has just completed a survey of primary school teachers in a central Queensland mining town influenced by large scale development. They were asked to identify student, teacher and school problems attributable to frequent student turnover, as well as to suggest ways to minimise any adverse effects of this turnover. Other schools are to be surveyed and an analysis of these results will be produced by Planning Branch at a later date. However, at this point

91

Provision of Education Facilities

It is worthwhile recording some of the comments made by teachers in relation to 'student' problems. These include:

> "Many students come without records or with vague reports that give no accurate description of what has been learned. So many do not know what reading book they have been using (parents usually don't either) and time is wasted trying to fit the student into established reading groups and other class groups".

> "It takes some children several weeks to settle in. Part of the problem arises when children find themselves behind or advanced in work. ...Many children have difficulty making new friends".

> "Social behaviour suffers due to lack of time to create friend-ships".

> "Children lack interest in school work as often they know they will only be in that area for a short time, particularly during construction phase ... Other students in the school are often disrupted by the arrival of new children and the need to adjust to them".

> "Children join classes throughout the year, bringing with them different books and pads. There appears such a large discrepancy not only interstate, but also within Queensland schools concerning standards and approaches to work. Emphasis in content also varies markedly. Thus a good month is required for the student to become 'settled in'."

These comments from teachers highlight some of the problems that they feel are faced by students changing schools regularly.

Summary of research findings on student turnover

Primary schools located in areas most recently influenced by resource development had higher than average rates of student turnover, around 30 per cent, compared to the more established mining towns, with 14 per cent. The State average is 11 per cent. Further, secondary schools have higher rates of student movement than in most primary schools, possible reflecting the lack of secondary options in these remote areas. Most of the migration in-flow to these areas is from other mining towns and urban centres in the region or from other regions in the State, rather than from interstate or overseas. For new mining or development areas like Emerald, Yarraman and Nanango, between 25 and 30 per cent of new enrolments at the beginning of the year had left by the end of June.

92

Table 5.7   Population parameters used in impact assessment studies.

Demographic factor/parameter (a)(b)(c)		Callide/Biloela	Wolfang/Clermont	Glenden	Export coal proposal Collinsville/Newlands/Abbot Point	Riverside/Moranbah	Tarong/Nanango, Yarraman	Theodore
Percentage married males in workforce (d)	con.	Power Stn. - 80%) Contract - ?) 45% Mine - 40%	40%	44%	30%	70%	Power Stn. - 40% Mine - 50%	25%
	oper.	Power Stn. - 90% Mine - 90%	70%	61%	80%	70%	Power Stn. - 80% Mine - 75%	80%
	serv. con.	90%	50%			40%		25%
	serv. oper.	90%	70%		80% (to 86%)	40%		80%
Dependent children per married male worker (d)	con.	0.6	0.5		0.75(0-1)	1.85	0-1	2.0
	oper.	1.8	1.8	1.85	2.2	1.85		2.0
	serv. con.	1.8	1.0					2.0
	serv. oper.	1.8	1.8		2.2			2.0
Service workforce as percentage of total/direct workforce	con.	13%	10%		15%	20%		
	oper.	13%	15%		15%	20%		
Percentage workforce imported from outside region	con.	Power Stn. - 100% Mine - 100%	100%	20% to 33%	MOST			100%
	oper.	Power Stn. = 90% Mine - 100%	100%					100%
	serv.		100%					
Date TAS report was produced		April 1982	April 1982	Sept. 1981	April 1980		Nov. 1980	March 1982 (draft)

Notes:

(a) In cases where percentages have not been quoted, they have had to be calculated from data contained in the IAS.

(b) Where parameters were unable to be calculated, the appropriate category was left blank.

(c) No report contained estimates of primary and secondary school-aged children.

(d) In some cases it was unclear as to whether the percentage of married males in the workforce referred to all married workers or just those with families.
con. = construction phase of porject; oper. = operational phase of project; serv. = service component of workforce.

Research Findings on Population and Workforce Structure

To date, emphasis has been placed on the setting up of the project, identifying the Department's information needs for planning of educational facilities in mining areas, selecting appropriate examples of towns and/or companies to be surveyed, and planning the methods of collection of data. As noted above, there has been a change in direction of the research, with less emphasis now being placed on the historical part of the survey, and some changes being made to the towns/companies to be surveyed. Although certain data still have to be collected, some initial findings have emerged.

COMPARISON OF EXISTING POPULATION PARAMETERS AND IMPLICATIONS FOR PLANNING OF FACILITIES

A comparison was made of demographic factors/parameters contained in selected impact assessment studies. These are summarized in Table 5.7, and it is clearly evident that there is a wide variation across their values, with little or no justification for these differences. For example, the percentage of married males in the construction workforce varies from 25 per cent to 80 per cent, while that for the operational phase varies from 60 per cent to 90 per cent. Similar variations are recorded for the service component of the workforce. Variations are also identified in the number of dependent children per married worker, ranging from 0 to 2.0 for the construction phase, and 1.8 to 2.2 for the operational phase. The service component of the workforce associated with a development, where it was able to be quantified, varied from 10 per cent to 20 per cent, and showed little variation between the construction and operational phases. Some reports were able to provide estimates of the percentage of workforce imported into the region and these varied from 20 per cent to 100 per cent, dependent on whether there was a project in the area or whether the project was new. This figure is essential for estimating population and school enrolments in existing areas, to avoid over-estimates or double counting.

Population parameters used by companies for their projections have been refined by the companies over a period of time, in the light of changing market conditions and further analysis. Thus, they may differ substantially from those used in the impact assessment studies. As an example, variations have occurred in the percentage of married males in the workforce for the Riverside project at Moranbah, where the percentage of married construction workers has been decreased from 70 per cent to approximately 40 per cent.[13] Similarly, refinement of other factors has also occurred. In certain cases, factors are now provided where previously they were not known, for example, the service component of the workforce at Glenden has been identified as 35 per cent where previously no figure was given.

Because data was available for Glenden, it has been chosen as an example to illustrate how changes in demographic factors occur,

94

Table 5.8   Comparison of IAS factors with planning branch
factors and other factors provided by company

Demographic factor/[a][b] parameter		Export coal proposal Collinsville/Newlands/ Abbot Point (IAS)	Town of Glendon outline report	Town of Glendon infrastructure package	Planning branch ratios	Comments
Percentage married males in workforce	c	30%	45–54%	46%	20%	It is often not clear what a company means by percentage of married male workers. Sometimes it refers to all married males; other times the accompanied married males only; and yet other times only the married workforce with families. For example, the 30% in column 1 refers to married workers with families on site. Note that percentages for the Infrastructure Package have been calculated from workforce numbers provided. Planning Branch also applies a factor (0.8–1.0) to obtain the proportion of married males that have families. In this case, the proportion is 1.0 because the town is isolated and workers would be accompanied by families. If the operation was located within reasonable distance of a large urban centre, then some married males would leave families behind during the week (0.8 would be used).
	o	80%	61%	68%	80%	
	s	80–86 (oper)		39–41%		
Dependent children per married male worker	c	0.75 (0–1)		Mine 0.53 Town 0.78	1.55	Planning Branch figure of 1.75 would be reached only when secondary facilities were provided in the town. Planning Branch uses a proportion of 0.60 of total dependent children as the number of school-aged children in years 1–10.
	o	2.2	1.85		1.75	
	s	2.2 (oper)				
School-aged children per married male worker (with families)	p				0.70–0.80	The proportion used by Planning Branch depends on whether the town is established or not. If established, the higher figure is used. Note that no data provided by company gives indication of student yield proportions.
	s				0.15–0.25	
	p+s				0.85–1.05	
	<p				0.70	
Service workforce as percentage of total/ direct workforce	c	15%/?	26/33	?/35%		The first percentage refers to the proportion of total workforce; the second refers to the percentage of direct workforce only.
	o	15%/?	26/35	?/35%		? has been inserted where appropriate data are missing.
Percentage workforce imported from outside region	c	most	30 33%			This figure is essential for estimating population and school enrolments in existing areas to avoid overestimates or double counting.
	o					

Notes:

(a) Workforce – c = construction phase, o = operational phase, s = service component.

(b) School-aged dependents – p = primary school-aged, s = secondary school-aged, p+s = primary plus secondary school-aged, <p = prior to school.

from the time an IAS is undertaken until operations commence. Table 5.8 summarizes these changes and provides comparative Planning Branch parameters. Of particular note are the changes that have occurred in both the proportion of married males in the workforce (30 per cent increased to 46 per cent for the construction phase and 80 per cent decreased to 68 per cent for the operational phase) and the number of dependent children per married worker (2.2 reduced to 1.85 for the operational phase).

Phase of development: variations in student yield/population parameters

When considering the question of numbers of school aged children, that is, student yields, it is clear that attempts to monitor the enrolment growth in mining towns are more difficult than originally thought. Student yield rates will be different in construction compared to operational phases, and they also vary as the economic base of the town becomes more complex.

Student yield rates, based on the number of students per married worker, have been calculated for various mining towns (Table 5.9). Yield rates for the construction phase have only been derived for recent projects, Nanango and Oaky Creek, as construction workforce data are unavailable for areas like Moranbah, Dysart and Blackwater. Some companies have not been co-operative. Nevertheless, this more recent experience indicates that the construction phase yield rates per married worker of just under 0.5 for primary school students and approximately 0.1 for secondary school students, providing a fairly accurate guide to school enrolment growth in that phase of a project. Note that Oaky Creek represents a new town whereas Nanango was an agriculturally based community before mining and related development activities began.

In the early operational phase primary yield rates based on the experience in Blackwater and Moranbah are in the approximate range 0.55 to 0.65 children per married worker, whereas when the mining operations are in "full swing" and the town is more developed then about 0.8 to 0.9 children per married worker are yielded. For secondary students, 0.15 to 0.20 children per married workers are yielded for the early operational phase, whereas around 0.30 children are yielded when operations are fully underway.

It is noted that the percentage of school aged children (that is, primary plus secondary children) in a mining town population is much higher than in the State as a whole. For example, it varied from 25 per cent for Clermont, to 33 per cent for Moranbah, compared to the State average of 20 per cent. Looking at the primary/secondary break-down also, it is clear that the proportion of primary school aged children in mining towns is significantly higher than for the State as a whole. As most of the growth in school enrolments, and consequently pressure on the provision of education facilities, occurs in the

96

Table 5.9: Number of Primary and Secondary Students per
Married Worker for Construction and Operational
Phases of a Project in Selected Areas

	Moranbah	Dysart	Blackwater	Oaky Creek	Nanango
Construction Phase					
Primary(a)	–	–	–	0.5	0.48
Secondary(b)	–	–	–	–	0.1
Operational Phase					
Primary(c)	0.53–0.79	0.24–0.86	0.63–0.87	–	–
Secondary(d)	0.30		0.34	–	–

Notes:

(a) For both these areas, but for Nanango in particular, these
yields are for married workers living in caravan parks.

(b) Again these are for students yielded from caravan parks.

(c) There are two values recorded. The first applies when the
project is in a transitional phase, that is, moving from
construction to operational. As the project becomes
entirely operational then the yield rate rises.

(d) Because secondary enrolments do not become a problem until
usually well after the construction phase, these values are
for when the operational activity is well advanced.

primary and pre-school sectors during the construction and early operational phase, it is imperative that reliable student yields be available for these phases of the project life.

SUMMARY AND CONCLUSIONS

Research undertaken by Planning Branch has demonstrated that there are deficiencies in the planning process, of a data organisational nature, for the provision of education and social infrastructure, in resource development. Four main problems emerge.

First, one of the major problems faced by government departments responsible for the provision of services such as education, health, welfare services etc. in resource communities is the frequent lack of appropriate and timely data on population structure, size, and turn-over. The information that is available and the associated assumptions they embody vary markedly, without much justification, between the different projects considered. Second, though "officially" most of the data necessary for planning purposes come from Impact Assessment Studies, because of data deficiencies, direct recourse to the companies concerned is often required. However, the degree of co-operation, as well as the ability to provide data, varies drastically between companies. Third, since companies in the past have been more concerned with the physical infrastructure side of a project and its costs, they simply do not have an easily assessable data base that is of use to departments providing social infrastructure. Fourth, there is a complete lack of any regional co-ordination in the provision of government services. Each project is considered as a separate entity in itself, when departments are requested to assess the future demand for their services. The fact that a number of different projects are occurring in the same town or region is totally ignored by those responsible for the co-ordination of planning activities.

This chapter has attempted to provide some insights into the difficulties faced by Planning Branch in the Department of Education when providing and maintaining school facilities in resource development areas, as well as to outline Planning Branch's efforts to overcome some of them. Accuracy in forecasting school enrolment profiles over time in mining areas is essential. For example, the opportunity cost (both to the Department and to the company) in having a school open six months too early or too late is substantial. This is compounded by the significantly higher construction costs per unit in non-metropolitan areas.

Attention was also focused on some of the problems facing the 'educators' once schools are provided in resource development areas and a number of useful findings regarding the size, composition and mobility patterns of mining town populations have emerged. For example, in new mining and associated development centres like Emerald, Yarraman and Nanango, between 25 and 30 per cent of new enrolments arriving at the beginning of the year had left by the end of June. In

Emerald Primary School, for instance, there have been 44 arrivals and 51 departures between the end of February and the end of June 1982 (Table 5.3). Therefore, with enrolments staying almost constant, in excess of one primary class has been replaced by another in a four month period. If this school had grown by 40 or so students an extra teacher would most likely be provided, but no explicit relief is given for a turnover of a similar magnitude.

The downturn in mining activity should <u>not</u> be accompanied by a corresponding fall in the type of research discussed in this chapter. It is only now that some appreciation of the demographic and economic impacts of development projects is being gained. There are a number of towns in Central Queensland that are good examples of new and established towns in the construction and/or operational phases of the projects life. It is essential that demographic changes in these areas be monitored for the next few years at least.

NOTES

1. The indirect effects, particularly employment and the associated population growth, of mining projects can be quite considerable. Some brief consideration is given to the size of direct and indirect employment multiplier effects later in the chapter. However, in the main this chapter concentrates on the direct population and resultant school enrolment changes associated with resource development, though the state—wide effects on the school system are arguably significant.

2. Their surveys of selected Western Australian new and old mining towns, as well as other established non—mining communities, in the mid 1970's enabled them to paint a fairly detailed picture of most aspects of community life in these areas.

3. Brealey and Newton found population turnover levels exceeding 100 per cent per annum in the initial years of a town's establishment.

4. Historically, the construction workforce has comprised a relatively young labour force with a higher than average proportion of single men and lower than average family component. By comparison, the operational component of the workforce has a significantly greater proportion being married with a larger than average family component.

5. It is also conveniently overlooked by some critics of the State education system, that it is the Government system which bears most of the responsibility for providing education facilities in resource communities, as well as in most other rapidly growing parts of the State.

6. More specifically, a larger population base is required before secondary schools are provided because the number of secon—

dary students yielded per unit of population is lower than for primary also since the secondary curriculum is more specialised a larger student base is required. A useful 'rule of thumb' is that it takes 3 'full size' primary schools, 800 to 1000 pupils, to support a 'full size' secondary school, 1000 to 1200 students.

7. For example, one particular company decided to delay by six months the planned commencement of the construction phase of the project, without informing the Education Department. Consequently, new primary school facilities were unoccupied for six months.

8. In an attempt to overcome these problems a major research effort has only recently been set in motion by Planning Branch to obtain historical, current and future data on population and workforce profiles from a number of companies involved in resource development in Queensland. The main aspects of this proposed research are discussed above.

9. Other State Government departments involved in the provision of social infrastructure in resource areas have a similar complaint.

10. A preliminary report titled "Student Movement Into and Within Queensland" by G.J. Butler, T.D. Schramm and D.A. Stephens is available on request from Planning Branch.

11. The actual timing of the survey is crucial. The survey gathers information on children enrolled at the school in question on 26 February 1982. Since we are primarily concerned with that segment of the school population which attended another school last year, then for all schools and regions to be legitimately compared on the basis of their number or percentage of new students, we need to be able to assume either (1) that all schools receive their full quota of new students no later than the 26th February or (2) that the proportion of the yearly intake of new students that a school receives by the 26th February is equal for all schools. Quite obviously neither of these assumptions will be satisfied. For instance, schools in fairly stable population growth areas will probably have received most of the new students that they will get for the year by 26 February. On the other hand, schools located in high population growth or high turnover areas will receive new students at regular or irregular intervals throughout the entire year. consequently, any comparison of the number of student migrants between regions, schools or groups of schools should only be made with this qualification in mind. However, a detailed study of the arrivals at and departures from selected schools for the entire year is being conducted by Planning Branch, the details of which are outlined below. This should enable us to minimise most of the problems associated with this aspect of the survey.

12. These children may belong to a transient group of people who follow mining related work from town to town.

13. Caution should be taken when using percentages of married males in the workforce, to avoid double counting. For example, the percentage of married males in the workforce drops as a town becomes more established, and more women enter the workforce. Figures of 44.8 per cent for Mt Isa and 66.9 per cent for Moranbah can be compared with percentages proposed in some IAS reports of as high as 90 per cent for the operational phase.

THE OVERSEAS EXPERIENCE OF

RESOURCE DEVELOPMENTS

MINERAL RESOURCE TRANSPORTATION AND FRONTIER INFRASTRUCTURE PROVISION IN CANADA

Iain Wallace

INTRODUCTION

Frontier mineral producers invariably face costs and obligations which comparable operations in more developed regions are not required to internalize. Provision of transportation infrastructure to link their mines to external markets is frequently the single most substantial expense of this nature. However, rapid inflation in the cost of capital projects during the past decade, compounded more recently by high interest rates and soft markets, has severely reduced the ability of mining companies to finance infrastructure investments. As a result, perennial questions about the degree to which, and the conditions under which, the public sector should share the costs of installing and operating necessary transportation facilities have assumed renewed importance. In Canada, discussion of these issues is particularly timely in the light of the publication by the federal government of a discussion Paper on mineral policy (Energy, Mines and Resources [EMR] Canada, 1982). My purpose in this chapter is to review the circumstances in which mineral-related transportation provision in frontier areas of Canada has been made in the past, to comment on the conclusions which the Government's discussion paper draws from this experience, and to outline a framework within which public sector evaluation of specific projects could proceed on a more consistent basis than has been evident hitherto.

BACKGROUND

Construction of frontier transportation infrastructure to support new mining ventures did not take place in Canada on a significant scale before 1950. Much of the mineral wealth of the Canadian Shield and the Western Cordillera had been made accessible to North American markets as a result of transcontinental railway construction in the period 1880–1920, but so long as the United States was relatively self-sufficient in mineral resources demand for Canadian production was limited (nickel being a notable exception). Sustained economic expansion after 1945, however, led to growing US mineral import demands which triggered a dramatic increase in the size and geographical extent of Canada's mining industry. US investors were attracted by the proximity

105

and political stability of their northern neighbour, and Canadians in turn welcomed the economic growth associated with expansion of the mineral sector, favouring it with taxation policies which tended to encourage investment. Moreover, postwar Canadian governments, both federal and (where relevant) provincial, displayed an active interest in promoting the social and economic development of northern frontier regions. Public sector aid to promote resource development and provision of the necessary infrastructure thus became politically acceptable at a time when market forces were already strongly supportive of the northwards expansion of the Canadian mining industry. One measure of the degree to which frontier mineral deposits became commercially and physically integrated into the continental market during the 1950s and 1960s is that over 4000 km of railway lines were built to gain access to new and prospective mines (Wallace, 1977).

By the early 1970s a number of factors combined to change considerably the outlook of a continuation for this frontier expansion of mining activity. The substantially expanded productive capacity of Canadian mines had largely met the medium-term needs of foreign buyers of mineral products. The federal government accepted the argument of the Carter Royal Commission on Taxation that the mining sector neither required nor deserved preferential treatment vis-a-vis, say, manufacturing. Public sentiment evidenced a growing nationalism which found particular focus in opposition to the dominant role of US corporations in many sectors of the Canadian economy (not that mining displayed the high level of foreign ownership found in the petroleum sector). The impact of resource developments on the environment and on indigenous society began to receive more critical public attention. Even before the onset of the "energy crisis", therefore, private sector appraisals of the attractiveness of exploiting Canada's frontier mineral resources were changing, as was the unqualified enthusiasm of governments for this form of development (Miller, 1980). Market conditions and policy stances remained generally negative through the balance of the decade.

By the early 1980s, however, against the background of a persistent global recession, the dilemma presented by resource-dependent frontier economies has once more become increasingly evident. In the Canadian north, mineral extraction is one of a very limited numer of activities by which a market-oriented regional economy can be sustained. The complete cessation, at least temporarily, of mining in the Yukon Territory, whose economy is very largely dependent on activity in this sector, is but the most critical event to prompt renewed federal interest in the institutional and market requirements of viable frontier mineral production. This interest comes at a time, however, when government deficits render the public sector poorly placed, even if disposed to assist frontier development projects. Provincial governments with frontier interests face similar limitations.

Current Federal Policy

The federal mineral policy discussion paper (EMR, 1982) devotes separate sections to "Infrastructure" (pp. 73-76) and to "Northern and Regional Development" (pp. 77-81). It notes that,

> "in new mining areas, especially remote ones, government is usually asked to provide or contribute towards the required infrastructure. In such cases, government decisions are very critical since they often determine whether or not a major project will go ahead...[for] in many cases, infrastructure accounts for a significant portion of the total capital cost of a new mining project."

Reviewing government involvement in two developments examined later in this paper (Pine Point, NWT and Cyprus Anvil, Yukon), it concludes that, "where feasible the infrastructure was provided on a cost-recovery basis;...[that] the companies were by no means the sole beneficiaries of the infrastructure provided" and that the initial private sector investment was followed by continuing capital expenditures to modernize and expand facilities. A somewhat defensive tone evident in this assessment is occasioned by "the fact that both projects were attractive investments for private industry, and even may have been commercially attractive with a lower infusion of public funds." The questions which are therefore raised are,

> "were the incentives provided by government in the form of infrastructure too lucrative? Since the government bore much of the downside risk, should it have insisted on sharing at least partially in the potential upside profits beyond a normal target rate-of-return? Should infra-structure support have been made conditional upon receiving firm guarantees from the companies regarding social objectives like industrial spinoffs, native employment etc?"

The discussion paper goes on to argue that, "since the realisation of social benefits is so crucial to the justification of the subsidisation of infrastructure, government should receive firm commitments from industry that these benefits will, in fact, be forthcoming when the deposit is developed". Where publicly funded infrastructure can be provided on a fully commercial, cost-recovery basis, of course, the private sector is not assumed to incur obligations of this sort.

Among the rationales for subsidizing the provision of infrastructure which the federal document explicitly rejects are those predicated, "simply for the sake of opening up a region, earning foreign exchange or creating jobs in sparsely populated areas. ...As a general principle, mineral developments should take place only if they can pay their way." The section on northern (territorial) development echoes this stance; "the general philosophy regarding mineral development on these lands is that market forces should determine the pace of exploration and

107

the viability of development." The discussion of infrastructure concludes that if government is to assist in its provision for frontier mineral projects, involvement should be in ways that minimize the risk to public capital and provide for sharing in the profits which are indirectly the result of such investment. Risk minimisation is associated with "multiple use of infrastructure", which implies provision "within a regional, rather than a single-mine context", and also "provision of sufficient data from the private sector to satisfy itself [the government] that the venture <u>will be successful</u>" (emphasis added). If the public sector provides infrastructure on this basis, then "repayment may be designed on a regional basis, rather than being borne entirely by the initial mine. Of course, the distribution of costs should recognize the value to the initial user of early availability."

Mining industry reaction to the discussion paper as a whole has been critical of what is seen as its disproportionate stress on the industry's social obligations at the expense of addressing more fundamental economic issues. Although the document's coverage of infrastructure has not been highlighted in corporate criticism, the position summarisd above clearly favours a severely limited public sector involvement in frontier mineral projects which require substantial infrastructure investment, especially when compared to government attitudes in the 1960s. An earlier internal report of EMR Canada explicitly singles out the initial high profits derived from the Pine Point project as having "soured the traditional view of goverment infrastructure support to mine development as a generally acceptable practice" (EMR Canada, 1981, p.4). It is clear, however, that the government's stance on this whole issue remains ambiguous in the context of specific requests for assistance. One of the complications impeding the formulation of a coherent policy towards frontier infrastructure provision in Canada is that EMR's overall responsibility for national mineral policy has been allocated, with respect to the northern territories, to the Department of Indian Affairs and Northern Development (DIAND). The Minister responsible for DIAND is on record as being, "prepared to take the initiative to promote investment in key infrastructure and ... [to] take the long-term perspective in terms of recouping these costs" (Lazarovich <u>et al.</u>, 1983). The question remains of how much, and on what terms, public support is likely to be forthcoming.

Lazarovich <u>et al.</u>(1982) argue that, "a more systematic and comprehensive method of assessing government assistance for infrastructure development" is required. The "general principles" which they identify and those set out in the EMR discussion paper are identical. A conservative stance towards this form of spending is indicated, with the government's contribution to projects being "determined through an analysis of the social and economic costs and benefits." To this motherhood statement we can add the inference of the discussion paper that the accounting of social benefits will require, "firm commitments from industry" that these will be forthcoming. One must question the practical realism of policy based on such assumptions. If governments are, legitimately, concerned to get value for money from public spending on infrastructure and to minimise the riskiness of their investments, the incorporation into policy-making of a much more explicit analysis of the economic environment of particular mineral development proposals seems both feasible and necessary.

POLICY-RELEVANT PROJECT ATTRIBUTES

Public sector involvement in the provision of transportation infrastructure for frontier mining projects in Canada since 1950 reflects more a series of ad hoc decisions than the application of a consistent set of criteria for judging the necessity or extent of support. An analysis of the characteristics of some key developments suggests, however, that one can identify a limited number of variables which, if given explicit attention, could help frame a more consistent policy stance in the future. In the following paragraphs, these variables are first defined and then applied in a retrospective analysis of five frontier mining ventures which focuses their significance. They consist of attributes of the commercial and of the regional context of specific projects.

Features of the commercial context which have a bearing on arguments in support of state assistance towards the cost of transportation infrastructure are primarily: the international market structure of the mineral(s) involved, the institutional framework of the project, the geographical orientation of sales, and the projected volume (tonnage) of production. The essential elements of the regional context which complement these considerations are: location with respect to the ecumene, the extent of private sector initiative in infrastructure provision, and the prevailing level of economic development. No claim is made for the originality of these variables, but Canadian experience suggests that inadequate attention has been given to their significance as bases for a coherent policy towards mineral-related frontier infrastructure.

Canadian mineral producers are almost without exception price takers in world markets (Urquhart, 1978) and are, as a result, forced sooner or later to adjust their prices and volume of output in accordance with global demand. Even where, as is the case for some base metals, they enjoy an element of price leadership within North America, so long as they remain constrained by the dictates of commercial production (even if owned by the public sector), they are not immune to the cyclical prosperity characteristic of the industry, nor to the need to match competing suppliers in major markets. Despite the EMR's talk of, "firm commitments from industry", therefore, there will always be an element of risk associated with state expenditure on mineral-related frontier infrastructure.

The degree, and hence the political acceptability, of this risk can be more accurately estimated if the institutional framework of a project is explicitly acknowledged. Canadian mineral production takes place within four broad categories of corporate relationships, two of

which promise greater stability of output than the other two. The ver-
tically-integrated iron mines of North American steel producers represent
a distinct category in terms of relative stability of output over a period
long enough for infrastructure investments to be recovered. Canadian
firms producing under long-term (ten years or more) export contracts,
or together with foreign equity partners assuming marketing responsibilities,
represent a second group generally associated with continuity of shipments. Production at mines owned by Canadian-based integrated
processors with limited captive markets in downstream industries is
somewhat less predictable; and independent mines dependent on
short-term supply contracts are clearly least able to guarantee the
utilisation of associated infrastructure.

The reason for identifying the geographical orientation of sales
as a separate variable is that it points attention to specific characteristics of a project's market. For instance, Canadian mineral shipments to Japan, although meeting strong competition from Australia and
other Pacific Rim suppliers, enjoy greater stability as a result of
Japan's deliberate policy of diversifying raw material sourcing than they
would in its absence. The rationale for considering tonnage of production in the context of infrastructure provision is primarily for its
bearing on the economic and technical feasibility of alternative transportation systems.

Of the variables defining the regional context of frontier mineral
transportation infrastructure, the location of a project with respect to
the potential ecumene determines the likelihood of additional traffic
being generated by renewable resource-based industries. The extent
of private sector investment in, and hence the nature and extent of
demand on the public purse for, infrastructure provision is largely
determined by the commercial variables associated with a specific
project, but the state's willingness to commit funds will reflect a
broader assessment of the economic development strategy which best
meets its objectives for the region. At least four public sector
responses have been evident in Canada over the past thirty years:
leave the private sector responsible for meeting its own transportation
needs; provide transport assistance with the explicit goal of fostering
resource development; respond on the basis of a project's contribution to the attainment of other policy objectives; respond in order
to sustain the viability of a mineral-dependent economy threatened
with severe decline.

PROJECTS IN CONTEXT

The thrust of this chapter is that the reflections on state involvement
in providing transportation infrastructure to support frontier mining in
Canada that help shape the federal government's recent mineral policy
discussion paper draw less insight from past experience than they
might. Specifically, they do not identify, in the way that has just been
attempted, key variables which could provide the basis for more
consistent evaluation by policy-makers of the merits of public support

to specific projects. In this section, therefore, five frontier mineral developments are reviewed to illustrate the utility of the proposed framework of analysis for assessing their policy implications.

The development by the Iron Ore Company of Canada (IOCC) of iron mines in the Quebec/Labrador region in the early 1950s, with subsequent expansions, is the largest frontier mineral development project to have been undertaken in Canada to date and the prime example of one whose infrastructure was supplied almost entirely by the private sector. To gain access to the ore at Schefferville, IOCC had to construct a 575 km rail line to a deep-water terminal at Sept Iles. This single-purpose transportation system, necessary to extract large tonnages from a site well beyond the ecumene, accounted for approximately half of the initial capital investment in the project. Formed by a consortium of major US steel corporations to open up an entirely new source of captive ore to replace declining shipments from properties in the Lake Superior region, IOCC was the forerunner of the dramatic expansion of the Canadian mining industry brought about by the resource needs of the dynamic and hegemonic USA economy in the 1950s and 1960s. Although the mineral transportation infrastructure laid down in Quebec/Labrador was complemented within five years by the construction of the St. Lawrence Seaway at public expense (on an intended cost-recovery basis), IOCC's investment did not hinge on a firm guarantee that the Seaway would be built within a given time frame. The willingness of the private sector to assume the substantial cost of providing a regional transportation system reflected both the financial strength of the project sponsors and the economies of scale inherent in a multi-million tonne operation. By the mid-1970s, the economic environment of the US steel industry had changed radically, and the cost of much less extensive infrastructure constituted a decidedly negative factor in the evaluation of frontier iron ore resources elsewhere in Canada (Wallace, 1977).

The Pine Point lead-zinc development has already been cited for its influence on the evolution of Canadian government attitudes to frontier mineral infrastructure provision. The EMR discussion paper (1982, p.75) notes that the $75 million (1964) invested by the public sector to build the 690 km Great Slave Lake Railway to connect the mine to the continental railway system represented 66 per cent of the total initial capital costs of the project, and other publicly-funded infrastructure reduced the private sector's share to 22 per cent. "In essence, the provision of infrastructure by the government raised the [mining] company's before-tax rate-of-return from 19 to 91 per cent." This excessively generous level of public assistance, which was scarcely questioned in Parliament at the time (Macpherson, 1978), was undoubtedly a reflection of claims made for the railway, that it would open up a whole new region of the ecumene for economic development and, in particular, play a strategic role in facilitating and cheapening access to the Mackenzie River and the western Arctic. Gibson (1978, p.21) argues that:

111

"Pine Point ore was not immediately needed to supply Cominco's smelter in Trial, B.C.; the company could therefore afford to go through the slower process of persuading the federal government to build a railway to Pine Point. Very little persuasion was necessary."

The agreement between the mining company and the Canadian National Railways (CNR), which built and operates the line to Pine Point, contained a traffic guarantee of 215,000 tons per annum for a ten-year period, and on this basis a basic freight rate was agreed which tapered considerably for additional shipments. In fact, roughly three times the guaranteed tonnage was shipped during the decade. Moreover, the mine agreed to a "special charge" calculated with reference to the value of mineral shipments, for a ten-year starting in 1968. This $20 million deferred contribution to the capital cost of the railway, which was to have been collected by CNR and returned to the federal government, appears never to have been levied (Wallace, 1977). So although the Great Slave Lake Railway has indeed served the variety of social and economic objectives anticipated by its proponents, it justifies the reputation for embarassingly uncritical public sector infrastructure assistance to frontier mining which hindsight attaches to the project.

The northeast British Columbia coal project, scheduled to begin commercial shipments in December 1983, is comparable in scale to the Quebec/Labrador iron ore developments but presents a much more complex set of policy issues. Total costs of $2.8 billion (1982) include over $1 billion of public spending on infrastructure. The largest component of this is the approximately $490 million being spent by the British Columbia Railway (BCR) to construct a 130 km branch line across the grain of the Western Cordillera to link the coalfields to the existing railway network. When fully operational, in 1985, the project will involve two mines shipping at least 7.7 mllion tonnes of metallurgical coal under 15-year contracts to Japanese buyers. In the economic climate of the early 1980s, two medium-sized Canadian mining companies, even with foreign equity partners and long-term contracts, could not afford to provide the necessary infrastructure without public sector asistance. If the BCR had been forced to recover its capital and financing costs fully in the coal freight rate, it would have had to charge over $16 per tonne, in place of the $4.85 (reduced to $3.85 until March 1989) which has been agreed as its average rate over the 250 km from the mines to the CNR interchange at Prince George.

The question of what level of public support the project was to receive, and through what channels, was muddied by a notable absence of federal-provincial harmony with respect to the issues involved. This contrasted with the clear-cut objectives of the Japanese negotiators who had the specific goal of opening up a second source of supply of Canadian coal, independent of the major existing producers in southeastern British Columbia and their associated transportation infrastructure. The Canadian government was interested in developing a major Pacific coast port to relieve pressure on Vancouver. The British Columbia government sought the stimulus to sustained economic development in a frontier region which the coal project could provide. It was also aware of the positive impact which the coal traffic would have on BCR finances. Nevertheless, despite these complementary interests, "the two governments not only failed to act as coordinators of the project but often stood in each other's way and let their differences jeopardize the contract and delay its culmination" (Tafler, 1981, p.30).

Cost-recovery of provincial infrastructure investment will be achieved by imposing two surcharges on mine output, one to recover outlays on townsite, power and regional highway provision, the other, a per-tonne levy on coal shipments, to recover the railway costs. If inflation during the 1990s averages nine per cent per year, the surcharge on traffic currently contracted for will repay the public investment by the time the contracts expire. The government has indicated that additional mines which are expected to open in the region during the next decade "can expect to pay the surcharge on coal moving over the branchline and any revenues generated can be applied to provide a return and/or shorten the payback period." (Government of British Columbia, 1982, p.13). During 1981, the two mining companies requested an initial five-year freight rate reduction of $2.00 per tonne, which the railways (BCR and CNR) agreed to grant. As a result, the "development rate" which was claimed to be necessary "to sell the deal to Japan" is non-compensatory and provides a public sector subsidy to the mines' customers. It will not be offered to coal shipments in excess of volume initially contracted.

Mining operations in the Yukon Territory currently raise in an acute form the infrastructure issues associated with sustaining economically marginal production in a resource-based frontier economy. Although the region's narrow-gauge rail link to the Pacific coast was built as a private sector initiative during the 1890s gold rush, the modern mining history of the territory dates from the 1960s. Output expanded in response to favourable market conditions, strongly supported by an active government program of road construction to create a basic network of access roads to potential resource developments. The economics of transportation in the Yukon dictated that mineral traffic from these mines be trucked to the railhead at Whitehorse, from where the White Pass and Yukon Railway (WPYR) provided an integrated multimodal service to Vancouver via Skagway. The largest mineral producer, Cyprus Anvil, began its lead-zinc operations in 1969.

The viability of the WPYR which, unlike most Canadian railways, had survived the years without any form of government assistance, began to be threatened in the late 1970s by reductions in the mineral traffic on which it had come to depend. Loss of asbestos traffic in 1978 reduced WPYR's annual gross revenues by 18 per cent, with a noticeable impact on the railway's earnings (Canadian Transport Commission [CTC], 1980). A freight contract with Cyprus Anvil which

113

commenced the same year soon proved to be non–compensatory and the WPYR felt obliged to appeal to the federal government for financial assistance. This was refused in April 1979, "partly because the long-range outlook for the railway is very good ... Anticipated developments in the early 1980s will certainly benefit the railway to an unprecedented degree" (EMR Canada, 1980, p.43). Nevertheless, the granting of federal aid was reconsidered six months later in light of the railway's serious financial difficulties.

Cyprus Anvil is cited in EMR (1982, p.75) as an example of public infrastructure assistance which represents "the more usual experience in base–metal mining" in contrast to the Pine Point project. Government investment "raised the company's expected lifetime rate-of-return only from 11.5 to 15 per cent." The document does not reveal, however, that the government also gave a contractual guarantee to Cyprus Anvil of access to tidewater for shipment of its ore. A CTC inquiry occasioned by the WPYR's request for government assistance concluded that the railway "has been obliged to underwrite the move-ment of ore from Cyprus Anvil's often troubled operation at Faro and additionally, has been obliged to act in a way that honours and supports" the federal government's guarantee of tidewater access (CTC, 1980, p.194). By 1980 it was quite clear that "Cypris Anvil ore is central to the survival of the railway", and that the mining company "is entirely dependent on the railway in present circumstances" Some compromise of previous positions was required if both entities were to remain viable, and in 1981 the federal and territorial governments agreed to provide WPYR with a $6 million interest–free loan for twenty years, while Cyprus Anvil agreed to a higher, compensatory, rate.

Nevertheless, the current global recession has exposed the shallow optimism of the 1979 federal diagnosis of the WPYR's future and of the Yukon mining economy which supports it. The Cyprus Anvil mine closed, initially for two months, in June 1982, in response to continued weak metal markets. In September the closure was extended to April 1983 and the mine applied to Ottawa for a $15 million aid package. The WPYR closed down as a result of losing 80 per cent of its remaining tonnage and half its revenue. Fearing the loss of a quarter of its inhabitants by the spring of 1983 in view of the complete collapse of the territorial mining industry, the Yukon government also sought federal aid. Resumption of operations at Cyprus Anvil is recog-nised as being central to any effective short–term strategy to revive the Yukon economy and the WPYR, but bargaining between the interest-ed parties has been complicated by a labour contract dispute at the mine and the cancellation by Japanese buyers of one of the two major contracts covering its output (Financial Post, Toronto, 20 Nov., 1982). The form and extent of federal aid had not been made public at the time of writing.

This sequence of events calls into question the adequacy of the EMR's analysis of frontier mineral infrastructure issues. In the medium term, the federal government is committed to maintain some

114

configuration of mining activity in the Yukon as the economic base of the Territory. But the region is characterised by high operating costs and medium—sized base metal operations selling primarily offshore in competitive markets. In the hope of securing expanded and more stable production, the federal authorities responsible for mineral development policy (DIAND) are currently encouraging the co—ordinated development of a cluster of prospective mines in the MacMillan Pass area (Lazarovich et al., 1983). This regionalised approach is regarded as one which more readily justifies public sector assistance in extending the existing transportation infrastructure and which, by increasing the volume of traffic on the WPYR, would assure the railway of adequate revenue. How successful attempts to synchronise investment by unrelated producers facing varied market conditions will prove remains to be seen, but this strategy represents one approach to risksharing by the state and private enterprise.

A different approach is evident in the high arctic, a region where, although mineral development is embryonic, it is certain to increase in scope. The pioneeering mine, Nanisivik, was opened on Baffin Island in 1976 by a group combining Canadian and European capital, assisted by the federal government. The principal innovation of this project was the government's decision to treat its investment in projectspecific infrastructure as earning and 18 per cent equity participation. Federal interests in promoting this venture were diverse (Fish, 1979). They included the desire to demonstrate the feasibility of commercial mineral development in the far north, to gain experience of arctic shipping, and to provide opportunities for training native Inuit in mining sector skills.

Cominco's Polaris mine, a similar lead—zinc operation on Little Cornwallis Island, opened in 1982, was funded entirely by the corporation. Its principal innovation was to have the concentrator, power plant, and related units built on a barge in southern Canada and towed to the mine site, where it is permanently berthed. A point of conflict with the federal government arose with respect to transportation. The company expressed strong opposition to Ottawa's proclaimed intention to limit all shipping in Arctic waters after 1985 to Canadianregistered vessels, arguing that to be deprived of access to shipping on the international market and forced to accept the anticipated higher cost of domestic vessels was an unjustifiable burden on the remote operation. A compromise has currently been reached in that Polaris is committed to ship half its output in Canadian ships. Both these mines have been made possible by developments in arctic shipping which provide a summer season of adequate duration to export the annual production of base metal concentrates (about 150,000 t and 250,000 t respectively) from coastal sites. Marine access is crucial to the viability of projects in this region, and mineral transportation infrastructure is essentially confined, therefore, to docking facilities.

CONCLUSION

The degree and nature of state assistance to be provided to private sector mining ventures requiring transportation infrastructure investment in frontier regions will ultimately remain a matter of political judgement. Calculations of the social benefit derived from a specific project cannot reasonably be expected to be immune from the riskiness inherent in its commercial and regional environment. Public authorities who have a legitimate interest in ensuring that risks are minimised and shared equitably with the private sector would be well advised to create frameworks for policy implementation which give explicit attention to the variables identified in this chapter, whose significance has been briefly illustrated in the context of selected Canadian frontier developments.

7

OK TEDI: LESSONS HARDLY LEARNT

R.T. Jackson

INTRODUCTION

Much of the growing body of literature on the impact of mining in the third world seems to be dominated by two characteristics: its primary focus is upon the direct economic impact of mining projects at a national scale, and, secondly, it is generally optimistic. Much of this optimism is based on several positive suggestions made by the writers concerned with improving the third world nations' share of mining profits (Emerson, 1980), negotiating positions (Reid, 1981), and access to finance (Radetzki and Zorn, 1979) or expertise (Bosson and Varion, 1977; Cobbe, 1979). Even those writers who attack the mining industry are optimistic in the sense that they do not doubt its profitability; their concern is that a greater share of the profits should accrue to the host nation in question (Ilunkamba, 1980).

Nowadays, third world governments who have done their homework are in a far better position than they were a decade ago to negotiate with mining companies interested in projects in their territory. Certainly this has proved to be the case in Papua New Guinea whose representatives have renegotiated one major project (Bougainville Copper) and bargained over a new one (Ok Tedi) with skill and success in recent years.

For such countries, the problems of negotiating general issues appear to be well on the way to solution. However, several other major issues remain problematic. Firstly, any mining project, once established, needs to be supplied over a number of years; the value of such supplies may equal or exceed the value of the profits of such a project or the income generated by it for the third world country's government. The question of how to plan for the integration of such demands into the national economy for the benefit of the host nation is not a new one but it is one increasingly worth examining. While this chapter cannot answer the question, it will try to describe some of the difficulties of integration of indirect mining benefits into a national economy. The case treated is the Ok Tedi copper/gold/ molybdenum project of Papua New Guinea.

In the second part of the chapter we deal with a less frequent focus of attention in the literature: the complex question of to what degree benefits derived from a mining project should go to the mining region itself or to the national exchequer for general development expenditure. Of course local politics, local administrative arrangements and local economic history may tend to deprive any individual case study of any pretension to universal application. Nevertheless, the questions here raised for Papua New Guinea have also been raised in quite different settings. For example, Spooner (1981), referring to the Orkney and Shetland Islands has queried 'whether such [peripheral] regions with their often fragile communities and environments, are adequately compensated for social and environmental disruption'. This question of balance in the geographical allocation of benefits is, of course, only part of a wider question: how do governments which encourage mining because of the money it brings in to the national exchequer then proceed to spend that money? Johnson (1981), in his generally optimistic survey of achievements by the Botswana government, in negotiating direct national economic benefits with mining companies, ends with the warning: 'the most serious problem in the government's overall strategy to achieve social justice is that the planned re–investment [of mining revenues] in other sectors, particularly in rural development, appears to be lagging'. Precisely the same could be said in the case of Papua New Guinea. However, in this chapter, I shall examine one specific aspect of this broad topic of government's re–investment policies: to what extent should such re–investment be directed at the mining area itself?

BACKGROUND TO THE OK TEDI PROJECT (OTP)

This case study deals with the copper/gold/molybdenum deposits of Mt. Fubilan which is located in the headwaters of the Ok Tedi[1] amongst the Star Mountains of Papua New Guinea (PNG). Construction work for the mine, which will, by 1989, have cost at least US$1,400 million, commenced in August 1981 with the building of a pioneer road between the new mining town of Tabubil and a river port, 150 km away on the Fly River, at Kiunga the existing local administrative headquarters. The deposits were first discovered by Kennecott Pacific geologists in July 1968, but Kennecott withdrew from negotiations with the PNG Government in March 1975.[2] In 1976 a consortium led by Broken Hill Proprietary (BHP), which is easily the largest Australian-owned company, took over the project. BHP now owns 30 per cent of the Ok Tedi Mining Ltd (OTML) as does Amoco Minerals, a US company, whilst the PNG Government and a mini–consortium of three West German companies each effectively hold 20 per cent. Production of gold is planned to commence in 1984, of copper in 1986, and of molybdenum in 1989. The value of production will obviously depend upon metal prices but should total somewhere in the range US$8–12 billion. Through company tax, resource rental tax, personal tax, dividend withholding tax, and dividends the PNG Government hopes to retain between two–thirds and three–quarters of all profits from the mining project; between 1986 and 2010, US$4 billion is expected to flow into the government exchequer via the Mineral Resources Stabilisation Fund

118

(MRSF). The MRSF was set up as a regulatory device to handle flows to government of receipts from Bougainville Copper Limited (BCL). Its essential purpose was to prevent government spending all revenue from BCL in years of high metal prices, thus reserving substantial sums for budgeting in poor years such as 1981 and 1982. The MRSF has, generally, succeeded in this task.

The Ok Tedi project has been on a variety of drawing boards now for fourteen years which, superficially, might suggest that there has been ample time available to satisfy even the most demanding social or environmental planner. In addition, those planning for Ok Tedi have had the example of BCL before them throughout this period. The BCL project has received considerable attention in the literature and has created very severe problems for PNG's planners in economic, social and environmental fields and thus also in the wider political and legal spheres (Jackson, 1979). BCL's problems arose partly because it moved so quickly from discovery to production (in approximately six years) that it could readily be argued that inadequate time was available for serious planning. However, in addition, BCL was 'non-planned' before Independence and before the present planning structure was established. Given the BCL example and the panoply of not only national but also provincial planning structures available since Independence, one could reasonably expect that the planning for Ok Tedi would have been better prepared.

The Ok Tedi project has several other points of interest. Firstly it is located in the Star Mountains only a few kilometres from the country's border with the Indonesian province of Irian Jaya. The border zone is a sensitive area in view of continued armed Melanesian guerilla activity against Indonesian rule in Irian Jaya. Secondly, the Ok Tedi project is located in one of the least effectively incorporated parts of the country. The first exploration patrol in this area took place in 1963, only five years before Kennecott's arrival; indeed, most of the details on the area's newly issued 1:100,000 topographic maps were filled in by Kennecott. Whilst the project area in the mountains only came under government control two decades ago, the lowlands of Western Province immediately to the south were mapped and incorporated into the colonial state many decades earlier. But then, once incorporated, such areas were neglected as being of no interest, neglected to such a degree that for some years, by gentlemen's agreement, Dutch officers and missionaries administered and evangelised large portions of the northern parts of Western Province. Thus, in a sense, the planners had an almost virgin field to cultivate. Not only that but given the almost total lack of development in the general area, the 30,000 or so people of the affected region north of Kiuna, were desperately anxious for the mine to go ahead. Thus the field was not merely virgin, it was also made up of very pliable human elements.

Major obstacles to good planning at the local level did, of course, exist and not the least of these are the area's very rugged environment and extremely wet climate, and its extreme isolation.

Access to Kiunga is either by plane, or by a tortuous 850 km journey up the Fly River. However, now that the project has started, and for the rest of its planned 30-year life span, transport costs are rapidly being reduced and regularity of service is vastly improved.

The people of the area are divisible into at least three groups. The Star Mountains' people, the Min, have spread outwards from the Telefomin area of the West Sepik Province into both the Western Province and Irian Jaya. They are principally taro cultivators and gatherers. One Min sub-group, the Wopkaïmin are the owners of the mine site itself. Another sub-group, the Faiwolmin who at the time of European contact were at war with the Wopkaimin, occupy the land on which the mining township of Tabubil is presently being built. Tabubil is expected to house upwards of 8,000 persons by 1990.

In the foothills to the southwest of the mountains live the Ningerum who have traditionally cultivated both root crops and bananas as well as gathering sago. It is on Ningerum land that the mine's tailings dam will be built. In the plains to the south-east of the mountains live the Aekyom and Yonggam, the former being principally sago gatherers, the latter supplementing sago with banana cultivation. The Aekyom enthusiastically tried to adopt rubber cultivation during the 1960s and whilst only a few of the more southerly villages, accessible from Kiunga, succeeded, this innovation did lead to a revolution in Aekyom settlement patterns (Jackson and Budai Tapari, 1977; Hyndman, 1979). Previously, settlement was in family hamlets which shifted between favoured sago processing sites. With the search for economic development through rubber, large villages were established along the gentle ridge top of Kianga-Ningerum track well away from most sago areas and often on other groups' traditional land. The road from Tabubil to the project river port at Kiunga will run through this band of spontaneous resettlement.

In general terms the Min, Ningerum, Aekyom and the Yonggom were amongst the poorest people in PNG when judged in terms of cash income earning opportunities and provison by government of social services. Apart from rubber, no commercial cash crops were grown by them and their major way of earning cash was to migrate elsewhere.

THE NATIONAL PLANNING PROBLEM:
TAPPING THE PROJECT'S INDIRECT BENEFITS

The national government of Papua New Guinea's first priority in negotiating the development of the Ok Tedi mine with, first, Kennecott and later, the BHP-led consortium was the maximisation of government revenue from the project. This stemmed directly from the government's view of mining's role in national development, viz. mining in itself is regarded as not necessarily developmental but, by raising large amounts of revenue, it enables government to budget for projects which are in line with national goals and directive principles. The high priority given to revenue maximisation also stemmed, however, from the government's experiences with BCL. The original Bougainville mining agreement had been finalised, before self-government and Independence, by the Australian colonial administration. Local opposition to mining on Bougainville, unlike the later Ok Tedi case, had been rather widespread but an agreement had nonetheless been pushed through. BCL had argued, in the course of negotiation, that the mine seemed likely to be a marginal proposition economically and had obtained a variety of tax concessions from the Administration (Garnaut, 1981). However, in early 1974, BCL announced that its profit during 1973 (its first full year of operations) had been $A158 million, which was at that time the largest profit ever announced by an Australian-listed company. Such a profit was partly made possible by an upsurge of copper and gold prices during 1973 but clearly the concessions granted earlier under the pretext of 'marginality' were considered by the emerging PNG politicians as totally unnecessary if not fraudulent.

Subsequent renegotiation of the agreement in 1974 abolished most of the concessions and resulted in government receiving from 1973 onward upwards of 60 per cent of all BCL profits. However, it is relevant to note that renegotiation concerned the national government's share of revenue and that it changed little as far as local and provincial benefits were concerned (Bedford and Mamak, 1974). That lack of improved status has doomed both provincial/national government relations to this day.

In 1976 the BHP-led consortium took over responsibility for the Ok Tedi project on the basis of an agreement most of whose pages deal with problems of taxation. For three years up to 1979 the BHP-led consortium continued to stress the marginal nature of the project and in general, most government officials tended to agree with that evaluation. However, when gold prices began to soar in 1979 Ok Tedi suddenly took on a very different status – as one of the very best mining prospects anywhere in the world (Jackson, 1982). Despite government's reservations on the consortium's proposals for training and environmental matters (which the consortium then revised and improved at government's insistence), progress towards a final agreement was rapid and in the decade of negotiations between government and the mining companies the emphasis was very heavily upon the share of mining revenues passed on to government.

In general it does seem as if those negotiations resulted in the government achieving this primary aim. If profits from the project are close to the estimated total of $US5.8 billion, then on paper the government will receive upwards of 60 per cent of such profits. However, mining revenues are not the only revenues generated by the project. The total value of metals in Mt. Fubilan is, roughly, $US10 billion. Mine construction will cost $US1.5 billion, wages during the life of the mine $US0.7 billion and other maintenance costs upwards of $2 billion. Thus, over 40 per cent of the metal values will end up as project costs. This, in fact, is a larger total than that of projected government receipts from mining revenues. Whilst the principal aim of government may have been achieved, to what extent has government also managed to tap these large indirect benefits of the project? To what extent will Ok Tedi be integrated into the PNG economy? And, what planning has been done to achieve this?

Overall the simple answer to all three questions is: very little. A variety of reasons can be adduced to explain this situation. Firstly, given the BCL experience it is not at all surprising that the government gave top priority to ensuring that the sharing of mining revenues was weighted in its favour. But given the state's limited manpower resources much less attention could be given to the matter of indirect benefits.

Secondly, there is the obvious fact that before the mining project can be integrated there has to be a project. Until late 1979 there was always doubt as to whether Ok Tedi would ever shed its marginal status. Planners, burdened with the day-to-day management problems of development throughout PNG, were able to devote little attention to the question of internal project linkages until 1980 by which time insufficient time remained for adequate planning.

Thirdly, and arising out of the preceding point, as with all mining projects, plans for Ok Tedi changed constantly throughout the negotiating period. This point is of major significance and requires some elaboration. What might have appeared to the outsider to be very minor technical changes in the project would later turn out to have had a revolutionary effect on its whole design. A change in economically viable ore content measuring one part in a million might mean the gain (or loss) of 500 more employees or might indeed mean the life or death of the whole project. A rearrangement of financing arrangements or production schedules might result in doubling the size of the mine town at Tabubil.

For example, early in 1979 the consortium came up with a 'staging' concept for mine construction and production whereby gold would be mined and processed first and only later would copper extraction begin. This would both reduce early construction costs and allow later costs to be financed from early production. A simple enough idea, but one which meant that the whole project became very much more attractive even before gold prices started to soar — and had to be redesigned. A second example is that, at the time of writing, no location has yet been chosen for the site of the project's ocean terminal. If a remote site is chosen, integration of the project with the national economy will become extremely difficult; if Port Moresby, the capital, were selected, as is possible, considerably greater potential might be available for integration. Under such circumstances, the planners need to be extraodinarily flexible.

Fourthly, the generally weak development of manufacturing industry in Papua New Guinea might suggest that even if physical linkages made opportunities available few could be taken up (Jackson, 1981). Certainly

it is true that the bulk of mine needs – heavy transport, fuels, highly specialised equipment –will, for the foreseeable future need to be
imported. Nevertheless on this point it does appear that inadequate
attention was paid to local potential – by government if not by some
private firms. Even if local supplies in fact contained a high import
component the potential in terms of local employment in such areas
as office equipment supplies, foodstuffs, construction steel, insurance,
housing materials, furnishings etc. would seem worthy of serious investigation. Furthermore, whilst it may be unrealistic to expect the development of mining supply industries in a country with only one major
project, realism takes a small step forward when there are two such
projects. There is a fair probability that several further major mining
ventures might be developed in PNG during the next two decades.[3]
Under such circumstances then the development of a mining supply
industry certainly seems plausible.

Fifthly, such a development would require a change in government
policy towards mining. The present policy, as stated above, is to regard
mining as a means of raising revenue for development rather than as
intrinsically developmental. In a sense, it is this policy more than
any other factor which dissuaded planners from serious investigation
of linkages between Ok Tedi and the economy as a whole. The policy
as it stands has much to commend it: it implies a determination by
government to develop as it sees fit and not be drawn into too great
a dependence on an industry infamous for its fluctuating revenues,
low employment to capital ratios, and environmental impact. But as long
as the policy remains in force then it will give little encouragement to
the development of mining as an integral part of the economy in which
case the policy could be interpreted as encouraging the natural
tendency of mining projects to become enclaves, and as writing off
PNG's claim to any major share ot such project's indirect benefits.

When we combine all the above reasons: relative priorities, a
rapidly changing decision-making environment, inhibiting policy directives
and lack of time, we can understand why government's input into the
process of integrating the project into the national economy was small.

The majority of any further direct links between the project and
the national economy are likely to come about less as a result of
government planning than through the project company's tender award
system which gives preferences to companies based in PNG and with
local equity. There will, then, be some flow of indirect benefits from
the project to the general economy, but not as a result of any great
effort on the part of government.

The lesson PNG learnt from the Bougainville experience was the
need to ensure the getting of the greatest share of mining revenue.
It showed that it had absorbed that lesson reasonably well in dealing
with Ok Tedi. But, in turn, one of the lessons from Ok Tedi is the
need to examine means of tapping the indirect benefits. The nature
of the mining industry's own planning processes, subject as they are

123

to rapidly changing circumstances, might suggest that the simplest way of doing this is to incorporate into the mining agreement clauses which formally encourage the companies to favour locally based companies when tenders for supply of goods and servics are called. Beyond this, however, if the longer term strategy of Papua New Guinea seriously intends to incorporate several other mining projects then a more intimate involvement in the planning of domestic industries would seem desirable.

DIRECT REGIONAL BENEFITS OR
OVERALL NATIONAL DEVELOPMENT?

Right from the start, the government's attitudes on the question of balance between national and regional gains have been confused. Whilst attempts were made to generate direct local benefits, ambivalence became evident when these conflicted with national aims. The 1976 agreement between the government and mining company did entail several clauses which, it was hoped would help to ensure certain benefits for the development of the mining region. Specifically, the Telefomin District of the West Sepik Province and the Kiunga District of the Western Province were:

> to be given preference, where possible, by the consortium's employment policy; and

> to be given preferential treatment by the consortium in any business development assistance provided by them.

Benefits for the whole of the two provinces concerned were not built into the agreement. With a view to obtaining baseline data for the further planning and implementing of such worthy objectives, the present writer was commissioned by government departments to report on the general development of the region up to 1977. Despite the patchy nature of the data which these reports made available to them, the government negotiators pressed very hard to ensure that the final agreements followed and amplified the guidelines for local participation laid down in 1976. However, in the end, it must be said that whatever efforts were put into negotiations the benefits experienced by local people so far do not match such efforts.

Some of the reasons for such a situation are rather obvious ones. It is in the nature of big mine construction that it starts with a bang and is finished as quickly as possible. Almost all mine construction is farmed out to specialist firms usually on contracts with stiff penalty clauses for any delay in completion and bonus payments as a lure for early completion. Such firms cannot afford to take much notice of local people unless such people are trained and available as part of the construction workforce. In the Ok Tedi case, construction commenced in August 1981, thirteen years after the ore body's discovery, yet no more than a handful of the area's thirty thousand inhabitants had received training to qualify them for anything more than labouring work with the project. Much of the responsibility for such a situation lies with the lack of adequate planning by the government itself and, more especially, with the lack of implementation of such plans. Three interrelated factors may be mentioned as contributing to such inadequacies: (a) an unwillingness by government to finance infrastructure in the mining area prior to a firm agreement with the mining consortium to proceed with the project; (b) the dilemma the national government faced trying to maximise mining revenue whilst also having to finance developments in the mining areas; and (c) a lack of co-ordination both between national government departments and between national and provincial governments involved.

The Government's 'wait and see' policy

The PNG government's guidelines on mining investment date, in the main, from 1973 in the early days of self-government. These guidelines state inter alia that all mining projects should provide their own infrastructure. Whilst the policy was, and remains, a reasonable one it tended to have the effect of holding back what otherwise might have been normal government infrastructure investment in the mining area. In the short term this made sense — it seemed wise to wait and see what form of infrastructure mining would need and would bring, rather than to spend money on developments which would possibly be made obsolete in a very short time. But since 13 years elapsed between discovery of the orebody and the first phase of mine construction such a policy led to considerable frustration in the region.

From per capita data relating to the period 1969-1971 Kent-Wilson estimated relative levels of general development for each of the 79 sub-districts in Papua New Guinea on a relative scale ranging from 0 to 100. On this scale the crude mean for all sub-districts was 29.3 whilst the scores for Kiunga and Telefomin sub-districts were 17.6 and 6.0 respectively. The criteria used by Kent-Wilson included cash cropping production, health facilities, government staffing, school enrolment, accessibility and local government. Telefomin scored far below the crude mean on all criteria and Kiunga only scored above the crude mean on health facilities; significantly, all health facilities in the Kiunga area were at that time provided by missions and not the government. Of vital significance was the fact that at the time of Kent-Wilson's survey there was no secondary school in either sub-district. Those students who gained entry to such schools had to travel as boarders to schools several hundred miles away from home. As a result, whilst the average, in 1977, for Papua New Guinea was one secondary school student for every 77 persons, that for Kiunga was 1:141 and for Telefomin 1:250. This was of particular significance since, aside from labouring work, employment on the project generally requires a minimum education qualification of four years at high school.

Only after many years of lobbying and the raising by local people of K16,000 towards it, did the government agree in February 1977 to proceed with the construction of a high school at Kiunga. The first graduates of the school are now being produced. As far as Telefomin is concerned, a high school was set up in 1980 but adequate funds for it have never been made available and there is some danger that it may have to close shortly.

In health matters delay was even greater since it was thought even more desirable to wait and see what mining requirements would be before further facilities were provided. In any case, government could argue that health provision in the area was above standard for the country as a whole - even though this was a result of mission rather than government efforts.

Economic development was also affected negatively during the thirteen year exploration period. Agricultural development in the area had long been made difficult by its remoteness; indeed at the time of Kent-Wilson's survey cash crop production from the area was nil. Agricultural extension workers who were trying to encourage plantings of rubber and chilli were, obviously, constantly faced with the dilemma of trying to carry out their work in an area which, at any moment, might find most of its labour force abandoning cash crops for mine-related employment. Development of market garden projects suffered from the disadvantage of lack of markets as long as mining did not proceed and government agencies in this area specifically instructed their field agents to leave such matters to various missionaries. Preparation of the people for mine-related business activities was much less well organised. Not until 1979 when the mining agreement was virtually completed was a very junior Business Development officer sent to the area. Before that no Business Development extension agent had been supplied on the grounds that until mining plans were known any effort would be wasted. The same logic was applied to road construction, electricity supply, telephone systems, housing and town planning. Whilst in Port Moresby, Ok Tedi took up millions of man-hours of work, in the project area the advice was, wait a little longer; it was advice given for 13 years.

The net result of this policy was therefore the generation of frustration and feelings of neglect amongst the local people and, when the decision to mine was eventually taken, to leave them in a very weak position to take advantage of the concessionary clauses won for them in the 1976 Agreement with the mining consortium. These problems partly arose from the lack of precision in the national mining policy: whilst it is indeed reasonable that projects should provide their own infrastructure this should not excuse government from the need to provide infrastructure which the regional population would need whether or not mining were to take place. Since the mining area was one of the least developed areas of the country with minimal infrastructural provision (by government), and since one of the stated national aims of PNG was and is to move towards greater regional equality in the provision of opportunities for development such a policy, with hindsight, would seem to have been in error.

Regional development vs revenue maximisation

The fundamental interest of the national government in the Ok Tedi Project was to maximise national revenues. As the major financial beneficiary of the project it, therefore, stood to lose most revenue as a result of any expenditure by the project (let alone direct spending by itself) on the local region. This applied not only to direct project expenditure on training or land compensation, for example, but also on indirect expenditure such as subsidisation of local production of market garden crops. Thus any expenditure on local or regional development in the mining area would reduce total revenue to the national government. Two other factors helped to sharpen this conflict of interest in the Ok Tedi case. Firstly, the decision to proceed with the project came in early 1981 at a time which saw the beginning of a still unended period of reduced export earnings for PNG. Throughout 1981, prices for all the country's exports remained very depressed: prices in 1981 expressed as a percentage of average prices 1970-79 (at 1980 constant prices) included: copra 52.4 per cent, coffee 62.8 per cent, cocoa 64.5 per cent, palm oil 67.8 per cent and copper 60.2 per cent whilst gold prices steadily slumped throughout the year (PNG National Planning Office, 1981). During 1981, therefore government revenue was under very severe pressure and by 1982 government expenditure had to be cut back in many areas. Revenue maximisation from Ok Tedi took on even more importance as a result, whilst the opposition at central government levels to expenditure in the local area increased.

Secondly, a separatist movement emerged in the mine region whose aim was to have a new province declared for the area (the North Fly) as a separate entity from the pre-existing and much larger Western Province. Whilst this movement came into being in the mid-sixties its presence only began to be felt seriously by the government in Port Moresby in 1979. Since then, and particularly since the decision to mine was taken, the group has made various demands for development planning funds separate from those of Western Province in general, demands which the national government, in view of its expected great dependence in future upon Ok Tedi resources, has partially met. In a sense, the North Fly separatists' argument gains much of its weight as a result of the 'wait-and-see' policy described earlier. However, in the absence of any thought-out policy on the question of balance between regional and national benefits, when the crisis came no national answers could be given to the secessionists' demands.

Revenue pressures and the emergence of political pressure groups within the mining region have thus intensified the government's dilemma. Its response to the dilemma has been a sharp one, verbally if not, so far, in political practice, for the 1982 Budget papers refer to major resource project areas as follows:

"Experience of recent years has shown that the full costs of major projects need to be taken into account when assessing

127

viability. Too often the costs of secondary infrastructure and
services necessitated by the project are not included in the
initial economic assessment. This results in government paying
these costs as direct subsidies to the project. In general a
very high standard of non-essential support has been provided.
However, general welfare and development services, no matter
how desirable, should not be confused with economic projects.
The resource projects should bear only the cost of essential
support, while associated development proposals should compete
with other expenditure demands under the other objectives".
(Emphasis added.)

In the Ok Tedi context, this statement contains at least one direct
untruth and shows signs of being little more than a knee-jerk reaction
devoid of political reality. The logic of PNG mining policy is that project
revenues should be maximised to enable government, through its
central planning agencies, to finance development throughout the
country according to national development principles. However, from the
regional point of view there are two weaknesses to the argument.
Firstly, for peripheral areas which are fortunate enough to possess
economic mineral (or other) resources, such resources are seen as
the only way the region will attract attention and development. This is
clearly true in the Ok Tedi case: the North Fly has been part of Papua
New Guinea for 98 years now and for 90 years it remained almost
totally ignored by government in Port Moresby. Only Ok Tedi and Port
Moresby's great hopes for Ok Tedi have given the North Fly people
any political weight at all. They must gain maximum benefit now whilst
they, albeit fortuitously, occupy centre stage in the country's economic
affairs, and before they slip out of the spotlight as Ok Tedi is mined
out. They regard themselves (and by any objective standards their view
is justified by the facts) as having been neglected for many decades
and regard appeals by the central government to allow its resources
to be used for the benefit of all the country as being not entirely
fair.

Secondly, and more basically, there is the question raised by
Johnson (1981) and mentioned earlier in the context of Botswana: the
logic of the government's argument for its role as re-distributor of
revenues gained from the exploitation of local resources is hardly
borne out by its past record in such re-investment. Local interests
would be justified in suspecting that their share of such a redistribution would be small. Empirical research has indicated reasonably
clearly that national expenditure in PNG since 1970 has not been
redistributive in a geographic sense and that regional disparities have,
if anything, grown rather than been reduced (Barry and Jackson, 1981;
Hinchcliffe, 1979). The most recent government comment on this matter
was contained in the 1982 National Public Expenditure Plan which
states that "it makes no sense to encourage the development of all
rural areas. In the past this emphasis on rural areas has been taken
to mean the direct subsidisation of rural enterprises and districts,
irrespective of their long term viability. It must be accepted that

128

population and activity will naturally shift to areas of greatest economic potential" (PNG National Planning Office, 1981). This statement
would appear to signal a significant shift in government policy away from
an area in which it has had little success in the past. From the view-
point of leaders of the people in the Ok Tedi mining area it merely
strengthens their determination to get what benefits they can rather than
see them go to urban areas or into politically-inspired projects elsewhere. If the policy is now to be of selective investment only in
'viable' regions, then such people are well aware of their own, long-
term peripheral position in respect of such policy aims.

A further implication of such a policy is that other regions which
currently might be regarded as being 'non-viable' and thus liable to
little government assistance now, may, in future, themselves be
discovered to be in possession of major mineral resources. Indeed,
this is highly likely given the nature of known mineral resource distribution in PNG. Once again the regional economic and political problems
experienced at Ok Tedi might be expected to arise as previously
neglected areas take on national economic significance.

We are left, therefore, with the rather unusual conclusion that,
given Papua New Guinea's rich mineral resources and the example
of the rags—to—riches Ok Tedi story, not only would a continuation and
strengthening of the regional equality policy be socially just but it could
also ensure that future, often unexpected mining projects were not
faced with unrealistically high demands from people who justifiably felt
themselves to have been neglected by the development planners. A
degree of regional equality in basic infrastructure is, in other words,
of great significance to the future mining industry of the country, and
revenue maximisation goals must be tempered by this fact.

Lack of co—ordinated planning

It is difficult to be precise and at the same time not be libellous
in describing the grounds for stating that co—ordinated planning for the
OTP was conspicuously absent. Lack of co—ordination stemmed from
at least three sources: the inability of national government and
provincial government to work out what each should plan and implement; lack of co-operation between the various national government
departments involved, and the general lack of knowledge amongst both
national and provincial government officers of conditions and aspi-
rations in the project areas.

From 1975 onwards the national government of PNG has decentra-
lised to 19 provincial governments a variety of functions whose exact
number differ from province to province but which in virtually every
case include responsibility for health, education other than post-
secondary schools, agricultural development and land matters. The Fly
River Provincial Government (FRPG) of the Western Province in which
the Ok Tedi Project is located is one of the poorest and least well
staffed of any in the country. Whilst it will directly benefit from the

project, insofar as it will receive 95 per cent of the 1.25 per cent of royalty on all exports by the project, its attitude all along was that without at least an advance on such revenues and, preferably, great increased recurrent annual grants from the national government it would not be able to fulfil its responsibilities to what it regarded as a project which was basically of national rather than merely provincial importance.

The national government for its part was, first, reluctant to spend project revenues in advance and, second, especially reluctant to do so via a provincial government whose professional competence many national public servants and politicians frankly doubted. Moreover, there was no easy way by which the national government could be assured that any finance given to the provincial government would actually be spent on the project region. The obvious solution would have appeared to have been the establishment of a special planning authority for the project area to temporarily takeover not only the FRPG's responsibilities in the area but also those of the West Sepik Provincial Government in the Telefomin area. Such a step, however, was vigorously lobbied against by those opposing the North Fly separatist group. Such opponents included not only people from the southern portion of Western Province but all those who did not wish to see any encouragement given to separatist tendencies. Since there is virtually no province in PNG without some sort of separatist movement such a solution had many opponents.

In the end, however, a 'half-baked' special planning authority did come into being — 'half-baked' because the 'authority' lacked bureaucrats with planning expertise. It was even quickly taken over almost entirely by North Fly separatist politicians. In short, disputes between national and provincial government over their role in the Ok Tedi project allowed the North Fly separatists to obtain a much more powerful influence in Ok Tedi matters than either party would have wished. Whilst this was, of course, an inadvertent victory for local involvement in the project, the lack of any planning expertise available to the local politicians and their current unwillingness to accept such expertise is likely to have less than optimal results for local people.

The second reason for a lack of co-ordinated planning in the OTP was the rivalry between different national government departments for control of the project's co-ordination. This resulted partly from the very nature of the project, partly because of personality clashes and partly through sheer-bloody-mindedness. Leaving aside the last two factors, the first is of some general interest. As a mining project gathers momentum so the relative focus of the project changes. In turn, the relative interests of different government departments in the project will vary. Thus, in the early stages of a project, the emphasis is on the exploration and proving of the ore deposit and at such a stage the government department of mines (Minerals and Energy in the PNG case) clearly has more need to keep a close eye on the project than almost any other government body. Once the project begins to take on a semblance of feasibility, the departments with responsibility for legal matters and finance would be expected to become more and more involved. Once feasibility seems to be proven then the departments responsible for physical planning, environment and labour become more interested. Of course, all these interests and others besides are present from the first; it is the relative strengths of such interest which vary. As with the problem of preparing the local project area for its role, here too a special 'task force' approach might seem appropriate. This would seem especially true in the staffing circumstances of the PNG bureaucracy in which many senior positions are still held by expatriates on three year contracts. Expatriate staff turnover therefore is very high whilst frequent transfers and rapid promotion of national staff further reduce the ability of particular departments to handle anything other than day to day matters. Such a turnover also ensures both a lack of continuity and a failure by government to build up its collective, accumulated skills and knowledge.

The lack of knowledge amongst top government negotiators of actual conditions in the mining area, immediately outside the confines of the mining camp itself also contributed to poor planning. There was a marked reluctance by the members of the government team organising the negotiating and planning of the project even to meet at Kiunga or Daru (and, vice versa, difficulty in getting provincial or local officials to Port Moresby meetings), let alone investigate personally – which meant, on foot – the reactions or the conditions of the local people. Far too much reliance was placed upon the observations of a small handful of individuals who were rather peripheral to the key processes. One result was that the national planning team's 'feel' for the area was negligible and when minor problems arose in the project area few people realised that they were problems with a potential for growth. One simple example of this ignorance must suffice: the 1976 Agreement between BHP and the government states, on several occasions, that the Telefomin sub-district is a part of Western Province. It is in fact in the West Sepik Province and has never been in Western Province.

CONCLUSIONS

In short the experience of the Ok Tedi poject so far justifies the optimism of those who argue that third world governments are now in a much better position than they were a decade ago to negotiate for themselves in major resource projects. But it also suggests that one of the chief reasons why PNG will not receive any great proportion of the indirect benefits of the project is simply because it assigned far greater significance to ensuring its share of direct benefits.

The state has created for itself a dilemma between its own revenue maximisation efforts and its responsibility to protect the interests of all the people in part of its electorate. Its renewed determination, as expressed in the 1982 Budget, to use such projects for the good of the whole country rather than for 'excessive' expenditure

131

in the project area will also have to be matched by a much more effective performance in its role of redistribution. In fact, even if its
performance in this role were far better than it has been, there are
numerous reasons why the government of PNG and others like it, might
find themselves mistaken in proceeding too vigorously with such a
policy. Amongst these we might mention the fact that for many such
project areas mining seems to be the only conceivable means of
achieving any form of progress towards satisfying the people's demands
for development within their own area. However, a far more practical,
if less moral, argument is simply that in weakly incorporated states, long
term revenue maximisation by central government is probably best
achieved by ensuring a contented population in the vicinity of all-too-
vulnerable mining projects.

'Resource rental taxes' (known by their opponents as additional
profits taxes) are now accepted increasingly by both governments and
mining companies alike (Garnaut and Clunies Ross, 1974). The fundamental logic of such a tax is that above and beyond a certain rate
of return on any resource project, additional profits are a reflection
of the 'accidentally' rich nature of the resource rather than of any
great efficiency by the exploring company. Such a tax ensures that the
greater part of any profits in excess of a reasonable rate of return
on a company's investment accrues to government. This, it can be
argued, is somewhat analogous to the position of the inhabitants of
an area which, through no merit (or fault) of their own, is found to
possess economically exploitable mineral (or other natural) resources.

In the Ok Tedi and the wider Papua New Guinea case, the
inhabitants are clearly investing something of their own – specifically
their land as well as, more generally, their way of life. Their 'reasonable rate of return' might well be a level of infrastructural services
equal to the level of the national average; their equivalent of the
company's minor share of additional profit might similarly be calculated
in terms of services over and above the national average.

Above all, the Ok Tedi case suggests that planners have done
their job well in determining their relationships and those of the
national government they serve with the investing companies. But they
have done very poorly in determining the same relationship with the
people of the project area.

132

NOTES

1. Since 'Ok' is the Star Mountains peoples' word for river, Ok Tedi River is tautological and avoided here.

2. Frieda River (copper), Ramu (nickel/cobalt), Porgera (gold), Misima Island (gold), Manus Island (copper), Kainantu (gold), Yandera (copper), Gulf Province (gas) are all regarded by the PNG National Planning Office as likely candidates. Most would require capital investments in excess of $US250 million some in excess of $US1 billion.

THE IMPACTS OF RESOURCE DEVELOPMENTS

IN THE HUNTER VALLEY, NEW SOUTH WALES

8
RESOURCE DEVELOPMENT AND ENVIRONMENTAL PLANNING: THE HUNTER VALLEY EXPERIENCE

Diana G. Day, and Richard A. Day

Considerable attention has been devoted to documenting the impact of coal based industrial developments in the Hunter Valley Region. Much of this work is in the form of specialist reports, impact statements and single agency development plans. However overviews have been published by Hunt (1978), Muswellbrook Shire Council (1980), Wise (1981), University of Newcastle (1981) and Day (1982a). This paper is concerned with reviewing the mechanisms employed in the planning, co-ordination and management of the development that took place. Approaches range from single agency and private sector development plans, through formal attempts at co-ordination under the general auspices of the New South Wales (NSW) Environmental Planning and Assessment Act (and associated legislation), to ad hoc state initiatives such as the creation of a co-ordinator of infrastructure development for the Hunter Region. The efficacy of these arrangements is appraised by reference to the general body of procedural planning theory.

DEVELOPMENTS IN THE HUNTER

Rapid expansion of underground and surface coal mining activities within the Hunter Valley in the late seventies was fostered in part by the 1973 and following OPEC oil price rises and the subsequent new comparative price advantage of coal as an energy source on world markets. Within New South Wales an anticipated accelerated growth in demand for electricity stemmed from enticements made by the Labour Government to the aluminium industry of large assured supplies of relatively cheap electricity which in turn boosted the requirements for electricity generation. Along with steadily increasing general electricity generation consumption, this heralded an increased demand for labour, in time of high unemployment. Construction of new power stations commenced at Bayswater in the central Hunter and Eraring at Lake Macquarie. Six Hunter power stations, five of which are in production, have a potential future cumulative capacity of 11,210 MW. Although Water Resources Commission budgeting for water supply to power stations in the Upper Hunter has included volumes for a further two power stations, it is not clear whether there are any plans for their development. Two possible sites in the Upper Hunter are under scrutiny by the New South Wales State Electricity Commission. A further possibility is to locate a further generating plant on Tuggerah Lake to the south of Newcastle.

137

Coal for the region's power stations is supplied from a number of Singleton North-West District and Newcastle District mines. For example, the new Eraring power station, with the second generating unit producing power on 29 November, 1982, is currently supplied by two underground collieries, Myuna and Cooranbong. The Mount Arthur North open-cut mine will provide around 8 million tonnes of steaming coal for Electricity Commission power stations by the late 1980's. This mine has gone to tender to reduce State Electricity Commission financial commitments with delayed deliveries until 1985/6 following a slow down of Bayswater and other power station developments.

New coal mining activities are located generally within the Single-ton and Muswellbrook Shires in the central Hunter, with further author-isation to the west. For example, the large Department of Mineral Resources authorisation area to the west of Muswellbrook is set aside for geological studies of coal suitability for conversion to liquid fuels. Further open-cut and underground mining occurs at Ulan to the far west. By 1985, at least 13 open-cut mines will be in full operation in the central Hunter Valley with these Northern coalfields already yielding a total raw coal production of 16.14 million tonnes in 1979/80. The Hunter Valley has 73 per cent of the State's measured and indicated coal resources of which a high percentage can be mined economically by open-cut technologies. These reserves should be a continuing significant focus for coal developments in NSW.

The Alcan Australian Ltd aluminium smelting plant at Kurri-Kurri at 90,000 tonnes capacity p.a. is the only completed plant within the Hunter. Major construction works for the Tomago Aluminium smelter (North of Newcastle), with 220,000 tonnes proposed capacity, are underway while the Lochinvar Aluminium project failed, due to the inability of BHP to find a partner for the $500 million venture. This has substantially reduced the need for large blocks of electricity.

Concomitant with these large scale resource developments, has been a rapid phase of urban growth, particularly within the Singleton Shire. Substantial revenue and capital sources are being used by Singleton Shire Council to meet local infrastructure needs for roads, sewerage, residential sites, recreation and parking. As a major land developer for the Shire, the Council has provided industrial land at the Mt Thorley Industrial Estate and, at Singleton Heights, a large reserve of residential land (Parker and Hirst, 1981).

Major coal based development projects in the Hunter Region entail a total investment of over $9,000 million (Perkins, 1982). Related infrastructure requirements within the Upper Hunter include major water storage and distribution systems, and road and rail networks. At the time of the accelerated power stations construction programme of 1980/81, it was envisaged that up to four power stations in the Upper Hunter would require about 62,000 ML per annum of fresh water by 1990 and around 100,000 ML per annum by 2005. With current water supply such provisions would have been unavailable. Further developments since the establishment of Glenbawn Dam (1958) are:

the Glennies Creek Dam now commencing storage in connection with Bayswater Power station development and with the potential for Newcatle Water Supply augmentation;

the pending enlargement of Glenbawn Dam in the mid–late 1980's; and

the probable diversion of Barnard River Water through the NE divide of the Hunter Valley and thence via the Hunter River for further regular water supply to power stations.

With a slow down of construction at Bayswater, completion of the Barnard diversion scheme has been deferred until late 1984. The phasing of Glenbawn Dam enlargement is also unclear. The New South Wales Water Resources Commission indicate the possibility of one or two additional major storages on Hunter tributaries before 2005 although this does not seem highly likely at present in view of restricted financing arrangements and a slightly reduced short term industrial demand. The construction of Tillegra Dam on the Williams River north of Newcastle would assure metropolitan Newcastle of a large additional capacity by the late 1980's, but the overall viability of this scheme is in doubt.

To a large degree, existing road and rail infrastructure have been utilized for coal transport with the completion of the Ulan–Sandy Hollow Railway line for transport of coal from Ulan mines to the coal loading facilities at the Port of Newcastle at a cost of near $70 million. Further development is in the form of spur lines such as the Saxonvale Rail Loop, the Mount Thorley Railway and proposed Wambo and BBC/United Rail Loop extensions. Surplus capacity on the double track railway line from Muswellbrook to the Port has, in line with government policy, facilitated quite intensive, 24 hour-a-day coal transport to Newcastle for storage and export at the two existing coal loading facilities. Future capacity of the Port will be increased by the construction of a new coal loader at Kooragang Island. Considerable coal movement is by road however, and continuous upgrading of the New England Highway and privately owned roads is in progress.

Since the introduction of the Environmental Planning and Assessment Act, 1979, a designated development application must be accompanied by an Environmental Impact Statement and it has been through these statements for major projects and through subsequent assessment that the details of projects and their perceived potential environmental effects have been made public. Almost 100 environmental impact statements for developments in the Hunter planning region are in progress or have been processed. These include aluminium smelters (three per cent), coal mines (31 per cent), coal related projects, for example, coal washery and rail loader (10 per cent) concrete batching plants (eight per cent), electricity generation and

139

distribution (six per cent), extractive industry (sand/gravel) (13 per cent), forestry (one per cent), marinas (six per cent), Port facilities (three per cent), railways (three per cent), roads (one per cent), water supply (three per cent) and other (12 per cent).

Such statements, their assessments and a number of public enquiries (e.g. the R.W. Miller and Co Pty Ltd, Mount Thorley open-cut mine enquiry) reveal a number of environmental concerns related to development in the Hunter embracing economic, social and biophysical areas. Examples are unemployment, scarce housing, diminished water quality, noise and air quality issues, water availability, landuse conflicts, land subsidence, and lack of visual and recreational amenity.

The following section examines how single development agency planning responded to the problems of major industrial expansion within the Hunter Valley.

DEVELOPMENT AGENCY PLANNING

Major public sector development agency planning strategies are not publicly exhibited and discussed in the manner of environmental plans. However they can be ascertained to varying degrees from a variety of sources, although it is often difficult to establish precisely how individual agencies plan development and how sensitivity and flexibility are incorporated into such plans. Information exchange with the public, and indeed sometimes between branches of an agency, is often poor.

In the Hunter Valley, some of the major public development groups involved in coal extraction are the Electricity Commission of New South Wales (SEC), the Hunter District Water Board, the Water Resources Commission, New South Wales (WRC), the State Rail Authority, the Department of Main Roads, the Maritime Services Board, the Public Works Department and the Department of Mineral Resources. To take an example, the activities of the SEC within the Hunter are most frequently determined from media coverage which conveys the dynamically changing situation of electricity supply provision. Recent environmental impact statements, such as for the Bayswater Power Station, the Barnard River Water Supply Project or the Mount Arthur North coal project, give summaries of the basic location, design and overall environmental impact of the projects. Studies of the impact of a project are frequently specific only to the development. For instance, implications for water quality downstream, or in relation to other projects, are only loosely addressed.

The WRC (1981) environmental impact statement on the Glenbawn Dam enlargement did synthesize development plans for that dam and other storages under the ambit of WRC control. However, it did not address in detail the proposed activities of the SEC in drawing water from a north-east catchment through to Glenbawn Dam and any of the questions such a diversion scheme would raise. WRC liaison with agricultural water users is frequent, in terms of press releases regard-

140

ing times of permitted pumping from surplus flows along the Hunter. Further, letters were sent to irrigators announcing details of the new water allocation and water ordering schemes. However the bulk of these communications tend to be in the form of short term advices rather than longer term policy change. The Department of Agriculture has had some input to the determination of water allocation volumes. However, written details on the introduction of such new schemes are difficult to find and information must be gleaned by a succession of personal interviews at the agencies concerned.

Agency development plans for the Hunter have been frequently described most clearly in meetings with the public, with selected interest groups and with official committees, such as the Hunter Planning Committee. For example, the SEC, the WRC and the State Rail Authority are frequently represented at public meetings concerned with industrial expansion and the Hunter environment. Outlines of recent construction timetabling are often given at such meetings, although sometimes the quality and quantity of information flow would seem insufficient even for a public audience. Many government groups are represented at the numerous public meetings and conferences held in the Hunter Valley over the past six years.

Annual reports are a further indication of some recent and future agency initiatives, although generally to the exclusion of all other agencies. It must be noted, however, that trends in policy change are frequently not specified at first, but embodied as an internalised information flow for relevant employees within that organisation. Future plans are almost always vaguely referenced in the annual report. For example, in the SEC 1981 Annual Report (p.9), relating to future developments it is stated that, 'investigations of possible sites for future power station development beyond the present programme continue.'

Further information regarding present and future activities of major development agencies is found in occasional publications, leaflets and the various Acts; for example, the 1973 Mining Act and the 1979 Glennies Creek Dam Act. Yet papers and explanatory documents are rarely issued and that part of the information base relating to agency development planning which is made public, or indeed conveyed to other agencies, may be substantially limited.

However it is apparent that there is both informal and more formal liaison between some development agencies. For example, the Hunter District Water Board, the WRC, the SEC and the Public Works Department are represented on the Water Utilisation Council. In association with this Council, the WRC has produced a sequence of plans and a more recent review of water resource development within the Hunter Region. It can be supposed that wide ranging informal and formal discussions occurred between the government groups in order to establish priorities for water storage schemes, delivery systems, management and financing of storages and agreement of completion dates for construction as well as considerations of adverse environmental impact. In the latest review of water requirements for the Hunter Region (WRC, 1982), as well as in preceding documents, estimates of water requirements are given for power generation, coal mining, coal liquefaction, other industry, urban and agriculture as well as for other use/losses. While it is quite difficult to establish how such potential usage estimates were derived, it is anticipated that information exchanges were made between development and other service agencies in order to arrive at best estimates of water requirement and mode of supply.

Yet, to a large extent individual agencies are primarily concerned with problems pertaining to their own development program. For example, the SEC initiated the Barnard River diversion scheme to provide for reasonably large, regular water supplies for Upper Hunter power stations which were in 1980/81 under a full phase of expansion, following the 1980 Accelerated Energy Development Program. The scheme would give the SEC almost immediate flexibility and independence in fresh water provision for cooling. This sense of urgency has lapsed with the cancellation of the Lochinvar smelter project and the shelving of expansions at the Kurri-Kurri Alcan smelter. Even so drought and reduced flows along the Hunter River in 1981 resulted in almost a cessation of river water pumping for Liddell Power Station for one year and, preparedness to lower the level of two of the station's circulating water pumps. This would have exacerbated the need for near future additional assured water supplies had not construction phases on Bayswater Power Station been delayed.

THE NEED FOR CO-ORDINATION

A number of resource development problems ranging from deficiencies in transport infrastructure through unmonitored environmental effects and poor communication between development agencies, private industry and the public, suggests the need for some more effective co-ordination of government initiated energy developments within the Hunter.

In terms of information flow, there can be varying perspectives on how acquainted the public are with development plans, their environmental impact and future management. Opinion varies on the type, amount and form of information required for decision-making. Even if agencies have the correct data available, it may not be in useful form and non-conveyance or piecemeal release of such information to the public can generate considerable feelings of ill-will. Frequently, information relevant to problem-solving may be held by those agencies which cannot apply it. Conversely decision-making bodies may not have the information base they require.

An example of this can be seen in poor co-ordination of the study of water quality for the Hunter. Those findings which do emerge are piecemeal and tend to be misinterpreted or viewed with disinterest by a number of groups.

142

The number of agencies collecting water quality data in the Hunter with varying degrees of rigour or interest is becoming formidable. Much of these data have not been integrated or analysed to give a regional perspective on the temporal and spatial variability of water quality and much of the data utilised for consultant's reports is highly suspect in terms of sampling frequency as well as site selection. The WRC has made the most comprehensive study of water quality to date.

It appears that much of this information should be more effectively disseminated to water users although this is often facilitated on a need to know basis. For example, the Department of Agriculture gives irrigators weekly river readings of salinity below Maitland. This allows for decision-making on whether or not irrigation of crops can take place.

With the earlier (1979–81) proposed rapid industrial expansion for power stations, smelters and mining there emerged a number of additional water supply schemes for the Upper Hunter. Such expansionist tendencies, with limited appeal in terms of co-ordinated water supply development, have now been tempered by the recent recession. This has tended to minimise co-ordination crises and has led to a closer consolidation of activities and liaison between government groups. For example, several new mining ventures have been delayed for one to two years, and this additional time may be useful in allowing further consideration of environmental management options for open-cut mines. One issue pertinent here is the interrelated management of overburden spoil and voids or depressions left after the completion of open mining. Initiatives embrace the possibility of transfer of spoil dumps to mined voids, although outcomes of further negotiations with industry are uncertain.

CO-ORDINATION AND CONTROL

Despite criticisms to the contrary, various attempts at co-ordinating development in the Hunter had already commenced by the early seventies, largely under the auspices of the forerunners of the New South Wales Department of Environment and Planning. Initial attempts at producing an outline regional plan for the Hunter (State Planning Authority of New South Wales, 1972) faltered in view of the limited prospects for substantial development. Nevertheless, from the beginning of 1977, as state government interest mounted, a substantial two year exercise in plan generation was mounted.

The preparation of the Hunter Regional Plan represents one of the most comprehensive exercises yet seen in Australia as regards the level of liaison and public discussion involved. A sophisticated conceptual framework was employed commencing with outline discussions in the first half of 1977. Initial goals and objectives were refined both through an extensive process of additional data collection (culminating in 23 working papers), and through a goals-achievements style weighting exercise involving the Hunter Regional Planning Committee, together with local planners and community representatives. A substantial draft plan

143

was issued in November, 1978 (Planning and Environment Commission NSW, 1978). This substantially took the form of a policy document and incorporated the types of information acquisition and liaison procedures foreshadowed in the 1979 Environmental Planning and Assessment Act.

During the 1977–1978 period, regional plan preparation undoubtedly acted as a major catalyst in enhancing both general and governmental awareness of the issues, developments and associated infrastructure and environmental issues facing the region. the original Regional Planning Committee comprised key representatives on local government and state instrumentalities. The quite generally perceived importance of this group's role, together with extensive liaison between the then Planning and Environment Commission and a very wide range of other government bodies, ensured a substantial breaking down of single purpose agency isolation.

The draft plan itself provided a substantial list of recommended policies meeting with at least the expressed approval of the responsible bodies concerned. By the late seventies New South Wales land use planning, or environmental planning as it was now termed, was at the crossroads. The new legislation took a broad view of "environment" defining it to include "all aspects of the surroundings of man, whether affecting him as an individual or in his social groupings". This opened the doors for much broader consideration of economic, social and biophysical aspects of planning not necessarily tied closely to land use. Yet the newly created Department of Environment and Planning was hardly a heavyweight in the New South Wales government league, and was in a relatively weak position to affect co-ordination, let alone coercion, in the management of overall development. In the event the plan played safe and is a mixture of some essentially mandatory policies with respect to clearly defined land use issues, coupled with much more open ended recommendations and statements of support in respect to the proposed activities of other government departments and instrumentalities. In no sense is the draft document a corporate attempt at phasing and budgeting the infrastructure developments of the region.

Perhaps for this reason the draft version of the Hunter Regional Plan played quite a limited role in the attempts to co-ordinate the pressures of the Hunter development boom in the late seventies and early eighties. At this time the final document was something less than eagerly awaited and entered the world with no more than a whimper in March, 1982 (Department of Environment and Planning NSW, 1982a). In its final form the statutory planning instrument comprises a series of policy statements reworked, but expressing, in general, the sentiments of the draft plan. These policies are essentially concerned with land use and, for the most part, worded sufficiently broadly both to obliterate the need for frequent revision and, therefore, to allow considerable flexibility with interpretation. It follows that any ongoing value of the plan will depend on the success with which the Department follows through with continued monitoring, additional research and implementation programmes. Evidence to date suggests these are proceeding, in which case effective land use requirements co-ordination may well be achieved though as a supplement, rather than integral part of the plan _per se_.

Passage of the 1979 Environmental Planning and Assessment Act also had the effect of including environmental impact assessment as an integral part of mainstream development control. In so far as 95 environmental impact statements had been submitted by September 1, 1982 (Department of Environment and Planning NSW, 1982b, 30-3), this aspect would seem successful. Yet it has been contended by the general manager of the aluminium division of BHP that the same smelter would have been built at Lochinvar regardless of whether there had been an EIS and public enquiry (Wise, 1981). Such an extreme comment highlights the suspicion that many environmental impact statements are little more than window dressing, despite the intent that such procedures will force sympathetic environmental considerations to operate throughout the design process. As at September 1, 1982 only two marinas and one commuter airport had been rejected out of the 95 applications submitted. While this may be taken as testimony of the environmental sensitivity of developers in the Hunter Region it also raised fears of a social and environmental sellout. A number of writers, for instance Dick, 1981 and Day, 1982b, have commented on the weakness of the environmental impact statement as a means of assessing cumulative development impacts while the involvement of the state government in both appraisal and decision is a particular problem under Part V of the Act dealing with government instrumentalities.

With problems enough of its own in attempting to co-ordinate land use requirements and in assessing environmental impacts, the Department of Environment and Planning was clearly not in a position to expedite overall co-ordination of rapidly expanding and changing development proposals and their regard to mounting criticism concerning lack of infrastructure co-ordination in the region, the NSW government, in September 1980, appointed a Hunter Region co-ordinator within the Premier's Department. His tasks may be defined as follows:

to alert various government bodies to development proposals;

to obtain from these bodies their programs for activity in the Hunter

to identify areas where information or activity is lacking and encourage examination of these by appropriate bodies; and

to support action to overcome these problems where necessary.

As the first co-ordinator, Mr David Easson, made clear, the task was essentially short term in nature in so far as once the liaison problems were solved operations should run smoothly. The ability to achieve this, while couched in modest terms, clearly resided in the co-ordinator being located at a high level in the Premier's Department in Sydney with direct access both to key politicians and civil servants. Easson sat on a number of local committees in the Hunter Region, in addition to visiting councils, regional offices of government departments, and major developers. The contribution of the Development Co-ordinator was thus not to identify problems but to ensure that awareness, action and funding were forthcoming from the relevant executive arm of government.

It can be appreciated that accusations of knee-jerk responses and inadequate co-ordination may readily be made in respect to the Hunter development boom. This in turn has led to calls for an independent Hunter Valley Planning Authority (Wise, 1981) and for rigorous benefit-cost orientated appraisals of Hunter development as a framework for rational decision-making (Perkins, 1982). The remainder of this chapter presents a critique of the degree of co-ordination that was achieved and comments on the likely feasibility of alternative approaches, prior to making recommendations on how the essentially ad hoc response experienced in the Hunter Region might be rendered more efficient in subsequent rapid development situations.

PLANNING THEORY

Although the range of procedural approaches available to practising planners — together with their limitations — are already quite well understood in theoretical terms, such perspectives are frequently dismissed in practice. It is argued that this can lead to belief in overly simplistic and ordered mechanisms for coping with change.

In the broadest terms, plan preparation hinges on fundamental, though sometimes implicit, assumptions about the nature of the organisational environments to be planned. Rational, comprehensive, synoptic planning ultimately seeks an overall strategy based on a sound understanding of all component variables. Alternatively, disjointed incrementalism, or muddling through, accepts the uncertain and imperfect understanding available and suggests that numerous ad hoc decisions on quite a broad policy front aimed at coping with currently perceived problems is both a satisfactory adaptation and an accurate description of reality. Decision-makers, well aware of the limitations of the synoptic approach, but unhappy with a complete retreat from the quest for overall perspective, have not surprisingly embraced the "mixed scanning" concept which seeks broad overview of key problems and variables as an ongoing framework for more detailed studies as required (Wedgwood – Oppenheim, Hart and Cobley, 1975).

The efficacy of these approaches relies heavily upon the relative stability and unitary nature of the organisational environments being planned, these factors in turn being partly related to scale. Stability is concerned with the rate at which developments are taking place while the unitary nature of the environment is concerned with the degree of variability between the aims and associated values of the various interest groups that will be affected by the decision-

146

making process. Characteristically, within group agreement on aims and objectives, together with a relatively stable, and thereby predictable, rate of development are attributes likely to be associated with local scale planning schemes such as a precinct development control plan. It is no accident that the time scale for commitment is generally short in these situations as this further reduces uncertainty. On the other hand regional planning exercises are likely to be characterised by a very broad range of action with widely disparate value systems, an uncertain environment and a long time span. Under such circumstances, it is reasonable to argue that any rigidly integrative scheme is doomed to failure and that the real choice lies between ad hoc incrementalism and some form of responsive and highly interactive mixed scanning system.

Theoretical guidance on the control of such complex systems (e.g. Chadwick, 1971) stresses concepts such as requisite variety, redundancy and, associated with this, high semi-lattice connectivity aimed at ensuring both that changes in the system will be readily picked up and that the information will be disseminated to the relevant action agencies. Translated into more practical terms, Wedgwood-Oppenheim, Hart and Cobley (1975) consider the establishment of a performance evaluation and policy review unit charged with overall co-ordination and dissemination of information flows and, in the United Kingdom context, directly responsible to the regional director of the Department of the Environment. The authors suggest that monitoring strategic plan performance per se is unlikely to be particularly rewarding, nor are large parametric data sets particularly effective. Instead, local authorities can be relied upon for comparatively early warning of emerging problems which may then lead to special data requirements often including considerable qualitative assessment. The unit's role is thus one of information acquisition, based on a variety of approaches. As regards dissemination, an annual wide ranging state of the region appraisal report is recommended and the unit as a whole is seen as the forum in which regional policy is debated and through which the flow of communications between participating public bodies is channelled. Approximately twelve short term professional staff are envisaged, selected for their analytical ability, energy, diplomacy and commitment; the leader having relatively high civil service status.

AN APPRAISAL

The question can now be posed: how does the Hunter experience relate to the various perspectives on regional co-ordination and management that have been put forward?

Prior to the mid-seventies very little overall co-ordination was apparent, various bodies being responsible for different services and tending to operate with little liaison beyond their intra-departmental development plans. Early attempts to create a general awareness of the region's problem and a resolve to tackle them as a whole can be seen in the renaissance of regional planning by the then State

Planning Authority in the early seventies. This type of activity increased in scale rapidly following the discussions on a fresh environmental, social and economic orientation to new land use planning legislation proposed initially in 1979. These new concepts borrowed heavily both from the abstract procedural perspectives of McLoughlin (1969) and from their administrative interpretation in terms of the English 1968 and 1971 Town and Country Planning Acts. Not surprisingly, this led to more than an implicit emphasis on goal and objective formulation, public participation, alternative evaluation and a broader perspective on the scope of planning concerns.

This flush of synoptic enthusiasm came to full flower in the Planning and Environment Commission's Hunter regional planning exercise. Such features as massive public involvement and the use of computer modelling and full goal-achievement matrix procedures in the evaluation of alternative land use strategies are now generally viewed with some scepticism in connection with exercises of this scale. However, the initiatives undertaken in the Hunter during 1977 and 1978 did much to draw the disparate agencies operating within the region towards a closer understanding of their likely role in the development process over the next few decades. In the event, the significance attached to recommendations based on alternative evaluation and objective ranking have been generalised to such an extent that considerable flexibility remains in interpretation. This in turn probably reflects the low levels of reliability of such systematic, grand index approaches. However, the catalytic effect of the exercise, and, in particular, the way it involved members of a broad spectrum of government departments, which in turn had to give further thought to their programs, represents a major achievement in laying out the factual and liaison framework for subsequent successful liaison.

In some ways the Hunter Regional Plan was overtaken by circumstances. Its preparation was commenced at a time when the organisational environment of the Hunter Region was relatively static and had been so for many years. Above average unemployment and a static, often declining, industrial base were generally recognised problems and in that sense there was a reasonable degree of unanimity regarding the purpose of a regional plan. Such static circumstances favour the synoptic approach which reinforces the community's unity of purpose and, in the case of a land use planning perspective, sets out the preferred locational pattern for development, whilst avoiding the complex issues of phasing over which statutory environmental planning has no mandate. However, once the general realisaton that the future of the Hunter lay in a revitalised coal economy was translated into action by the New South Wales Labor Government the organisational environment quickly assumed a dynamic nature requiring considerably enhanced management skills.

The traditional system comprising large numbers of quasi-autonomous agencies was inadequate for two reasons. Firstly, the generally informal liaison procedures could not guarantee that all interrelationships could be appreciated in time. Secondly, large scale private developers faced a multitude of, at times bureaucratically inefficient, consent agencies; thereby materially slowing down determinations and threatening to send the goose with the perceived golden egg elsewhere. Initial government reaction essentially viewed both these problems simply as threats to the establishment of industry. Thus in April, 1977 the Industrial Investment Unit was created in the Premier's Department with the brief of "co-ordinating planning and provision of infrastructure requirements of potential major development projects" and operating as a liaison unit between the New South Wales government departments and business organisations on industrial development matters" (Wise, 1980, p.12). At the same time, steps were taken to establish a single body able to co-ordinate all respective conditions and permissions a prospective developer would have to meet, a role eventually taken on board by the Department of Environment and Planning.

However two problems remained. Firstly, as serious development commenced, opposition and further ramifications began to emerge. For the purposes of regional planning two components of community value structures tend to be significant. These are, firstly, the dichotomy between what might loosely be called the free market, or libertarian, ethic and redistributive social equity considerations and, secondly, the dimension of development versus conservation. In reality both these components are rich in variation and complex in interation. Nevertheless, it follows that as development commenced in the Hunter, issues of who gains and who loses would begin to emerge and, coupled with this, concern with the detrimental effect that such development would have on the biophysical environment. An apocalyptical comment that gained some currency reduced land evaluation criteria for the Upper Hunter into land that has been mined, land suitable for mining and land being mined.

Political pressures stemming from equity and environmental lobbies created further complexities for overall co-ordination. A partial solution was the creation of an infrastructure co-ordinator in September, 1980 which served to create a more visible concern with the issues at hand. These were quickly expanded to include urban co-ordination (water, sewerage, utilities and serviced land) together with such social infrastructure as education, health and community services.

Yet this much more difficult task of co-ordination had to be played with kid gloves. While all purpose development agencies have a valuable role in the planning and construction of green field sites, and particularly new towns, such integration is impracticable for political, administrative and constructional reasons in a large, complicated existing developed area such as the Hunter. No state government would be prepared to delegate such huge discretionary powers nor would strongly individualistic departments be made to shift priorities and loyalties by a few paper decrees. In essence, what is required is a very high level of co-ordinatory diplomacy with direct access to the top of the political chain. The position of regional infrastructure

149

co-ordinator fulfilled this role and has obvious links with the performance evaluation and policy review unit expounded by Wegwood-
Oppenheim, Hart and Cobley (1975), though with less emphasis on the
information base.

The need for rapid and sensitive reaction by such co-ordinating
units is clearly demonstrated by the response to decline as well as
to expansion. The cancellation both of aluminium schemes and export
coal mine initiatives from 1981 onwards has wrought havoc with estimates for electric power capacity, associated water storage schemes,
harbour facilities and requirements for railway rolling stock. While
relatively static land use policy plans such as Hunter Regional Environmental Plan No. 1 (1982) can emerge relatively unscathed, major reactions are required to curtail infrastructure development. The rapid
manner in which this was achieved testifies to the improved level
of monitoring and co-ordination within the control system.

CONCLUSIONS AND RECOMMENDATIONS

It is easy to criticise the level of overall management and co-ordination achieved during the Hunter boom and to make facile, technocratic
recommendations for greater degrees of overall measurement, understanding and control. However, even brief reference to planning theory
indicates that the manner and speed with which the developments
occurred, against a previously static background and entrenched tradition of single purpose agency planning, precluded the possibility of
any overall agency having control. Instead, what occurred may be
regarded as quite a successful ad hoc response in terms of what the
benefit of a hindsight look at planning theory suggests is the only
appropriate response to managing a rapidly changing regional development boom. Co-ordination was eventually achieved, although problems
associated with a lack of public discussion and inadequate review
of cumulative environmental effects were not resolved adequately at
the time development pressures eased.

What is disappointing is the inability of the New South Wales
State government to formulate its co-ordinating machinery earlier. In this
regard the Department of Environment and Planning, only just established
during the heat of the boom, will hopefully reflect on what can be
learnt. In anything other than an initial data base and static situation,
unitary, synoptic regional planning responses are likely to be unsatisfactory, although a comprehensive review of land use factors may permit
development of a worthwhile general landuse development framework.
Beyond this the problem becomes one of co-ordinating all development
agencies to meet the changing, problem orientated objectives of the
region and the land use function serves only as relatively small, and
properly subservient, aspect of this overall enterprise.

There is no absolute mandate that this strategic, monitoring and
co-ordination role should fall to the Department of Environment and
Planning rather than say the Premier's Department. Nor does such a

process have much to do with statutory regional land use planning as as been amply demonstrated in the case of United Kingdom structure plans. However, the need exists for co-ordination and the network initially establishd by the Department of Environment and Planning in the early stages of its regional environmental planning exercise suggests that it would be in a good position – and by inclination most likely to want – to take on this role as an adjunct to simply monitoring its relatively simple land use implications. Such a responsibility should result in the regular, at least annual, publication of regional reports. They should be designed to stimulate discussion, in turn leading to policy recommendations direct to the highest levels of state government.

This chapter has stressed the need to acknowledge explicitly the significance of rapid and reliable information flow between the multitude of agencies likely to be involved in rapidly changing regional planning issues. However one other element is valuable and that is the proper application of substantive knowledge. Co-ordination was slow in coming because government did not appreciate adequately the range of issues and problems that even a superficial knowldge of the development process would readily indicate. Apart from the obvious plea for better educated and more forward thinking planners who, perhaps, will remember the Hunter boom as an interesting case study in co-ordination, value conflict and infrastructure ramifications – more detailed knowledge of the effects of what happened can be added to the environmental planner's arsenal. This requires substantive research of costs and benefits, social, environmental problems and the like. However, unheeded research is not worth the paper it is written on. It is of paramount importance that no efforts are spared in inserting results obtained into appropriate monitoring and management channels.

9

THE ECONOMICS OF WATER USE IN THE HUNTER VALLEY: PRESSURES FOR REALLOCATION

A.K. Dragun

INTRODUCTION

The provision of additional sources of water to meet rapidly expanding demands in a mature water economy (Randall, 1982) can provide society with a major economic quandary. On the one hand, a range of new and expensive dams and diversions may be under consideration to satisfy the growing requirements of industry, urbanisation and natural resource processing – where the value of the marginal product of water may be very high – while on the other hand, substantial volumes of water may already be provided to other activities – where the value of the marginal product is quite low. The usual scenario in this context is of course the contrast between the low value adding agricultural users, where water is generally provided at nominal cost, and the rapidly expanding industrial, urban and natural resource processing sectors, where the willingness to pay for water may be very high.

While water providing agencies struggle to raise the large capital construction sums required to meet the expanding needs of the mature water economy, the predominance of economic interest has been directed to the basic resource allocation issues. In this context, the focus of concern has been on the "institutional barriers" to efficient allocation of water resources and particularly the possibilities for overcoming such barriers through rational pricing and the establishment of water markets. The usual expectation is that the implementation of a market for water would enable users where the water productivity is high, to directly purchase the volume of the resource that they would require from other activities where the productivity of water is low. In such circumstances, transactions would be expected to occur where the willingness to pay of the first class of users would be higher than the value of the marginal product of water generated by the second class of users.

However, despite the substantial interest that has been expressed in water markets in Australia, it appears that the notion of water markets has not yet entered the calculus of governments and their water managing agencies in this country. At this stage no significant water market exists anywhere in the country and the input of an

Table 9.1   Hunter Valley: irrigation water use by source (ML), 1979

	Source	Irrigation	Riparian and Losses[3]
(1)	Hunter River, from Glenbawn Dam[1]		
	(a) Zone 1	32,000	10,500
	(b) Zone 2	12,000	10,000
	(c) Zone 3	27,500	16,500
	Sub Total	71,500[4]	37,000
(2)	Goulburn River	16,000	-
(3)	Wollombi Brook	7,500	-
(4)	Glennies Creek	2,000	-
(5)	Paterson River	6,000	13,000
(6)	Williams River	6,000	14,500
(7)	Groundwater[2]	60,000	-
	TOTAL	169,000	64,500

1.   Zone 1, from Glenbawn Dam to the junction of the Goulburn River, Zone 2 from the junction of the Goulburn River to above Wollombi Brook, Zone 3 from Wollombi Brook to Maitland.

2.   While a substantial proportion of the groundwater would be used for irrigation, some components would be used for stock watering and other agricultural uses. The WRC estimates are 4% to stock watering 29% to domestic and the balance to irrigation.

3.   Riparian allocations are specific entitlements provided to land owners adjacent to the water courses. Thus, subsequent to the construction of the three major dams in the region, the Glenbawn, the Lostock and the Chichester - riparian owners were necessarily provided with specific allotments under the conditions of the Water Act, 1912, (NSW).

4.   This value has been revised by the Water Resources Commission, to 74,000 ML, in the 1982 Review of Hunter Region Water requirements.

Sources

1.   Water Resources Commission of NSW, Preliminary Plan for Development of Water Resources in the Hunter River Basin, Sydney : January 1979.

2.   Water Resources Commission of NSW, Hunter Region : Water Requirements and Storage Proposals, 1982 Review. Sydney : May 1982.

3.   Water Resources Commission of NSW, Hunter Regional Plan, Working Paper No. 20, Groundwater, Sydney : NSW Planning and Environment Commission, 1977.

economic rationale into matters of water provision is found to be conspicuously lacking; it is limited to some marginal cost pricing input for the
metropolitan water services of Perth and lately the Hunter District Water
Board. Whilst this paper briefly considers the lack of success of the
market approach to water allocation in this country, the main theme
is to outline the current institutional and economic structure of water
provision in the Hunter Valley of New South Wales. Such a perspective
will provide insight on the non-advent of water markets and will also
be useful in delineating a benchmark for considering the benefits and
costs of water provision. Given the current structure of water provision, the major initiative will be to contemplate the possibility of achieving a more rational approach to water allocation in Australia. In this
context a second-best proposal is put forward in terms of an irrigation
block buy-back scheme to be followed by the implementation of a
marginal cost pricing program.

CHANGING PATERNS OF WATER USE IN A RAPIDLY
DEVELOPING REGIONAL ECONOMY

Agriculture

The problems of inefficient water allocation are vividly portrayed in the
Hunter Valley Region of New South Wales. The region has had a long
period of settlement – dating from the early 1820s – and for the most
part, the local economy has been developed on a substantial agricultural basis (Whitelaw, 1974; Fink, 1977; New South Wales Environment
and Planning Commission, 1977). Recent estimates of the importance
of agriculture to the region indicate that the total area committed to
agriculture is about two million hectares, whilst the value of agricultural production is in the vicinity of $100m (New South Wales Environment
and Planning Commission, p.18–19). Of the total area, it is estimated that
about 30,000 ha are irrigated with the major water sources being the
Hunter River itself, a range of major tributaries and the extensive groundwater systems within the region. The volumes of water used by agriculture are difficult to estimate as a consequence of the lack of control
on private diversions and pumps. As a general rule it is considered
that between six and seven megalitres is required to maintain one
hectare of irrigated crop or pasture, so that the upper bound of water
use by this sector could be between 180,000 and 200,000 ML per
year.

The major source of irrigation water in the region is Glenbawn
Dam on the Hunter River north-east of Scone from which 71,500 ML
was provided to agriculture in 1979. The Lostock Dam on the Paterson
River provides an additional 6,000 ML, with Chichester Dam on the
Chichester River yielding another 6,000 ML (Table 9.1). The actual
volumes of groundwater extracted tend to be unclear – again due to
the lack of controls – whilst the proportions of both groundwater and
the riparian allocation which are directed into irrigation agriculture are
uncertain. The actual area irrigated from the Hunter River, according
to latest figures is 15,187 ha whilst 13,605 ha is irrigated on
tributaries.[1]

155

By far the largest portion of this irrigated area is devoted to ture pasture in connection with dairying and lucerne growing for hay, with smaller portions of grape vines and vegetable crops (Australian Bureau of Statistics, unpublished tables).

The potential increased demand for irrigation water – delivered under the current institutional arrangements – is undeniably strong. At this stage it is difficult to evaluate the excess demand for irrigation water from individual requests to the water managing body due to drought disruptions and a de facto moratorium on new connections. However, it has been estimated that according to suitable land availability, the current authorised area could be expanded from 30,000 ha to in the vicinity of 58,500 ha by the year 2000 (Water Resources Commission of New South Wales, 1979, p.2). Such an expansion would require an additional 102,000 ML of water per year, bringing the total allocation to 211,000 ML per year. Most of this growth would have to be obtained from additional storage on the Hunter River. However, due to additional pressures on direct Hunter sources from other activities, the potential extra water availability to irrigation has been downgraded to a range of between 16,000 and 50,000 ML per year.[2]

Industry, Urban and Natural Resource Processing

Not only is the Hunter region well endowed with a substantial agricultural productive basis, but the region is underlain by probably the greatest concentration of coal resources on the continent. At this stage, resources measured in situ in the Singleton basin have been put at 12,000 million tonnes, with inferred resources possibly as high as 250,000 million tonnes (Joint Coal Board, 1982). Coal was first discovered in the Singleton region as early as 1830, with reports of exploitation and sale dating from 1850.[3] Overall development of coal resources within the region was initially very slow with only 2 M tons being produced in all of New South Wales prior to 1860. From 1870 to 1960 the average annual growth rate has been in the order of 5 per cent and thereafter up to 10 per cent.

By 1950 coal production in the Singleton region had reached nearly 1.5 M tonnes per year but was only 1.7 M tonnes ten years later. However, by 1970 production had reached 4.2 M tonnes and rose dramatically to reach 18.65 M tonnes/year by the financial year 1980–1981 (Joint Coal Board, 1982). The incentives for the rapid expansion of coal development within the region were many – both in a market context and in terms of improved technology. Firstly, a major thermal power station, Liddell, was commissioned over the years 1971 to 1973 generating a new demand for in the vicinity of 5.5 M tonnes/year. Subsequent to the "oil crisis", the demand for thermal coal for export – principally to Japan – has also grown dramatically. Finally, the rapid expansion of coal production within the region has been facilitated by significant improvements in surface mine technology which has enabled large tonnages of coal to be exploited cheaply and thus competitively on world markets (Dragun, 1982)

The portents for coal field expansion in the upper Hunter region during the next decade are substantial. Whilst total coal production was in the vicinity of 18.65 M tonnes in 1981, planned capacity by 1985 is 54.5 M tonnes, rising to 87.6 M tonnes by 1990 (Dragun, 1982, p.28). At this stage at least three new surface mines and possibly one under-ground mine are due to begin operation before 1985 and a further eight surface mines are under development consideration.[4] It is significant that while such new mines could provide in the vicinity of 14 M tonnes of additional coal by 1985 and 26 M tonnes by 1990, the largest portion of coal production expansion is planned to occur in existing mining operations.

While the new Bayswater Power Station will consume in the vicinity of six million tonnes of coal when it comes into operation later this decade, the majority of the additional planned capacity is destined for export — principally for thermal purposes and mostly to Japan. Since a good deal of the "soft coking coal" destined for export is moderately high in ash content, it is essential that coal for export is washed. Additionally, substantial volumes of water are required for the various production and rehabilitation phases of mine operation, including wash-house use, vehicle washing, dust suppress-ion, irrigation and so on. The Water Resources Commission (1982, p.3) has estimated that current water usage by the coal mining industry is about 7,000 ML per year with a potential for expansion to 14,500 ML per year by 1990 and 26,000 ML per year by the turn of the century. Such volumes could double if the planned coalfield expansion does come to fruition.

By far the most significant new user of water within the upper Hunter region is thermal power generation. The Liddell power station utilizes 25,000 ML of water per year whilst the Bayswater station, currently under construction, will deplete an additional 36,000 ML per year. The possibility of two additional Bayswater size stations has been mooted for the region by the turn of the century — but as yet no pro-posals have been forthcoming.[5] The Water Resources Commission (WRC) has estimated that water requirements for the electric power sector could be as large as 100,000 ML per year by the turn of the century (Day and Dragun, 1983).

In conjunction with the rapid coalfield expansion and power station construction, it is inevitable that water demands by the urban sector of the region will grow as well. The current population level of about 63,000 is expected to expand to a range of between 82,000 and 90,000 by 1986 and 94,000 to 108,000 by 1990 (Department of Environ-ment and Planning, 1981). In 1979 the Water Resources Commission reported urban water usage at a meagre 3,000 ML per year. Such consump-tion was achieved during a prolonged drought in the region and amounted to a per capita consumption level of only 49 kilolitres (Water Resources Commission, 1979). With population increases estima-ted in the order of 30–40 per cent by 1986, the WRC anticipates urban

157

Table 9.2   Irrigated crop areas: Upper Hunter Valley 1980–81

LOCAL GOVERNMENT UNIT	LUCERNE	PASTURE	CERIALS	VEGETABLES	CITRUS	GRAPES	OTHER FRUIT	OTHER CROPS	TOTAL IRRIGATION	SOURCE RIVER	FARM DAMS	TOWN WATER	GROUND WATER
Maitland	380 (199)	556 (473)	88 (74)	602 (685)				50 (4)	1676 (1455)	1497	9		150
Muswellbrook	2855 (2089)	1238 (1400)	1460 (1834)	41 (31)		826	85 (4)	143 (79)	6649 (5457)	4261	21	9	2382
Singleton	2113 (1377)	2006 (2010)	804 (1005)	339 (333)	48 (50)	83 (27)		164 (63)	5557 (4865)	4577	83	20	1073
Scone	1423 (942)	1819 (1618)	1058 (1208)	8 (8)		170	5 (5)	100 (82)	4583 (3863)	1878	504		2520
TOTAL	6772 (4607)	5619 (5501)	3410 (4121)	990 (1057)	50 (50)	1079 (27)	90 (9)	457 (228)	18465 (15600)	12213	617	29	6125

Source: Australian Bureau of Statistics

water requirements expanding by 300 per cent so that per capita consumption in the Hunter Valley would be brought in line with consumption levels at Newcastle and some other major urban centres. By the turn of the century the WRC has estimated that urban water requirements will increase by 950 per cent according to the 1979 Preliminary Plan and by 500 per cent according to the 1982 Review.[6]

WATER SUPPLY IN THE HUNTER VALLEY

The responsibility for water provision and management on the Hunter river and its tributaries above the tidal limit at Maitland – but including the Paterson and Allyn river systems – resides with the Water Resources Commission of New South Wales. At this stage the Commission operates two major storages in the area, the Glenbawn Dam and the Lostock Dam on the Paterson river. In addition Lake Liddell provides water storage for Elcoms' Liddell Power Station. It is also proposed that the new Glennies Creek Dam will be completed by 1983 to be operational by 1985–86. In the Upper Hunter Valley the Commission is responsible for providing water to irrigators, industrial users – including coal mines and power stations – and town users. The major source of water in the region is the Hunter river and its tributaries, with long term average annual flows recorded at Musswellbrook of 386,000 ML, at Singleton of 875,000 ML and at Maitland of 912,000 ML (Water Resources Commission, 1979). Currently, regulated flow on the Hunter river amounts to a little over 100,000 ML per year. Complementing the surface water resources, the valley also contains considerable groundwater resources, estimated in the order of 30,000,000 ML. Of this total, exploitable yield is estimated at 280,000 ML per year and currently in the vicinity of 60,000 ML of groundwater is actually extracted (Furner, 1981).

The basic characteristics of the existing water storages in the Upper Hunter Valley, together with a range of proposed storages, are illustrated in Table 9.2. It should be noted that a prolonged drought since 1979 has reduced inflows to the major storages resulting in the Water Resource Commission reducing stated safe yields. Thus, the safe yield for Glenbawn Dam has been reduced from 155,000 ML per year to only 103,000 ML per year at the moment. In a like manner the safe yield for the Glennies Creek Dam has been reduced from 99,000 ML per year to 64,500 (and the dam has yet to be completed!).

The Cost of Water Provision

To render all costs to a comparative basis a price index was used to yield all actual construction costs and estimates of construction costs to a June 1982 numeraire. Operating costs are for the last financial year and the values for potential storages are the Water Resource Commission's best estimates for the particular dam types in question. Relative to such operating costs, total costs are calculated by annuitising construction costs over thirty years at, firstly, a nominal opportunity cost rate of 13 per cent. The total average costs per megalitre are illustrated in Table 9.3. Subsequently, average and marginal costs are calculated for water supply in the Upper Hunter,

159

Table 9.3   Hunter Valley: water supply, average cost and marginal schedule

Source	Increment To Yield	Total Yield	Value of Annuity at 15% Increment	Total	Operating Costs Increment	Total	Total Costs	Average Cost	Marginal Cost
Glenbawn Dam	103000	103000	13754270	13754270	160000	160000	13914270	135.09	
Lostock Dam	29000	132000	2788350	16542620	65000	225000	16607620	125.82	98.39
Glennies Creek Dam	64500	196500	5936580	22479200	200000	425000	22679200	115.42	95.14
Glenbawn Enlargement	60000	256500	5336400	27815600	160000	585000	27975600	109.07	91.61
Barnard II	70000	326500	9338700	37154300	1400000	1985000	38554300	118.08	155.41
Rouchel	30000	356500	10005400	47160200	200000	2185000	47360200	132.85	340.20
Brushy	30000	386500	11340000	58500200	200000	2385000	58700200	151.88	384.67

including the potential storages, to establish the longer term supply characteristics of the region. It can be seen that whilst average and marginal costs are currently relatively constant — with a slight decline owing to the possible Glenbawn enlargement — both rise significantly beyond a system yield of 250,000 ML. The very sharply rising marginal costs illustrate the supply dilemma within the region.

FEES FOR WATER USE IN THE HUNTER VALLEY

Currently, the Water Resources Commission utilises a two tier fee structure for the majority of water users; the industrial and irrigation users. At this stage no fees are levied against domestic or town users and riparian users. Additionally, the fee structure for power stations is still under consideration. The fee to irrigators and industrial users involves firstly, an annual metering fee on water used, and secondly a five yearly licensing fee for area irrigated or volume of water diverted. It should be noted that the water fees in the Hunter Valley pertain to metering costs from private diversions directly from the Hunter River. As such the WRC does not provide infrastructure downstream of the respective storages and the responsibility for diversion rests solely with the individual user.

The current annual metering fee is 90 cents per megalitre for all water used by both irrigators and industrial users. The metering fee is differentiated in that the fee for the first half of the particular allocation is fixed and must be paid irrespective of whether water is used, whilst the fee is a flat 90 cents for each megalitre used over half the licensed allocation.[7] The volume of water allowable to irrigation is generally 6 ML per ha, with special allowances for permanent plantings. However, a volumetric allocation scheme has recently been introduced whereby general irrigation allocations would be proportionately reduced according to water availability. Industrial users, on the other hand are allocated volumes of water in accordance with their stated requirements.

The second aspect of the charges structure is a five yearly licensing fee. This fee is determined according to area irrigated and the pump capacity for industrial users. The licensing fees for irrigation and industrial users are as follows:

Table 9.4   Licensing fees

Irrigation		Industrial	
Area	Fee $	Pump Capacity	Fee $
4 ha	93.60	50 (lit/sec)	97.50
20 ha	187.20	70	119.40
162 ha	725.45	90	136.50
		120	156.00
		150	175.50
		200	204.75
		300	263.25

161

With the completion of the Glennies Creek Dam a major new phase of water use in the valley begins, as substantial portions of the available water are specifically allocated to industrial and domestic ends. The Glennies Creek Dam Act provides for 36,000 ML per year to be diverted to the Bayswater Power Station – currently under construction – and another 8,000 ML to the Hunter District Water Board.[8] While the final form of the fee arrangement for the Bayswater Power Station has yet to be finalised, the fee is expected to be the average cost of water from both the Glennies Creek and Glenbawn dams. This average cost will be calculated relative to historic construction costs but with a capital allowance of between 11 per cent and 13 per cent – the current state treasury rates – on original construction costs. Consequently, the water fee to the Bayswater Power Station should be in the range of $48 to $57 per megalitre –a distinct adjustment on tradition and possibly a portent for change.

THE VALUE OF WATER TO DIFFERENT USERS

The differential between the cost of providing water in the Upper Hunter Valley and the actual charges levied on such provisions, has been explicitly illustrated in the previous two sections. The point of significance at this stage is that all classes of water users are subjected to the same general structure of water charges – if charges are paid at all. Thus, the state of New South Wales carries a subsidy to the dimensions of the capital and operating costs of providing water to all entitled users. While the maintenance of such a subsidy is worthy of much comment, it is nevertheless of social concern that a service, which is provided as a public good, be utilised in such a manner that it yields the greatest social value. Accordingly, this section of the paper will review the benefits attributable to the major classes of water users in the Upper Hunter Valley.

Overall, by far the largest portion of current available water supply is allocated to agricultural ends (75 per cent) where the estimated values to water are significantly lower than the categories of coal washing and power stations. It is also significant that, with the exception of vegetable crops and grape production, the remaining irrigated crops all indicate water values a good deal less than the total cost of provision from Glenbawn Dam. The industrial activities, on the other hand, appear to yield water values substantially in excess of water cost (however the current level of industrial, and urban, water use is relatively minor).

Given the anomaly between the productivity of water in irrigated agriculture and the costs of water provision, it is difficult to rationalise the increased allocations that the WRC foresees to this sector by the turn of the century. In contrast to irrigation agriculture, the rapid expansion of the coal mining and thermal electricity sectors will necessitate the provision of substantial volumes of water – where the value of water is sufficiently high to generate significant social benefits beyond cost of water provision.

162

Economics of Water Use/Pressures for Reallocation

Table 9.5 The value of water in differrent uses

Use	($/ML) Value of Water	(ML) Current[3] Water Use	Estimated[5] Water Use Estimates 1990	WRC[5] 2000	2005
Agriculture		74000	74000	74000	124000
Dairying	88.36				
Lucerne Hay	78.73				
Vegetable Crops	168.75				
Grapes	216.00				
Coal Washing	500.00	7000	11000-14500	16000-21000	21000
Power Stations					
10%	972-2261	25000[1]	25000[1]	25000[1]	18000[2]
15%	1264-2949		18000-36000	36000-72000	100000
Urban		4000	6500-9500	7100-11000	18000
Total Regulated Water Use		85000	109500-134000	133100-178000	263000

Supply	Net yield[4]		
Current System Net Capacity (Glenbawn)	99000	99000	
			System[6] Total
Glennies Creek (Net addition)	52000	151000	
			System[6] Total
Augmented Barnard II	70000	221000	
			System[6] Total
Glenbawn Enlargement	60000	281000	

1. Currently 25000 ML/yr is diverted from surplus flow for the Liddell Power Station.

2. As the filling phase of the Glennies Creek Dam begins the WRC has accounted a reduction of surplus flow of 7000 ML/yr (indefinitely) from the current diversion to Liddell Power Station. This accounting slight of hand does not appear justified if the notion of safe yield has any relevance and also in the light of the fact that Glennies Creek never previously contributed to regulated flow in the Hunter river in any formal manner.

3. Sources
   (i) Water Resources Commission op cit
   (ii) Day, D.G., Water use issues in the Upper Hunter Valley. Canberra : CRES, ANU (CRES Working Paper CP/WP7) 1982

4. The net safe yields are calculated as water available for use with the elements of riparian allocations, losses and stream flow maintenance deducted. It should be noted that while the net safe yield of Glenbawn is quoted at 99000 ML/yr (155,000 ML/yr in WRC terminology) actual safe yield during 1982 has been downgraded to 47000 ML/yr (103,000 in WRC terminology).

5. Source : Dragun A.K. and D.G. Day, Water in the Hunter Valley : Demand, Supply and perspectives on management - (forthcoming)

6. The system totals are shown thus to illustrate the supply-demand interface according to the current pricing and allocation procedures.

163

The current and potential dimensions of the issue of water allocation in the Upper Hunter Valley are illustrated in Table 9.5.

THE POSSIBILITY OF RE-ALLOCATING EXISTING WATER SUPPLIES

As illustrated in a preceding section, significant disparities exist between the benefits generated by various classes of water users in the Upper Hunter Valley. Such disparities are manifested in several forms; firstly, in pricing terms where the costs of providing water greatly exceed the actual fees collected or the benefits generated and secondly, in an allocational setting whereby limited water stocks are provided to activities yielding relatively low benefits to the exclusion of other higher yielding activities. Relative to the discussion of Australian water resources, the first perspective is best seen in the work of Davidson (1969) whilst the latter is probably best captured in the more recent work of Randall (1982). In essence, the first line of work is motivated by a concern that irrigators throughout Australia are too generously subsidised by being given a very costly resource too cheaply. Since no justification of such a subsidisation can be established on grounds of economic efficiency, it is generally suggested that water pricing in terms of water provision costs could wipe out the income transfer. Such an approach to water pricing would also effect a re-allocation of water from lower to higher valued uses.

The alternative approach, probably best discussed in Randall's work, focusses directly on the possibility of establishing a market mechanism for water, so that water initially used in activities where the value of the marginal product is low may be transferred to other activities where the value is larger. Such a perspective is primarily concerned with developing a structure of working rules and transferable rights which would enable interested and potential water uses to transact in water much in the manner of many other commodities in the society. Questions of water pricing are not necessarily subsumed in this approach with users in new systems being required to meet total provision costs. On the other hand allowances may need to be made for existing users who have traditionally been responsible for only minor portions of water delivery costs.

To some extent the "market for water" approach tends to dominate the discussion of "efficient pricing" in the current literature from the point of view of resource misallocation in mature water economies. Thus, the initial and pressing conflict to be confronted is the competition for limited water stocks between existing low value generating users and new high value potential users — where additional water supplies can only be obtained with sharply rising costs.

To place both perspectives in methodological and practical balance it is now timely to consider the substantial elements of both in some detail.

The Efficient Pricing Approach

This general line of analysis is not unique to water provision, being developed and applied to a wide range of public utility situations – particularly in the electricity sector. The literature on pricing for public utilities or services is quite lengthy with a range of works devoted to conceptual pricing issues (Boiteux, 1969; Coase, 1946; Tyndall, 1951, Turvey, 1969; Littlechild, 1970; Kahn, 1970; Kay, 1971; Turvey, 1971; Ng and Weisser, 1974; Trebing, 1976; and Joskow, 1976), similar pricing issues in other public utilities (Houthakker, 1951; Turvey and Anderson, 1977; Kolsen, 1966; Cicchetti, 1977; and Hanke and Wentworth, 1981), and also the direct pricing methodologies for water supplying utilities (Hirshleifer et al; Turvey, 1976; Saunders, et al, 1977; Riley and Schever, 1979; Feldman et al, 1981; and Hanke, 1981).

Prices and Distribution

The pricing of utility services has been an area of much concern to economists for some considerable time. The fact that a great many governments have utilised various utilities to further redistributive or secondary objectives has been of significance in this context, but it has also been widely observed that pricing rules designed to equate revenue with costs or to generate certain revenue surpluses have had little grounding or regard for economic theory.

The particular concern within the orthodoxy in relation to often ad hoc pricing principles, is to consider long run optimal pricing rules ... 'to allocate productive resources between [the utility] and other activities in such a way that optimal quantities of [the utilities product] and other goods is obtained.' (Houthakker, 1951, p. 7). Generally, the objective is to establish conditions so that 'the price of the [utility service] in terms of other goods is equal to its marginal cost in terms of other goods' (Houthakker, 1951, p. 8).

While the basis of orthodox economic interest in public utility pricing is motivated from the perspective of resource allocation and to some extent by a concern for utility consumer subsidisation, it must be noted that different pricing structures generate a range of impacts for equity and the income distribution. Thus, as Tyndall notes ... 'the introduction of different types of price structure in our one regulated industry will produce widely different effects on the distribution of income' (1951, p. 343). Consequently, concern with a particular pattern of public utility subsidisation necessarily implies that one form of income distribution is preferred to another. The same conclusions must be drawn in the resource allocation context – the public utilities' decisions on pricing will have an impact on equity whether the utility in question actively recognises the fact or not.

Marginal Cost Pricing and Welfare Maximisation

In contrast to the declining cost case, the utility experiencing increasing costs will find itself in the invidious position of accruing certain

165

Figure 9.1   Utility pricing with increasing costs

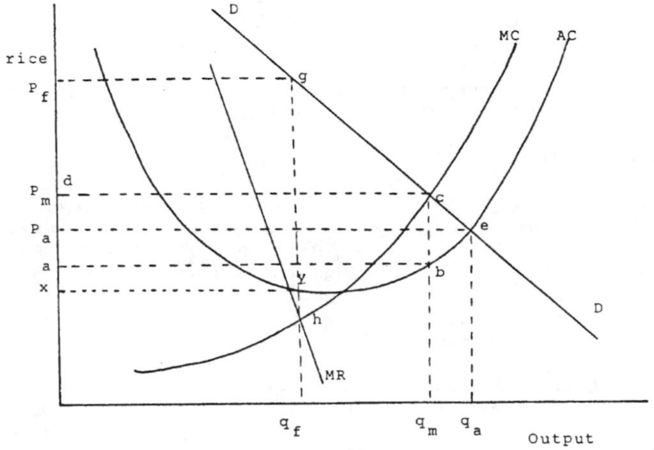

Notes

(i)   The marginal cost equilibrium is at c with Pm = MC.   This
        equilibrium yields utility output of qm and a surplus to the
        utility demonstrated by the area abcd.

(ii)   The average cost equilibrium is at the lower price of Pa
        generating the larger output of qa.   This situation is not
        optimal since the consumer willingness to pay for units in excess
        of qm is less than the marginal cost of production.

(iii)   To maximise utility profit $(xygP_f)$ price is set to Pf yielding
        output qf.

surpluses. As with the declining cost case though, pricing according to average cost is found not to be optimal. If price is set to marginal cost at price Pm the output is qm and it is observed that the utility accrues a profit to the dimensions of abcd (Figure 9.1). However if price is set to average cost at Pa the larger output qa is generated and it is found that revenue just covers normal costs. The price determined in this manner however, is not optimal since for every unit of output greater than qm – the marginal cost derived output – marginal cost exceeds the willingness of consumers to pay for the additional unit. Thus, social welfare is not maximised with the average cost price.

That the marginal cost price is the welfare maximising principle, according to the orthodox allocative view, is easily shown.

The social welfare derived from a particular utility service, W, may be defined as the difference between what the society would be willing to pay for the services, B, as against the total social cost of producing the utility service,

Thus, the objective function to be maximised is

$$W = B - C \tag{1}$$

Now, a society's willingness to pay for the utility output, P, may be defined in terms of a demand function for the output, f(q). Subsequently, the total benefits attributable to the utility service may be defined as the integral of this demand function, thus;

$$P = f(q) \tag{3}$$

and

$$B - \int P dq \tag{4}$$

It follows that the total social costs incurred in producing the utility output are a function of output so that the total social cost function is defined as;

$$C = h(q) \tag{5}$$

Consequently, the objective function outlined in equation (1) can be re-defined as;

$$W = \int P dq - h(q) \tag{6}$$

The welfare maximum can be established by differentiating this objective function with respect to output, thus we have;

$$\frac{dW}{dq} = P - h^1(q) \tag{7}$$

Thus $P = h^1(q)$ \hfill (8)

167

Hence for the welfare maximum the price of the utility service (P) should be equated with the marginal cost $(h^1(q))$ of producing that output.

Water Pricing in Relation to Reallocation

As has been described in previous sections, irrigators in the Upper Hunter Valley pay fees for water which bear little relation to the actual cost of provision. The impact of such circumstances is that the value of water in generating agricultural production is capitalised into the market values of irrigation land. According to the current interpretation of the Water Act, 1912, (New South Wales), irrigation water entitlements can not generally be alienated from particular irrigation blocks and subsequently the ability of water to generate income is included as an additional asset to the residual land.

The market values for flood plain land in the Hunter River Valley with an irrigation entitlement currently range between $2,500 per ha and $5,000 per ha whilst comparable land without an entitlement sells for between $500 and $1,000 per ha.[9] Such market values imply that the asset value of water is in the order of $2,000 to $4,000 per ha — a range which accords with the estimates of water value calculated in a previous section. The clear impact of the current irrigation water pricing policy in the upper valley is that an income transfer has been effected to the original landholders. Such a subsidy has generated expectations and investment decisions from original landholders, whilst new landholders would have paid the asset value of water in the market price of irrigated land. Subsequently, any approach to increase the price of water will generally result in a capital loss to individuals involved in the industry.

It appears that such a capital loss would probably not have any standing in the courts as a takings, but the social dislocation and need for rural re-adjustment of a marginal cost pricing approach to irrigation water may be politically unpalatable for the state government. In addition it should be noted that irrigation water pricing policies in the Hunter Valley will have an impact on the much larger irrigation districts throughout the state providing further dis-incentive for substantial price changes of water.

However, the situation for other water users in rural locations is quite different. It is becoming clear that whilst industrial and town water users in rural areas have not as yet been called upon to pay for water in relation to its cost of production, this picture is likely to change dramatically in the future. Given the precedence of the subsidy to agriculture and the continuing high cost of maintaining rural development programs initiated decades ago, it is unlikely that the responsible governments will yield to similar pressures from the developing urban and coal mining interests in the Hunter Valley, especially given the capacity of such sectors to pay for water resources. At this stage the water problem confronting urban and coal washing sectors is not likely to be one of pricing but is more significantly a question of availability of water. In the context of the values of water in the industrial and urban sectors – and the current levels of water consumption of these sectors – it could be expected that consumption of water would expand significantly if restrictions did not apply, even if the water were priced according to marginal cost criteria.

An indication that pricing will become of more relevance to the future use of water can be seen by considering the water allocation conditions provided for the Glennies Creek Dam. The Glennies Creek Dam Act, 1979, No. 126, (New South Wales), provides that 36,000 ML per year will be provided to the Elcom and a further 8,000 ML per year to the Hunter District Water Board. As the Glennies Creek Dam nears completion a tariff structure has been developed whereby Elcom pays for water in relation to the historic average cost of regulated water from the Hunter river. While this price bears little relation to the marginal cost of water in the valley, it is nevertheless 50 times the current price to private divertors in the valley.

The impact of this substantial price increase to Elcom will be felt directly by electricity consumers in the state as the additional costs of power generation are passed on. However, since Elcom averages electricity costs for units of the system, the additional water charges will be found to have negligible effects on tariffs. The full impact may be as little as 0.2 of one per cent for total system costs and as much as 0.5 of one per cent for generation costs.

Of more significant impact however, will be precedece of this new structure of prices for other industrial and possibly urban users of water in the valley. The commissioning of the Glennies Creek Dam will result in substantial additional volumes of water becoming available at a time when water provision to industry and urban users has been under considerable stress and where the pressures for expansion are strong. At this stage there appear to be few institutional, economic or political barriers to charging a price for water which does equate with the marginal cost of provision. Indeed the additional precedence of the "user-pay" water principle should facilitate a reconsideration of water pricing policies in this context.

As additional volumes of water become available in the Upper Hunter Valley, the justification for marginal cost pricing is strong in terms of the apparently quite high willingness to pay for water by both new industrial users and also urban users. Given the rapidly escalating water costs after the enlarged Glenbawn Dam project, it appears folly to precipitate a new regime of inefficient water use, especially in the context that a good deal of the industrial and urban demand has yet to come on line. A danger in the short-run is that surplus water may be allocated to irrigation according to past practices.

Overall the prospects of introducing a marginal cost pricing approach to new industrial and urban water in the valley appear positive in that consumers appear willing to pay such a price (and much more) if water supply will be provided. To a considerable extent the "development boom" that has been underway in the valley for the last ten years or so, has generally raised relative income levels so that public subsidisation of water supply is no longer justified. Also, since a good deal of the coal production from the area is exported, it appears that water subsidisation in the valley will also subsidise overseas consumers of coal – an additional perspective that the state government may find hard to support.

However, while a marginal cost pricing approach to new water provides a basis for water allocation to highest valued uses, pricing does not as yet offer a positive approach to re-allocating the vast quantity of water that is already tied to low value–adding irrigation. Fundamentally, the marginal cost pricing approach offers the possibility of obtaining more water – at a higher price and social cost – but cheap sources of water are available for exploitation and to obtain such water supplies alternative institutional approaches to water re-allocation need to be considered.

Markets for Water

The prospects and advantages of establishing markets for water have been long discussed in the economic literature. The possibility of allocating water resources through market mechanisms was an extremely popular subject in the United States literature in the early 1950s, as that country experienced a frontier phase of water development, and has recently re-emerged as a topical issue in the context of the mature water economy. To a considerable degree the interest in water markets has been directed to issues in the United States context with very little research available on the potential applications for water use in Australia. Substantially, the research interest has been pre-disposed to considering the "efficiency" advantages of market structures for water transactions with only passing reference to the general conceptual problems of instigating a market and very little attention given to developing an institutional framework to actually establish a water market.

To a significant extent the focus of economic interest in water markets has been normative – in terms of the orthodox view of allocative efficiency and the notion that competitive markets will achieve such efficiency – and also dominated by analysis of existing United States water institutions. This latter issue is of relevance in that a perusal of the relevant water laws in Australia as against the United States, quickly establishes that the Australian approach is legally and institutionally profoundly different so that direct comparisons of principles of water re-allocation are probably not relevant.

In what follows the general principles of water re-allocation through markets will be considered from the traditional perspective of efficiency, and also in terms of the standard theoretical difficulties encountered in applying a water market to practice. Subsequently, a

170

proposal for institutionalising a water market in the Australian setting
will be reconsidered and finally the prospects for institutional success
are drawn out in terms of the current status of water law in this
country.

Water Markets and Efficiency

The literature on theoretical and empirical aspects of efficiency
relative to water re-allocation through markets is extensive (Hirshleifer
et al; Hartman and Seastone, 1965a, 1965b and 1970; Meyers and Posner,
1971; Burness and Quirk, 1980a and 1980b; and Johnson et al, 1981).
The general theme of much of this literature is to conceptualise the
advantages of a competitive market approach to water re-allocation
where institutional criteria currently constrain the possibility and, in
some cases, to illustrate the efficiency gains of replacing traditional
water management institutions with market institutions.

Probably the most vivid account of the need for and advantages
of water markets is to be found in the normative work of Meyers and
Posner. The thrust of this report is that current water markets in the
western United States need to be improved from the perspective of
efficiency. The key here is that a degree of transfer of appropriative
water rights exists in the western states, but due to certain institutional barriers, such a system has been constrained from developing to
a "fully fledged" competitive market.[10] Meyers and Posner are concerned
with ... 'imperfections in law and institutions that interfere with the
market allocation of water resources'(p.iv). The general motivating theme
here is the need to modify existing laws and institutions to reduce
the costs of market transfers and to promote the allocation of limited
water resources to the highest valued uses. Support for the market
institution is established on three premises:

> tradition;

> the greater likelihood of maximising the
> productivity of resources; and

> less interference by government in people's
> lives.

The first premise is a "knee jerk" reaction according to the view
that if resources are re-allocated by markets in a range of alternative
commodity situations then water should be treated the same way. This
view mocks the traditional requirements of specifying externality free
transactions as well as a range of informational and public good
questions. The two additional premises are in fact normative sentiment
that firstly, markets will allocate resources efficiently, and secondly,
that less interference by government in people's lives is a desirable
goal. In this context no further comment will be forthcoming on these
premises. However, it will be useful to consider the re-allocational
mechanics of the market approach.

As was observed previously, a dilemma of the current pattern of water allocation in the Hunter Valley is that by far the largest portion of available water supply is allocated to irrigation, where the value of the marginal product is low. Against this a range of new water using activities have developed in the valley where the value of the marginal product is many magnitudes higher – but where society's only recourse appears to be to construct new water diversions at high cost to meet such demand. As has been variously illustrated, the values imputed to water in irrigation are far below the marginal cost of supply whilst the values imputed to industry and urban uses appear to be substantially in excess of such cost. Consequently, it would appear that a water transfer from irrigation to other uses in the valley – without reverting to the additional costs of increasing capacity – would generate net social benefits where previously a substantial social subsidy was in practice.

The proponents of the "market for water" approach envisage a process where such a transfer is achieved "automatically" and with a substantial degree of autonomy by participants. The essential motivation of the market operation in this context is that the value of the marginal product of the resource – water – should be equated in all uses. In a setting of a well defined volume of water, it would be envisaged that users, where the value of the marginal product of water is high, would be willing to pay a sum to other users where the value of the marginal product is low. The actual value of the transfer would be determined by the relative bargaining positions of the participants but it would normally be expected that users with low value of marginal product should be willing to receive a payment in line with the value of the income generated by water or slightly higher – as users with high value of marginal product would be willing to pay up to the equivalent value of income generated. In such a manner the value of the social product would be maximised.

Fundamentally, a market for water rights requires a range of institutional provisions. Firstly, individual property rights in water need to be clearly defined with respect to the usual characteristics of quantity, quality, point of delivery and time of delivery. Additionally such rights should contain provisions for payment of utility costs and directions for delivery under conditions of restriction. Tenure of such rights should be for a sufficiently long time frame to enable commercial decisions to come to fruition and actual rights allocations should be for a significantly small portion of total water supply for ease of transaction and from the perspective of user scale of operation. Finally, water rights should be alienable from particular uses and should not be conditionally attached to particular users.

The overall perspective is to define water in terms analagous to a wide range of other resources and commodities where market transfers are practised. Accordingly users of water will be in a position to make the correct commercial and technological decision on water use in relation to other factor and final product prices. In such a manner .. 'a system of marketable water entitlements would effectively price water at its opportunity cost to the user' (Randall, 1982, p.29).

An additional feature which may be recognised in favour of the market approach, is the question of the transactions costs involved with administering water use and providing for transfers. Hartman and Seastone (1965a) have been instrumental in highlighting the effectiveness and efficiency desparities of judicial and administered approaches to water re-allocation. In a similar vein the market approach appears to avoid a considerable degree of the administrative costs of water re-allocation and would appear to direct whatever costs that are borne in water transfers to the individual participants.

As was mentioned early in this section, a great deal of the interest in the possibility of water markets and water rights has been conceived within the institutional settings of the United States – and particularly the western states of the United States. However, Randall 1982 has recently proposed a structure of water property rights applicable to an Australian institutional setting. Broadly, Randalls' prescription for transferrable water rights in Australia, is in accord with the general trends established in the United States literature. The basic provisions (1982, p.36-47) are as follows:

entitlements should be "created" for some arbitrarily large period – with delivery by given years if requested;

deliveries of water should be specified according to season of delivery and in relation to some rotation or schedule convenient to the water authority;

the entitlements may be transferred at any time during the tenure of the right and additionally, may be rented or leased according to requirements;

rights should be specified for some small portion of total supply in relation to notions of uncertainty. Alternatively, different classes of rights may be defined according to probabilities of delivery;

water rights would be vested in individuals independently of land;

rights should specify the location of delivery and would require the water authority to approve such locational changes;

changes in costs relating to delivery should be bone by users; and

charging structures and provisions for amendment of such charges should be conveyed with deeds of water rights.

Additionally, Randall observes that a moratorium should be put in place for established irrigators relative to ongoing commitments by such users. Such a moratorium would preclude dramatic changes in tariff policy and provide for ongoing rehabilitation works. Users of water from new projects would not be exempt from the implementation of rationalised utility approaches to tariff structures. Overall, Randall observes that a market for water rights would re-allocate some of the water supplies from low valued irrigation to the higher valued industrial and urban uses and, at the same time, provide compensation to irrigators for past capital investment.

Water Markets: Some Difficulties

While economists have written much on the advantages of market transfer in the re-allocation of water resources, the fact of the matter is that very few such markets have been instigated. As McPherson observed in a paper in 1956, ... "The fact that such a (water) market does not exist suggests that determining the price of water competitively presents economic and/or institutional problems that have not yet been resolved" (p.1259). It appears that such a view remains just as relevant today, as it was more than twenty five years ago. It is also notable that despite the historical developments of water law in the United States — whereby the eastern states were tied to riparian notions whilst the west developed the prior appropriation structure of rights — there have been significant innovations towards a water permit approach with some comparability to the Australian approach (Davis, 1968; Maloney and Asners, 1974).

Probably the most conspicuous cause for concern with water markets is the ability to account external costs of water use. It is probably true that economic concern with matters of water quality has produced as many innovative ideas on improving water quality as has the concern with water re-allocation. At this stage, it is not clear how the liabilities for external damage under one water use would be transferred to other users — presumably generating other classes of external damage.

In a somewhat related vein, the questions of secondary benefits and fixed public infrastructure represent additional obstacles to be accounted for before a market institution could be implemented. While a water market may compensate the holders of water rights out of irrigation, it is clear that other enterprises as well as local communities associated with irrigation — usually classified by secondary benefits — may suffer significant income losses. Such issues, being of an equity nature and not necessarily involving efficiency, have been given low economic priority but at the same time, they are the benefits which probably influenced politicians to support the irrigation scheme in the first place. The question of redundant public infrastructure on the other hand, is probably best accommodated by requiring new users to meet additional costs of modified deliveries.

A range of minor difficulties and objections remain, but will not be dealt with here. However, a major institutional factor militating against the implementation of a water market in circumstances such as in the Hunter Valley of New South Wales – or in Australia in general, will be discussed subsequent to considering the equity and structural impacts of a water market.

The Impacts of a Water Market

As briefly addressed in the preceding section, a market for water rights whilst compensating the holders of water rights, could cause the decline of local communities and enterprises associated with irrigation. However, to a considerable extent, such a criticism may not be relevant in the Hunter Valley. To a very substantial degree, the local communities and towns which were once the major market and rural centres are today mining boomtowns. Additionally, questions pertaining to public infrastructure to regulate and direct water flow are not particularly relevant since all water provided to irrigation is actually abstracted by private diversions from the riverbed or from the adjacent interconnected groundwater system.

Questions pertaining to the environmental costs of different water uses remain to be addressed, but it could be that due to the contained nature of the industrial uses of coal washing and power station cooling, there may actually be less water use related contamination of the Hunter river and the adjoining river flats than presently occurs with irrigation. However, it is not clear how the environmental costs which have emerged through irrigation practices will be accounted for (Dragun, 1982). Of particular concern in this context is a general increase in salinity of irrigation and adjacent farm lands – where the extent of the costs are difficult to evaluate and the interdependence between cause and effect are not clear. Temporal elements will also be of relevance here.

The Implementation of Markets:
A Small Matter of the Law and of Precedence

While it generally appears that a water market in the Hunter Valley could provide a very useful re-allocative function, one major hurdle remains to be overcome. According to the Water Act, 1912 (New South Wales) and the equivalent water related acts in other states, individual property rights to water do not –and cannot – exist. Rather, water is a resource in the public domain which may be used by certain individuals for particular purposes – but which may not be alienated by any individuals. The actual provisions of water use and management are provided for under the varous conditions of the act, as matters of governmental administration without recognizing any aspects of ownership.

To establish the foundations of a water market private property rights will have to be defined in water with particular attention to exclusion, alienation and transfer arrangements. Such a prospect raises a range of issues;

(1) Why should a private excludable notion of a property right be preferred to any other form of property right? Other legal strucures which may be of relevance include notions of public property rights, collective rights, common property rights, tenure in common and public trust or public jurisdiction. As different legal structures yield different equity outcomes, they are not comparable in efficiency terms, thus sentiment in favour of any structure must be normative.

(2) Are private property rights in a resource such as water, legally definable? Private property rights in a commodity in the usual sense need to be rigorously definable in terms of physical characteristics – such as quantity and quality dimensions, but also according to delivery conditions. The property rights also have to be well defined in terms of interdependencies between individuals, especially in the context of externalities.

(3) If private property rights are to be defined, how are such rights to be distributed and under what conditions? There has been some discussion that existing water users should be given property rights in water gratis, whilst new users might obtain property rights through an auction. While the auction process may yield some public compensation, it appears that excluded individuals no longer have any interest in water use and management.

(4) How would the implementation of a water market in the Hunter Valley impact on water use elsewhere in the state? While there may be a substantial rationale for a water market in the Hunter Valley, there appears to be very little interest elsewhere in the state, particularly in the irrigation districts where the largest volumes of water are used. The significant legal changes which would be required to implement a water market in the Hunter Valley may not be justified for this setting alone and such legal changes may not be necessary or acceptable at the state level.

(5) The precedent of a water market in the Hunter Valley will generate significant implications for the use of a wide range of other natural resources, where the current legislative practices have much in common. Significant resources in this context include: coal, other energy resource, minerals, fish, wildlife, the atmosphere and to some extent, forestry. In very practical terms, the implementation of a water market would provide a case for considering a wide range of similar applications in situations currently deemed to be inappropriate or politically unacceptable. A particular case in point here is the recent passing of the Coal Acquisition Act, 1981 (New South Wales), which was designed to yield all control of coal to the state.

The general conclusions on the possibility of implementing a water market in the Hunter Valley are that whilst there might be considerable normative sentiment in support of such a proposal, there does appear to exist a range of positive reasons why such a market will not be operationalised in the foreseeable future. Chief of such positive reasons is the very long legal tradition which currently governs the allocation and management of water resources within the state and also the more pragmatic questions of the precedence of a particular water market to the management of other water resources within the state as well as a wide range of other natural resources.

An Irrigation Land Buy—Back: As A Compromise Solution

While the more traditional approaches to water re—allocation appear to offer little relief to a pressing social problem in the Hunter Valley, it may be necessary to resort to a pragmatic second best approach to yield some compromise. While the first best solutions of the market and pricing approaches appear to provide clear cut and ongoing solutions to the water re—allocation problem, they have in turn been humbled by not unreasonable institutional provisions and pragmatic political questions. On the other hand, a pragmatic approach which may satisfy some of the institutional and political criteria, may provide some relief to the allocational problem, but without the ongoing dynamics or finesse of the other approaches.

The possibility of an irrigation buy—back certainly fits into this pragmatic style, providing an administrative lever whereby resources currently committed to an activity, where the value of the marginal product is low, can be diverted to other activities where the value is higher. The buy—back is unlikely to confront any of the legal and institutional "obstacles" which humble the market approach and would probably attract political support when the cost savings of the buy—back as against a major capacity supplementation scheme become clear. However, it should be clear that the buy—back is an administrative tool subject to transaction costs and at the same time, having little in common with the re—allocative dynamics of the market approach.

Background on the Buy—back Approach

While the possibility of an irrigation land buy—back does not appear to have been raised in the literature in relation to water re—allocation problems, the notion has been of some use in other renewable resource situations, particularly in the discussions of marine fisheries. The context of application of the buy—back in the marine fishery is focussed on the efficiency of exploitation of a given fish stock, but otherwise the approach provides useful insights as to how a major structural change in resource use may be achieved by avoiding intractable institutional and political questions.

Basically, the fishery buy-back has been utilised in recently restricted marine fisheries where the existing level of fishing effort was considered to be too great in terms of the efficiency of exploiting the original fish stock (Campbell et al (N.D.); Bell, 1978; Newton, 1978; Gunther and Winter, 1978; and Copes, 1978). To achieve a fleet of the desired size, an administrative procedure was established to give certain fishermen an incentive to leave a particular fishery. Usual practice would be to pay fishermen a commercial assessment on boat and license, plus a gratuity and then subsequently auction the boat for scrap or some non-fishing activity. Thus, by providing an incentive for some fishermen to leave the fishery – presumably the least efficient fishermen would be the first to leave – the efficiency of effort utilisation is increased as is the peformance of the fishery.

While the fishery buy-back was designed to reduce the allocation of resources employed in exploiting a given fish stock, there appears to be no reason why the principle could not be used to re-allocate water resources between different users to increase social product. A buy-back applied to water re-allocation would operate by focussing on the irrigation land rather than any water entitlement – thus the major institutional hurdle of property rights in water is avoided. The Government of the day could utilise its powers of eminent domain to purchase sufficient irrigation land with water licences equivalent to meet an emerging industrial or urban demand.

Once such irrigation land had been purchased, the water licences could simply be forfeited and a surplus of available water would be established in the system. Such a surplus could then be allocated to high priority industrial and urban users as new licences. Subsequent to the purchase of the original irrigation land, the actual process of forfeiting the irrigation licence and drafting a new licence for those high priority users, is a straightforward administrative matter.

The actual land purchase process could be organised on a tender-offer basis or could operate by removing the less value adding activities such as hay production and cereal growing first. Relevant criteria could also include land condition and location, where a secondary objective should be the consolidation of small irrigation blocks to a larger viable dryland unit. Subsequently, the larger dryland unit could be re-sold to recoup some of the original purchasing expenses.

Currently, less productive irrigated pasture – lucerne and hay type land is selling in the valley for a range of $2,500 per hectare to $3,000 per hectare, whilst the better river flats suited to vegetable cropping bring in the range of $4,000 per hectare to $5,000 per hectare. If the less productive irrigation land, in the range of $2,500 per hectare to $3,000 per hectare, were purchased to establish a surplus for re-allocation to high priority users, some 12,700 hectare would be required to yield the equivalent expected water supply of the proposed Glenbawn enlargement.[11] In contrast to the current estimated cost of the Glenbawn enlargement of $40M, such a buy-back would have net costs of between $25M and $30M assuming land resale value of between $500 per hectare and $1,000 per hectare. At the higher range of land prices, the total net cost would be equivalent to the capital cost of the Glenbawn enlargement.

However, it is not clear that the substantial capacity contribution of the enlarged Glenbawn Dam will be fully utilised by industrial and urban users for some considerable time; with the ultimate irony that a good deal of the short to medium term surplus water could be diverted into new irrigation. The advantage of the buy-back proposal is that it could be operationalised for smaller increments of supply to meet emerging high priority demand. Thus, the water supply system will not be burdened by under-used capacity, with high initial capital cost provision and also a re-adjustment in the agricultural community can occur gradually.

It would also be convenient and timely if the water managing authority were to invoke a suitable tariff system with the new water allocations (such as a tariff system including the transaction costs of implementing the buy-back). In practice the net land purchase costs would be the capital costs of providing incremental capacity. However it should be noted that the original cost of the water is much higher. Effectively, the buy-back should be viewed as the cost of the original decision to subsidise water to irrigation and the price of water to all new users should be determined according to the marginal cost struct-ure of the system.

The general impacts of the buy-back proposal would be quite similar to the water market approach. Again, the initial irrigation water users would be compensated to stop using water. Whilst such compen sation clearly provides a windfall gain to some of the original irrigators, the process returns subsequent land buyers the equivalent purchase price they would have paid to enter irrigation agriculture. The flexibility of the buy-back would probably not be as great as the water market approach in that continued adjustments would not occur. The buy-back would have to be re-operationalised as a block, as new increments of demand emerged.

While a water market would provide a continual process of re-allocation —and would also facilitate the continuation of high valued irrigation — an evolution to the stage where all users were paying tariffs in relation to the marginal cost of provision would put pressure on the addition of new capacity as a resource to further re-allocation of a fixed stock of water. Thus re-allocation is only significant until all users are paying the marginal costs of provision whereupon new demands can be accommodated by capacity additions and the approp-riate pricing policies.

SOME CONCLUDING COMMENTS

The current allocation of water resources in the Hunter Valley clearly represents a significant economic and political dilemma. The bulk of the region's regulated water supplies are employed in an activity where the social welfare loss is substantial. According to current principles of water provision and management there is little recourse but to let the social subsidy to irrigation continue whilst a range of high value demands have recently emerged in the region. These high value uses will have to be provided for by further costly additions to water supply capacity.

The possibility of re–allocating the region's limited water supplies by the use of conventional markets is rendered inordinately difficult because of the basic structure of water law in Australia. Changes in such law, whilst conceptually quite straightforward, are practically impossible in the light of natural resource management at the state level as well as basic pragmatic politics. An approach which achieves much of what a water market would do is the irrigation land buy–back. This approach appears to suffer few of the institutional disadvantages evident for water markets and has the decided political advantage of being slightly cheaper than straightforward supply construction programs.

NOTES

1. Water Resources Commission of New South Wales, personal communications.

2. Water Resources Commission of New South Wales. Whilst the Plan of 1979 allocated an additional 102,000 ML per year to irrigation by the year 2002, the 1982 Review downgrades additional irrigation potential to 50,000 ML in a high growth scenario and only 16,000 ML in low growth. This perspective seems strange as the conflict arising from extra growth is the tradeoff between industrial and irrigation requirements rather than any complimentary effect. The confusion apparent in the Water Resources Commission's attitude to irrigation water is graphically illustrated in the statement that ... 'If no further dams are built on Hunter River tributaries in the study period, releases for irrigation purposes would not be required along these tributaries' (page 4).

3. The Sydney Gazette of June 15th 1830 reported that coal had been discovered on the property of a Mr Yeoman at Hunter River near Singleton. In terms of coal mining, The Maitland Mercury does report the sale of coal in Singleton (July 6th 1850) and the Muswellbrook Colliery came into operation during the 1850s as one of the first collieries in the district, see Roberston Research (1981), Coal had been discovered at Newcastle as early as 1791 with intermitent exploitation reported until 1831 when the Australian Agricultural Company was granted the privilege of mining all known coal sources in New South Wales, see J. Hunt (1977).

180

4. The mines most likely to begin operation before 1985 are Mount Arthur North, Glendell and the underground and surface mines of United. Other mines under consideration for the same time or shortly after include surface mines at Bloomfield, Glennies Creek, Howick South, Bayswater, Hunter Valley No. 2 and possibly Buchanan Lemington North as well as the underground operations of Black Hill and Barix, ibid.

5. At this stage the Electricity Commission of New South Wales has reported substantial consumer demand reaction to a series of recent rate increases. Such demand reaction has motivated the Commission to postpone the construction of existing proposals with ramifications for the construction of future thermal power stations in the Hunter Valley – see the Financial Review 17/8/82 and 19/8/82.

6. Given population projections to 1986, the WRC's estimate of water requirement by the urban sector is equivalent to a per capita consumption range of 133 to 145 KL per year, which is roughly equivalent to current consumption levels for Newcastle and Adelaide, for example. The values for 2001 amount to a per capita consumption range of 292–335 KL/year (1979 Preliminary Plan) and 166–192 KL/year (1982 Review).

7. The licensing fee has just been increased – with much controversy. The original fee was 55 cents per ML for the first 3 ML per hectare used in irrigation, or for the first half of an industrial allocation, and 30.5 cents per ML for all additional water used.

8. It is common knowledge that the HDWB is not keen to take the 8,000 ML from the Glennies Creek Dam, preferring instead to develop a major dam on the Williams River – Tillegra Dam. Water quality and management control appear to be the major considerations in this context.

9. Information on market prices of irrigated and non-irrigated land in the Hunter Valley flood plain was obtained through personal survey of regional estate agents with verification through the New South Wales Valuer Generals Office, Newcastle. A complication to assessing land values in this context is that some land with components of irrigated flood plain has been sub-divided for hobby farms. However, this effect is negated to a substantial degree on the majority of flood plain land where a prohibition on building exists.

10. In the western United States, appropriate water rights – water rights generally established according to the precedence of the first users – are contrasted to the more traditional notion of riparian occupiers in the east.

11. Assuming an average water use of 4.7 ML/ha this area should be equivalent to 60,000 ML, the additional safe yield of the Glen-bawn enlargement.

10

ENVIRONMENTAL ASSESSMENT IN REGIONAL DEVELOPMENT WITH REFERENCE TO THE ATMOSPHERIC ENVIRONMENT OF THE HUNTER VALLEY

N.J. Daly and A.J. Jakeman[*]

PART 1: RISK ASSESSMENT

Since their inception in Australia, environmental impact assessments have relied heavily on quantitative techniques to estimate the magnitude of specified impacts. This is especially true in assessing the quality of the atmospheric environment where prepared assessments focus greatly on the use of packaged computer models to predict precise contours of pollutant concentration over some set of averaging times and input conditions. Such models and their usages are typified by recent assessments of the impacts of Hunter Valley Power Stations (Electricity Commission of New South Wales, 1979) and Aluminium Smelters (State Pollution Control Commission, 1980).

As awareness has grown of the complexity of environmental systems and the uncertainty of the data collected from them, the concept of probability of occurrences of events has assumed increased importance. This has led to attempts to apply probabilistic theories to the evaluation of environmental effects. The application of models to the calculation of frequency distributions of potential ozone as a guide to the formulation of oxidant controls (Daly, 1978, 1979) and the statistical modelling of distributions of events (Daly and Jakeman, 1982) are specific responses to these general requirements.

In recent times the drive to employ probabilistic techniques has been formalised in the process of risk assessment. The term has been chosen to distinguish the process of impact assessment, and is described as a means of extending the concept of environmental assessment. Environmental risk has been defined by Whyte and Burton,

* The authors wish to indicate that N.J. Daly was the principal author of PART I of of this chapter and A.J. Jakeman was principal author for PART II. The authors would also like to express their gratitude to Dr P.J.B. Duffy of the Canadian Federal Environmental Review. Office for helpful discussions and to J.A. Butt for his assistance in preparing the manuscript.

Figure 10.1   Environmental risk state-of-knowledge profile

MANAGEMENT
CAPABILITIES

Do we know anything?
Are probability estimates available
Are measurements available?
- field
- laboratory
Has it been modelled?
Was this anticipated?
Who knows about this
Where has there been similar experience
What is likely public/ political response?
What resources do we need to find out/respond?
- emergency response
- legislative authority
- technical/equipment
- manpower
- financial
What resources do we have?
- emergency response
- legislative authority
- technical/equipment
- manpower
- financial
Which government agencies have jurisdiction and capabilities in these areas?

ENVIRONMENTAL RISK
CHARACTERISTICS

SOURCE
- what are sources/causes
- who is responsible
- what are initiating events
- when do they occur
- where do they occur
- what events have already happened

PATHWAYS
- what are environmental pathways
- how fast does risk travel/ develop
- what transformations take place (chemical/physical)
- does risk diffuse or remain focused

EFFECTS
- what are/will be beneficial effects
- what are harmful effects
- are effects reversible/ irreversible
- are effects chronic/acute
- are effects teratogenic/ mutagenic
- what are dose-effect relationships
- where are effects felt (geographically)
- what are harmful environmental effects
- what evidence for synergistic effects

SOURCE: Whyte and Burton (1980)

184

(1980, p.1) as "the probability value of an undesirable event and its consequences that arise from a spontaneous natural origin or from a human action that is transmitted through the environment". In mathematical terms, risk is the probability multiplied by the consequence of an event. Therefore, the difference between impact assessment and risk assessment is that "impact assessments are concerned with events that are reasonably certain to occur, while risk assessment is concerned with events that may possibly occur" (p.1). And it should be stressed that, "the difference between certain and probabilistic events appears not in the nature of the events themselves but in the human understanding and description of the processes involved" (Whyte and Burton, 1980, p.1).

The first step in risk management is obviously the identification of the state of knowledge and risks of the system under study (Figure 10.1). The other steps are the quantitative estimation of risk which is usually performed by scientists and risk evaluation, which is carried out by decision makers. The paper deals mainly with the estimation and evaluation phases. It is the aim of Part I to accomplish the following:

examine current procedures, particularly in New South Wales, for the assessment of developmental impacts, thereby making pertinent criticisms to motivate the adoption of risk assessment as a framework for a more integrative assessment procedure;

review the risk assessment framework;

describe the risk system and the nature of its component subsystems, with particular reference to the atmospheric environment;

propose a philosophy for the modelling of the risk system, which not only satisfies the probabilistic requirements of the risk assessment procedure but also is sympathetic to the complex nature of the risk system and the quality associated data; and

suggest that the information basis from which the environmental standards approach is derived for impact assessment can be used more comprehensively as the major tool in the management of risk.

In Part 2 of the paper, a case is made for the use in environmental impact assessment of specific statistical models which have a low degree of ambiguity in the definition of their parameter values. Specific criticisms are made of the applicability and application of the current packaged computer models used by consultant and regulatory bodies.

ASSESSMENT IN THE AUSTRALIAN CONTEXT

Environmental assessment generally follows pathways of the type shown

185

in Figure 10.2 which is a simplified summary of procedures recommended by the Government of Canada (1981). Within Australia this type of assessment is also required and is enforced by legislation at both State and Federal level. The planning and pollution measures associated with assessment in Australia have been comprehensively reviewed by Fowler (1982).

The basic intent of the legislative requirements is that the environmental effects of all aspects of proposed developments be determined in advance. In the Australian context however, there are three separate processes by which these effects are evaluated and managed. These three processes are briefly described in the following sections.

Environmental Impact Assessment

Environmental Impact Assessment (EIS) of developments in New South Wales are required under the Environment, Planning and Assessment Act of 1979 which became effective in 1980. Previous procedures for assessment were administered by the State Pollution Control Commission (SPCC). The developments from early concepts of legislation are described by Fowler (1982).

For the purpose of the Act in New South Wales, the factors to be taken into account when the likely impact of an activity is being evaluated are:

any environmental impact on a community;

a transformation of a locality;

any environmental impact on the ecosystems of the locality;

a diminution of the aesthetic, recreational, scientific or other environmental quality or value of a locality;

any effect upon a locality, place or building having aesthetic, anthropological, archaeological, architectural, cultural, historical, scientific or social significance or other special value for present or future generations;

any endangering of any species of fauna or flora;

any long-term effects on the environment;

any degradation of the quality of the environment;

186

any risk to the safety of the environment;

any curtailing of the range of beneficial uses
of the environment;

any pollution of the environment;

any environmental problems associated with the
disposal of waste;

Figure 10.2   Recommended pathway for Environmental Impact
Assessment

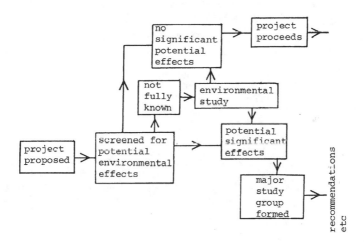

any increased demands on resources, natural or otherwise, which are, or are likely to become, in short supply; and

any cumulative environmental effect with other existing or likely future activities.

Criteria for evaluating each of these factors are not specified. Nevertheless, it is obvious that to address most of them adequately requires a substantial data base over a representative time period. It is a weakness of the procedure that the gathering of such a base is rarely possible on the time scale allocated for the impact assessment. Consequently, the state of knowledge of sources, pathways, dosages and effects (Figure 10.1) contains many negative entries in the "don't know anything" and "probability estimates" categories, although paradoxically, deterministic models may have been used to generate isopleths of pollutant concentrations around sources.

Clean Air Acts

Within Australia generally, control of pollution levels is exercised by the licensing of premises to emit wastes. Within New South Wales these controls are specified by the Clean Air Acts of 1958 and 1961. Licensing follows the philosophy of "best practicable means" (Court et al., 1981) which tends to be expressed in the requirement that emissions be limited to the levels achievable by modern plant being run efficiently.

Unfortunately, there is no evidence to show that the application of best practicable means involves comprehensive calculation and comparison of risks. Consequently, application of the requirements of the Clean Air Acts does not in itself guarantee that degradation of the environment does not occur.

Environmental Standards

The quality of the atmospheric environment is evaluated in many countries in terms of Air Quality Standards (AQS). AQS are intended primarily to protect public health, although secondary standards may be set or recommended to protect public welfare, a concept defined to include effects on vegetation, materials, visibility, climate, and some aesthetic factors.

In general, AQS take the form of a concentration of pollutant average over a specified time, and not to be exceeded for more than a specified annual frequency. The intention of the standard is to identify and prescribe a threshold concentration which, if crossed, poses a probability of damage to an "at risk" receptor. Both the probability accepted in the standard, and the at risk community to be protected are judgements which should reflect community goals. The averaging time of a standard is, in the ideal case, determined by the uptake rate of the receptor, and is therefore pollutant and receptor specific. The frequency at which the threshold may be crossed is again a judgement which should relate to community goals. A description of United States National Air Quality goals appears in the Federal Register (1971).

In Australia, AQS are used to evaluate the quality of the atmospheric environment with respect to public health, and are recommended by the National Health and Medical Research Council. In most cases, the adopted goals conform with those recommended by the World Health Organisation (WHO).

It should be noted that a development may satisfy the EIS requirements, conform with license requirements of the Clean Air Acts, and still cause, or contribute to violations of AQS if it is sited in a region of limited environmental capacity.

One major deficiency of the AQS is that they focus attention on individual pollutants and do not, except for special cases such as the combined sulphur dioxide–suspended particulate matter standard, consider interactive or cumulative effects. This deficiency is also present in the Clean Air Acts where attention is focussed on individual emission rates, and pollutants are considered as if each were in isolation. The cumulative effects addressed in the EIS are not included in the philosophies of Clean Air Acts and AQS.

REGIONAL ENVIRONMENTAL MANAGEMENT:
THE RISK ASSESSMENT FRAMEWORK

The EIS requirements, the Clean Air Acts, and AQS form the administrative structure within which the quality of the regional environment can be assessed and managed. However, to date, each of these techniques has seemingly operated as if it were in isolation. Fowler (1982) has also concluded that there is yet to develop any philosophy or common approach with respect to the integration of environmental impact assessment procedures and related development control.

Effective environmental management requires inter alia the development of an integrative philosophy. At present two basic philosophies are in widespread use and both have been alluded to earlier. These are the environmental standards approach; and the best practicable means approach.

The first approach is embodied in the legislative requirement that the effects of a development do not bring about violation of environmental standards. The most comprehensively documented example of such an approach is the legislative history of the US Clean Air Act amendment (United States Library of Congress, Environmental Policy Division, 1974). The most commonly encountered example is afforded by the rigidly enforced quality standards for domestic water supplies.

The best practicable means approach is less clearly defined than the standards approach and seeks to apply judgements framed within the context of each individual case. The approach is sometimes

189

Figure 10.3   The framework for assessing environmental risk

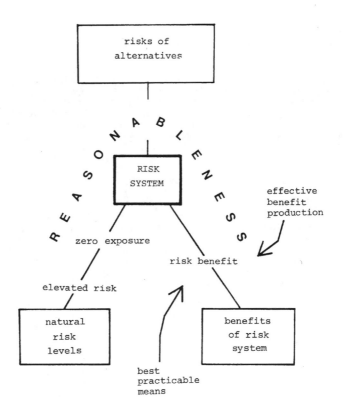

one which allows high benefits to outweigh environmental risks. The classic case is the toleration of an industry with high pollution levels because it brings needed employment to a region. The approach concentrates on the costs of controls and the benefits of the system of risk, but has not produced a methodology for assessing the risk system itself and the associated environmental costs.

Each of these management policies deals with only part of the environmental management problem. It is proposed that the risk assessment framework depicted in Figure 10.3 provide a basis for inclusion of the requirements of each. The framework in Figure 10.3 is adapted from that of Whyte and Burton (1980). Application of the framework requires consideration of the state of knowledge and the risk characteristics in each of the four risk systems identified in Figure 10.3. The objectives are to assign reliable estimates of the probabilities of risk for each.

Originally included within the framework of Whyte and Burton (1980) is the balancing of environmental risk against other (societal) risk. This aspect is omitted here for convenience as it is preferred to leave this non-environmental issue to others and make comparisons just with the levels of alternative (environmental) risks. However, since the consideration of risk is relativistic, it would not be objective to omit evaluation of the risk from natural levels. Clearly, the alternative risk systems component can be evaluated in the same way as the major risk system under consideration. Application of the risk assessment framework as an integrative philosophy also requires evaluation of how the probability of risk increases as benefits of the risk increase. These aspects are now discussed in more detail.

The Risk System

The system of cause and effect for risk evaluation can conveniently be decomposed into a number of subsystems. Figure 10.4 shows the breakdown into the following types:

the polluting subsystem caused by human activity;

the mechanisms of transport which "carry" the pollution to receptor sites; and

the subsystem containing the receptors on which there is the eventual environmental impact.

The above categorisation is general. For example, in some systems, human activity may cause impacts directly. Certainly, the breakdown is most relevant to atmospheric and aquatic systems.

To manage environmental risk effectively it is necessary to model successfully the process linking the polluting human activity right through to the environmental effects. In this way, the intermediate and

191

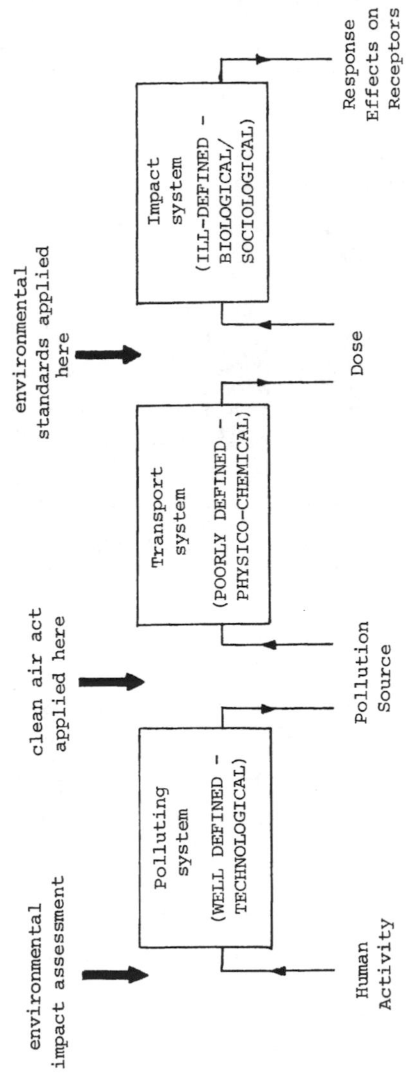

Figure 10.4   The risk system and its component subsystem types

final effects of potential levels of human activity can be gauged.

This modelling will often involve relating input or causal variables in a subsystem to output or response variables via a set of mathematical expressions or equations containing known and/or unknown system parameters. Clearly, once these unknown paramters are estimated satisfactorily, the response of the subsystem to a range of real or hypothesized inputs can be obtained. Thus, in considering the transport model, the aim is to provide input scenarios to the impact system. As we shall see, successful modelling of the impact system yields dose-response curves. These curves provide the basic information on the risk system, which, when interfaced with the Benefits of the Risk System, enables judicious choices of policy options for land use planning and the setting of environmental quality.

Risk of Alternatives

The risk of alternatives in the environmental assessment of plans for regional development is mainly concerned with the choice of alternative locations for specific developments, and the choice of alternative developments for specific locations. These are land use options which can be evaluated as individual risk systems within the risk assessment framework. Evaluation of the risks will clearly have to consider the full range of impacts of the particular proposals on the risk receptors including the probability of risk due to cumulative effects.

Benefits of Risk System

The benefits of a risk system are usually presented in the form of firm estimates based on an economic study. It may be, however, that the uncertainties are larger than appreciated if the view (Howard, 1982) that economic prediction is a very inexact science is valid. To the extent that the risk system can be defined by probability estimates, the data are available to enable policy makers to estimate the appropriate balance between benefits and risks.

There is a tendency to achieve this balancing of cost-benefit by assigning dollar values to the risks. The difficulties of evaluating environmental qualities for which no market exists and which lie beyond the possibilities of sensible valuation have been considered by Saddler (1970). In particular, approaches have been made which use interview techniques to establish "willingness to pay" to obviate environmental pollution. The technique is limited by serious deficiencies (Waddell, 1974). These include:

lack of knowledge on the part of the responder of the technical nature and range of damage forms;

the "Free Rider" problem;

the fact that citizens of polluted areas are less inclined to attempt to control pollution than those of less polluted areas; and

the finding that attitudes were likely to have been formed by and are subject to, change due to mass media definitions.

Despite these deficiencies, results of "willingness to pay" surveys are reported in forms such as: 65 per cent of respondents would pay $5 or more; 85 per cent of respondents would pay $1 or more; willingness to pay is an average $17.66 (Australian Environment Council, 1982)

These studies place an unrealistic and misleading emphasis on precise values for poorly defined and non quantifiable systems, and tend to ignore essential concepts of confidence and error limits on those values.

Natural Risks

Natural risks are well covered by the methodology adopted in setting standards. The procedure is to determine the distribution of natural levels of pollutants of concern and to select standards at some level which is not experienced in nature, and which provides a small probability of an adverse effect. The analysis in terms of dose-response relationships and frequency distribution of damages includes the Natural Risk System in the total assessment or risk.

MODELLING THE RISK SYSTEM

It is useful here to characterise the nature of the different risk subsystems so that the appropriate philosophical basis for a practical modelling approach can be adopted. The approach is a statistical one which satisfies the requirements of risk assessment. It is expanded upon in Part II where deficiencies in the applicability of the current modelling procedures are also discussed and the application of the alternative statistical approach is described.

Nature of the risk subsystems

In order to categorise the commonality and differences among the three subsystems which make up the system for risk evaluation, it is pertinent to invoke the ill-defined systems concept formalised succinctly by Young (1978). Basically, a system is ill-defined if the mathematical relationships linking system inputs, parameters and outputs (collectively called variables) possess a level of complexity which cannot be investigated precisely because it is difficult to perform the necessary planned experiments to obtain the data needed to identify all of these relationships. In the case of environmental systems, passive monitoring is often the only way data can be collected.

Therefore, the data from ill-defined systems have an associated level of uncertainty which arises not only from sampling and measurement errors but from this passivity also. The data are the inseparable product of a range of system mechanisms and, characteristically, the effects of individual mechanisms cannot be observed for long enough periods of time to be quantified with high precision.

The interested reader is referred to Young (1978, 1983a, 1983b) and Jakeman (1982) where these concepts are illuminated by way of examples encountered in their modelling of environmental systems.

Within the above context, the polluting component of the risk system shown in Figure 10.4 is usually well-defined. The relationships between variables may or may not be complex but they are generally capable of quite precise quantification since technological systems are designed to behave as they do. Therefore, predicting accurate model outputs of pollution source or input to the transport system requires no special treatment here. The comments on modelling for risk assessment in the remainder of these papers obviously relate, for the most part, to the more complex transport and impact system.

The ability to describe physico-chemical transport systems successfully within the environment varies. A fortuitous example is the transport of non-reactive pollutants down a river system. Transport within such a system can be explained very satisfactorily for risk assessment purposes but certainly not exactly (Jakeman and Young, 1980). However, the majority of transport processes possess at least a poor level of definition. These especially include water and airshed systems when reactive pollutants are being considered.

In fact, one of the most ill-defined of these systems is the transport and deposition of inert dust from open cut coal mines. Butt et al (1982a) provide the detailed reasons for the problems in such a system by experimentation. These reasons include the physical nature of the mine system as well as the sampling errors inherent in collecting relevant data.

On a more general note, it is widely accepted that the transport of any air pollutants under meteorological conditions of very low wind speeds, recirculations and fumigations cannot be satisfactorily described by currently available techniques of dispersion modelling (Feldstein, 1976). Clearly, to include these mechanisms in a model would involve a level of mathematical sophistication that would be difficult to verify.

Almost invariably within the risk system, the impact subsystem suffers the weakest definition. Furthermore, for a given system, the definition will deteriorate as consideration of impacts changes from flora to fauna to the human species. Thus it is usually easier to describe, at least empirically, the relationships between dosage and effects in plants than in humans. However, even on plants, it appears difficult to conduct experiments which are representative of true field conditions. With animals and especially humans, the complexity of description increases because sociological effects impinge. The effects

195

on humans, for example, are additionally influenced by their attitude to the pollutant. Alternative techniques for dealing with management of risk in some of these cases are discussed by Butt et al (1982b, 1983c).

The construction of dose-responsive curves to describe the impact system and consequently set environmental standards as chosen points on such curves has concentrated mainly on humans. It therefore rests largely on evidence from epidemiological studies since it is unethical to perform highly investigative clinical experiments. A classic and comprehensive example involves the analysis and constant review of data for the setting of the British standard for ambient dust concentrations in underground coal mines (Jacobsen et al 1970, 1971).

In the next section, the basis of our modelling philosophy is briefly described. This is enlarged upon in Part II where further rationale of the philosophy is provided. While the general comments are applicable to the impact system, the emphasis is placed on the environmental transport system. It is especially in this area that modelling techniques, which are used to obtain information for environmental impact statements in particular and for environmental planning in general, can be comprehensively improved.

Basis of a Modelling Approach

A great deal of the modelling of environmental systems has shown little regard for the real objectives of the modelling exercise. At one extreme, models have been applied which attempt to reproduce reality in fine detail, thereby satisfying any objective that management may care to investigate. On the other hand, over-simplistic models have also been used to produce long-averaged predictions without accompanying statistics to indicate the reliability of the means. These tend not to satisfy any substantial objective. One feature that both these approaches have in common is that they are mostly used deterministically. A deterministic model implicitly assumes that its mathematical links between system mechanisms are sufficiently accurate to produce predictions without the need for any form of error bounds on them.

It is proposed here that the models used for predicting ill-defined system outputs:

be specific to the objectives that management requires; and

possess a useful statistical or stochastic basis so that levels of reliability can be attached to the estimated model parameters and hence the model predictions.

It is instructive to demonstrate how such model types are consistent with the risk assessment approach. Consider a hypothetical polluting human activity of fixed intensity. It is usually straightforward

Figure 10.5   Schematic diagram sharing likelihood of dosage
to receptor areas of a fixed level of human
activity

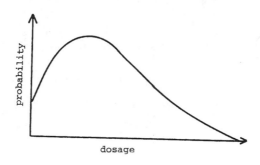

Figure 10.6   Schematic diagram showing mean and standard
error only of dose from Figure 10.4 as level of
human activity changes

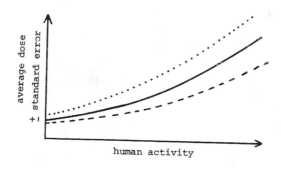

to calculate the source pollution from the technological system. From a statistical model of the transport system, the probabilities of levels of dosages to receptor areas can be assigned. The result is a curve of the form stylised in Figure 10.5. This procedure can be repeated for the full range of intensity of the human activity. The results can be summarised in a curve of the form in Figure 10.6 where only two statistics for each of the curves belonging to the suite of curves of Figure 10.5 are displayed. They are the mean and standard error of Figure 10.5 for each level of polluting activity. The standard error bounds are arbitrary but they usually will be larger than portrayed when models are applied to input data not generally encountered in practice, that is for very high source levels.

For the impact system, the dose–response curves obtained from modelling are ideally probabilistic and the discussion of frequency distribution of damages below provides a good example. Thus, a given dose has a certain response on average for a certain percentage of the population. Figure 10.7 elucidates the likely range of a dosage from Figure 10.6. Figure 10.5, if more detail is required, yields the corresponding range of response.

STANDARDS AND RISK ASSESSMENTS

It is the purpose of this section firstly to stress that modelling of the impact system, yields or can be extended to yield, dose–effect information crucial to the risk assessment procedure. Standards are chosen from this information to guarantee a low probability of a certain risk to "at–risk" receptors (see Shy et al., 1970). However, further analysis of the dose–effect data may enable identification of the rate of risk as pollutant concentration increases above the standard.

A good example of useful methodology which enables risk assessment is given by the analysis of dose–effect data for health damages caused by photochemical oxidants. Although this has been discussed elsewhere (Daly, 1981), it is informative to summarise the salient aspects here. The other aim of this section is to indicate a negative feature of environmental standards in the risk assessment procedure. As presently framed, they do not handle exhaustively the problems of cumulative effects of pollutants nor the problem of aesthetic environmental damages.

Frequency Distribution of Damages

Leung et al. (1975) examined dose–response relationships for health effects due to oxidants and conducted a delphi survey of medical professionals familiar with air pollution health effects. Each professional was asked to estimate the level at which 0, 10, 50 and 90 per cent of 14 population subgroups would experience each of three levels of effects. The health impairments were found to be described by the equation

Figure 10.7   Schematic diagram showing the likely range of
impacts as the bounds of dosage change

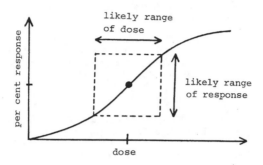

Figure 10.8   Frequency distribution of health damages as a
function of oxidant concentration

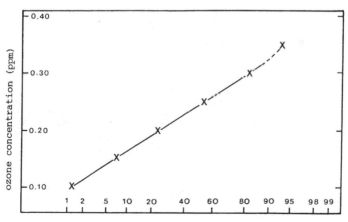

per cent of per capita damage below stated level

$$\ln \left\{ \frac{F}{1 - F} \right\} = A + B \ln (Ox) \qquad (1)$$

where F is the fraction of population affected, (Ox) is the concentration of oxidant, and A and B are parameters giving the intercept and slope for each function.

Bradley et al. (1977) weighted each subgroup by an estimate of the relative size of the group in California and weighted each of the levels of health impairment by a factor based upon estimated medical costs and productivity loss for that level. The 42 functions were combined to give a composite damage function as a function of pollutant concentration.

Further analysis (Daly, 1981) showed that the proportion of per capita damages is normally distributed about the mean oxidant levels. Thus, plots of the cumulative frequency of the per capita damage are a linear function of the one-hour average concentrations of oxidant and are shown in Figure 10.8.

The figure clearly shows how the per cent of damage increases as ozone concentrations increase. The damage increase is rapid, and it can be seen that about seven per cent of damage occurs below 0.15 ppm ozone, while about 22 per cent occurs below 0.20 ppm. The additional five ppm has produced an additional 15 per cent of damages; similarly about 50 per cent of damages occur between 0.15 and 0.25 ppm.

This analysis of the frequency distribution of damages provides estimates of the probabilities of damages associated with various levels. These estimates can then be fed into the state of knowledge of effects (Figure 10.1) to be used in conjunction with model predictions to define the risk system.

The methodology above is one which can be applied generally. The steps required are the identification of the damage effects, the development of dose-effect relationships and the identification of the form of distribution of damage with increase in pollutant concentration. Insufficient attention seems to have been paid to this approach which offers a means of assigning probability estimates to the likelihood of particular damages to specified receptors from given exposures.

Cumulative and Synergistic Effects

Examination of cumulative and synergistic effects is called for in EIS requirements and specified in the environmental characteristics listed in Figure 10.1. In practice these are either not considered or deemed to be too onerous or complicated to execute (Court et al, 1981). Despite this judgement there is a body of evidence which shows the need to consider the combined effects of pollutants. Thus, for example, Ehrlich et al (1977) have shown that on humans ozone and nitrogen dioxide have additive effects during a single exposure, and may have a synergistic effect for multiple exposure. Mizoguchi et al (1977) showed in studies with humans that symptoms such as cough, sore throats and eye irritation correlate significantly with combined pairs of pollutants. Corresponding effects are found with materials damage.

Greenaway (1982) has critically reviewed pollutant interactions with plants and classified the effects of the combinations into the three categories:

additive – a combined action of two or more agents equal to the sum of each of the agents used alone;

antagonistic – a combined effect of two or more agents that is less than the sum of each of the agents used alone; and

synergistic – a combined effect of the agents that is greater than the sum of each of the agents used alone.

The breakdown of the effects of the pollutant combinations on a range of plant functions ranging from foliar injury to enzyme activity and reproduction showed (Greenaway, 1982) that 12.4 per cent of interactions are antagonistic, 43.4 per cent are additive, and 44.2 per cent are synergistic. Thus, on the basis of these data, the probability of the considered pollutant combinations having additive or synergistic effects is about 0.87 which represents a major environmental input. Such effects are not considered by Clean Air Acts, AQS or best practicable means and are only given token treatment in some EIS.

Aesthetic Damages

Like cumulative effects, aesthetic damages are addressed in the EIS requirements but protection is not provided by AQS nor envisaged in the Clean Air Acts. A notable exception does occur in Victoria where there is a standard for visibility. Nevertheless, appropriate standards are difficult to specify objectively since the risk characterisation and knowledge profile of Figure 10.1 are poorly defined. The use of environmental attitude surveys (Butt et al, 1982a), however, does provide a means of assigning a relative rank order or selected aesthetic environmental factors and does seem capable of generating relative estimates of the probability of concern.

CONCLUSIONS

The Risk Assessment framework of Figure 10.3 offers a methodology which enables the environmental standards approach to be used in conjunction with suitable forms of Benefit Analysis. The advantages of this approach lie in the nature of standards. Standards are objective, are based on scientific analyses which aim to establish a threshold designed primarily to protect public health, and secondarily to protect public welfare, and are reassessed as additional evidence becomes available (US Federal Register, 1979; Heuss et al., 1971).

The framework requires that the standards approach be broadened to report more of the dose-response curve than at present. Such broadening would enable estimates of the probability of the various damages to be considered and balanced against the benefits of the proposals.

The balancing can only be effective if the knowledge profile of the environmental system is adequate. Accordingly the check list of Figure 10.1 needs to be considered for all at risk environmental components such as health, materials, vegetation, and intangibles like aesthetics. The cumulative and additive effects of emissions which have been largely neglected also need to be included in the analysis.

Implementation of the above tasks require a body of well organised environmental studies. The requirements are seen as:

The development of a land use plan which enables development and location alternatives to be considered;

Construction of a regional inventory of receptors and their damage profiles;

Development of Dose-Response curves for receptors to enable probability of damage estimates; and

Continued development of probabilistic models for use in risk estimation.

Many of these tasks are presently undertaken, but in an ad-hoc way. Without these data, neither the AQS approach nor best practicable means can be managed. With these data, both can be integrated into the Risk Assessment framework.

PART 2: MODELLING

INTRODUCTION

In Part 1 of this paper, the framework of risk assessment was used to develop an integrative approach to environmental management. Crucial to the approach is a modelling methodology which is appropriate for risk estimation. A philosophical basis for such a methodology was presented and a broad class of models described simply as specific and statistical proposed for risk system estimation. The class was demonstrated to satisfy the probabilistic requirements of risk assessment which recognises that a degree of uncertainty is associated with human understanding of environmental systems.

Part 2 of the paper elucidates the characteristics of the proposed modelling methodology and considers its advantages. The unsuitability of deterministic modelling is discussed and corroborated with two examples which are fairly representative of the treatment given modelling in many environmental impact statements. The comparative disadvantage seen of the proposed methodology is that its statistical nature makes some parameters site or location dependent. It is argued that this is only an apparent disadvantage since it requires that model estimation and validation should be undertaken in a comprehensive manner. These phases of model building and checking should also be carried out comprehensively for deterministic modelling.

RATIONALE FOR SPECIFIC STATISTICAL MODELLING

The merit of specific models is the following: since they are constructed to satisfy defined objectives, they can be simpler in structure and/or more economical in the number of system variables invoked than the more detailed models. For example, the usual objective in planning for air quality management is the determination of the number of occasions per year on which a given standard is exceeded. Therefore, it is often sufficient to be able to produce output predictions from a model in the form of probability distributions of concentrations for the relevant averaging time(s). This simple yet informative form of output negates the need for a model which predicts, more demandingly, concentrations sequentially in time from sequential input data.

A simplified model output requires only those major variables (input and system parameters) which drive the system to provide this form of output. Young (1978) goes a step further than this and hypothesises the existence in practice of a law of large systems which assumes that a system has certain dominant modes of observable behaviour which can be explained by a small number of causal factors.

The advantages of a simpler model lie not only in the convenience of having to monitor and/or incorporate fewer variables. More importantly, a more efficient model structure implies less ambiguity in model parameter estimates obtained from the input—output data base. It is well known from statistics that the variance of a model parameters and the 'simpler' the model structure, the lower the variances on the estimated parameters. And more refined model definition naturally leads to more accurate model predictions.

Despite the advantages of specific models of ill—defined systems, the specificity property alone does not guarantee certainty of model predictions. After all, by circumventing the horrendous problems of having to reproduce the reality of events in their finest detail, the need has been created to establish the reliability of the new model form. To account for the uncertainty associated with the model formulation, and implicitly that of the accompanying data, the model parameters must be given statistical properties. This is accomplished by appropriate choice of estimation method which basically relies on the minimisation of some assumed cost function or error in the model formulation. At this stage the possible range of values is obtained for each of the driving model parameters that is capable of producing the type of output data observed. Ideally, each parameter has this reliability defined as a probability distribution or, at worst, there is a standard deviation associated with the mean value. The precise type of parameter definition depends on the type of model and estimation employed.

It should be stressed that this approach does not override the need for the essential steps of model validation to check the adequacy of the model through its predictive ability on data sets. Poor performance indicates that checks be made on the amount, quality and best intensity of data used in the estimation phase. The predictive ability of a model is intrinsically dependent on the data used to develop it so that performance can only be commensurate with the properties of the best available data. On the other hand, additional investigation is necessary to ascertain whether further driving variables and enhanced parametric structure are required to explain the system better. The attraction to avoid is the inclusion of excessive model structure which is incompatible with the level of certainty in the data. Ambiguous system definition leads to better performance in terms of explaining the output data upon which the estimation was carried out. However, such performance will be severely diminished on other data sets.

There is, of course, a large body of techniques available to aid in the preliminary, intermediate and final stages of identification of the major causal variable driving a system. these range from simple statistical tools like multiple regression analysis (Anderson, 1958) through to recursive time series analysis (Young 1974; Young and Jakeman 1979, 1980; Jakeman and Young, 1979, 1983; Young et al., 1980; Jakeman et al., 1980; Jakeman and Sheridan, 1982).

APPLICABILITY OF DETERMINISTIC MODELLING TO ENVIRONMENTAL MANAGEMENT

Since the modelling literature on environmental systems has concentrated too much on detailed, or averaged, mechanistic and deterministic descriptions of transport processes, it is conceivable why the work of consultancies, management and regulatory bodies for environmental asssessment has followed this mainstream trend. Of course, the justification for researchers attempting such descriptions is the desire to provide general models which can be used off-the-shelf to fit any situation within the very broad framework for which the model was designed. In the United States, this is encouraged in the extreme where the use of all-purpose computer packages approved by the Environmental Protection Agency makes the work and results of environmental impact assessment easier to evaluate formally.

However, the reliability of these models for systems which are ill-defined is questioned here as is the faithfulness of their practical application. Some examples from the Hunter Valley are pertinent.

Dustfall

Because of the encouragement to use off-the-shelf models, the prediction of dust levels from open cut coal mines is proceeding according to poor but sophisticated state-of-the-art dispersion techniques. It is acknowledged for the most highly developed computer package for this problem that errors can creep in at an alarming rate (Pedco, 1978; ERT, 1979). Butt et al. (1982a) conservatively estimate that such a detailed model can produce predictions only to within an accuracy factor of eight when the required input inventory data are available. However, comprehensive inventory data have not yet been established in the Hunter Valley to provide input to such a model. To compound the problem, the deterministic nature of this type of model ensures that no grasp can be obtained on the level of error in the predictions whether that error be from poor input data or from inaccurate system definition.

Fluorides

The modelling of emission transport from proposed aluminium smelting has proceeded in the main according to simplistic yet still mechanistic versions of dispersion models. Gaussian plume models have been used to describe ambient fluoride around smelters, basically allowing only wind speed and direction data to drive the system. Other important meteorological factors like non-neutral atmospheric stability categories have to all intents been ignored. Another common practice is to feed into the model both average wind speed over 45 degree sectors and constant allowable emissions. In all the EIS presented, the averaging time has not been lower than one month.

Outputs of a model on a monthly, or even weekly, basis have little relevance to air quality standards which should exist down to a time scale of hours. Indeed, it may be the lower frequency conditions of high fugitive emissions and/or poor atmospheric dispersal which yield the most impacting concentrations.

It is also probably fair to say that the end result of too long-term averaging is a set of concentration contours around a source which are merely relative reflections of the average wind rose data imposed on the model. Their relativity often ensues from scaling of model predictions according to a restricted set of observations at one or two sites.

APPLICATION OF SPECIFIC STATISTICAL MODELLING TO ENVIRONMENTAL MANAGEMENT

Application of the specific statistical modelling philosophy to overcome the inadequacies of general off-the-shelf packages must take into consideration whether management is required for an airshed with or without comprehensive monitored data available. In most instances like the Hunter Valley, assessment is required of extended development in old regions where some amount of pollution data from installed sources already exist. However, assessment is sometimes required of the likely impacts of development in a region previously untouched. Gladstone in Queensland is a good recent example of this.

Consider, initially, the case where pollution data are available. A particular statistical model in such a system contains system parameters which are location dependent. For example, distributions of ground level concentrations of a pollutant transported from a constant emission source have been shown to correlate extremely well with distributions of wind speed measurements (Daly and Steele, 1976). The correlation constant estimated in such a case is related to the emission strength in a linear fashion as well as the topography of the area and other minor agglomerated meteorological influences. With such a model, it is a simple matter to predict with an accompanying accuracy the consequences of increasing the source strength or of imposing different wind regimes on that system for which the model was built (Daly and Jakeman, 1982).

In the case where relevant pollution data are not available in a region, the specific models remain basically the same in structure as those verified in regions with similar characteristics, although some of the structure may vary. At this stage of statistical model development, the possible range of parametric values is unknown since not enough statistical modelling has yet been done to provide this information.

As an interim measure, stochastic simulation provides a useful tool for investigation of the likely range of pollution levels for a new developing region. A particularly good example of this type of simulation is given by Hornberger and Spear (1980) and Spear and Hornberger (1980) for a water quality problem. However, in this case, some output data were available. Whitehead and Young (1979) and Mahendrarajah et al. (1982) demonstrate the basic steps in such a simulation using specific statistical models of two hydrological systems.

Used effectively here, the technique involves simulating output for the best a priori models (mechanistic or otherwise) of the system under investigation using selected inputs and random samples from the probability distribution of system parameters. When sufficient samples are taken, the end result is an aggregate of output with a mean and standard deviation which provide information on the likely range of behaviour of the system for the selected inputs.

MODELLING CONCLUSIONS

Mechanistic modelling work should continue on ill-defined systems to improve gradually, at least to a limit point, their level of definition. After all, this type of modelling helps the physical understanding of systems and ultimately provides valuable information to the specific statistical modeller. In the meantime, much effort should concentrate on building suites of models with individual objectives as opposed to more general models which accomplish too large a range of objectives.

Some of the parameters to be inserted in the specific models by users will be statistical, however, rather than measurable physical parameters and hence will be site dependent. In a developed region, these parameters can be estimated at least partly from existing data. Thus, estimation and validation will involve more conceptual effort than has been applied in the past. But any realistic modelling exercise should involve these phases. Statistical modelling will actually help to ensure they are carried out, whereas users of deterministic package models have tended to take comfort in the illusion that an "experts" physical perception of reality, when well documented in the literature, is an appropriate one.

For environmental models in virgin areas, stochastic simulation modelling is important to provide ball-park answers. However, the use of specific models in a variety of locations will gradually build up a wealth of information for application to new regions. Values of the statistical parameters found in each case study can be documented with relevant physical parameters operating in the location at the time of the study. In this way, upper and lower bounds and perhaps even probability distributions of the values of those parameters relevant to the new region can be ascertained. Obviously, the bounds on parameters are likely to be larger than those for established developed regions. In either case, the result is, as it always should be for ill-defined systems, a prediction with a level of uncertainty dependent on the level of uncertainty in the input variables and parametric system structure.

11

THE IMPACT OF THE COAL-BASED DEVELOPMENTS IN THE HUNTER VALLEY ON THE REGIONAL LABOUR MARKET

Frances Perkins

INTRODUCTION

The current and proposed investment of approximately $3 billion in coal mines in the Upper Hunter, $1.5 billion in coal washing and mineral processing industries and $5 billion in related economic infrastructure, will be accompanied by a considerable increase in the demand for labour in the Hunter Region.

Numerous publicly available and confidential studies of this projected labour demand have been carried out by the relevant New South Wales and Commonwealth government departments as well as by Hunter-based bodies.[1] However, as a considerable number of major projects have been formally cancelled or postponed recently and several more are now unlikely to proceed, most of these studies have to a greater or lesser extent been overtaken by events. Furthermore, because these reports often fail to specify which individual projects they assume will proceed, it is not possible to update their calculations of total employment growth as the investment plans of major developers are changed.

Consequently, this paper attempts to make an independent assessment of the likely level, industrial distribution and occupational structure of the demand for labour which will be generated directly and indirectly as a result of the new developments taking place in the Hunter Valley . This growth in labour demand is then examined in the context of the existing labour market situation, in order to assess the likely impact of the new developments on unemployment and skilled labour availability in the region. The market cost of this labour, to project developers and government authorities, as well as its social opportunity cost to the community, also is estimated approximately to form an input into the broader study, outlined in Perkins (1982), of the overall costs and benefits of the new coal-based developments in the Hunter region to the Australian community.

209

Table 11.1   Occupational status of the Hunter regional
labour force, 1976 and 1981

In the Labour Force -	Male	Female	Total	Prop of Work-force%	Prop of Popula-tion %	1976 Male	Female	1981 Total	Prop % Work-force	Prop of Popula-tion %
Employed: Wage or Salary Earner	97252	44983	142235	82.5	33.9	111369	54549	165918	83.5	36.2
Self Employed)	12259	5259	17519	10.2	4.2	8387	3601	11988	6.0	2.6
Employer)						5701	2442	8143	4.1	1.8
Helper unpaid	333	1500	1833	1.1	0.4	254	1169	1423	0.7	0.3
Total	109844	51742	161587	93.7	38.5	125711	61761	187472	94.3	40.8
Unemployed:	6874	3987	10861	6.3	2.6	5469	5847	11316	5.7	2.5
% of total unemployed	(63.3)	(36.7)	(100.0)			(48.3)	(51.7)	(100.0)		
Total Labour Force	116718	55729	172448	100.0	41.1	131180	676008	198788	100.0	43.3
Total Population	209344	210024	419368	-	100.0	229823	223899	458722	-	100.0
Participation rate (as % of pop. aged >15 yrs)	76.7	35.9	56.1	-	-	76.2	39.0	57.5	-	-

Source: ABS, 1976 and 1981 Census

210

Table 11.2   Sectoral distribution of employment, Hunter Region, 1976 and 1981

Industry	1976				1981			
	Males	Females	Persons	Prop %	Males	Females	Persons	Prop %
Agriculture etc								
agriculture, Agric Svcs	5050	2265	7311	4.5	4320	1871	6191	3.3
forestry, fishing, hunting	754	66	822	0.5	807	92	899	0.5
Total	5804	2333	8137	4.7	5127	1963	7090	3.8
Mining	7373	153	7526	4.7	9924	247	10171	5.4
Manufacturing								
food, drink, tobacco	3738	1593	5332	3.3	2860	1693	4553	2.4
textiles, clothing	979	1906	2885	1.8	891	1843	2734	1.5
wood, furniture	1410	172	1582	1.0	1356	185	1541	0.8
metal prods, machinery	24297	1883	26180	16.2	24535	2060	26595	14.2
other and undefined	3070	692	3762	2.3	3790	848	4638	2.5
Total	33494	6247	39741	24.6	33432	6629	40061	21.4
Electricity, Gas, Water-								
electricity, gas prodn	2743	259	3002	1.9	4228	357	4585	2.4
water, sewr, drainage	1237	116	1353	0.8	1423	161	1584	0.8
Total	3980	375	4354	2.7	5651	518	6169	3.3
Construction	9787	911	10698	6.6	13356	1354	14710	7.8
Wholesale, Retail Trade-								
wholesale trade and undf	5012	1579	6591	4.1	5280	1866	7146	3.8
retail trade	10410	10874	21284	13.2	9912	11222	21134	11.3
Total	15422	12452	27874	17.3	15192	13088	28280	15.1
Transport, storage-								
road transport	3063	560	3623	2.2	3675	636	4311	2.3
rail transport	2801	63	2864	1.8	3144	92	3236	1.7
water and air transport	1140	75	1215	0.8	1466	101	1567	0.8
stor, othr transport undf	351	119	470	0.3	330	189	519	0.3
Total	7355	817	8172	5.1	8615	1018	9633	5.1
Communication	1706	581	2287	1.4	1950	645	2595	1.4
Fin, Propty, Bus Svcs	4088	3737	7825	4.8	5896	5952	11848	6.3
Public Admin, Defence	5495	1847	7342	4.5	6151	1503	7654	4.1
Community Services								
health	2377	7361	9738	6.0	2900	8631	11531	6.2
education	3315	4976	8291	5.1	3991	6207	10198	5.4
other and undefined	1950	1016	2967	1.8	2161	1278	3439	1.8
Total	7642	13353	22996	12.9	9052	16116	25168	13.4
Rec. Persnl, Oth Svcs-								
enternt, recn svcs	703	647	1350	0.8	912	607	1519	0.8
restaurants, hotels, clubs	2150	3240	5390	3.3	2316	3960	6276	3.3
other and undefined	362	968	1329	0.8	388	1150	1538	0.8
Total	3214	4855	8069	5.0	3616	5717	9333	5.0
M/N Not Class and Not Stated	4485	4082	8566	5.3	7749	7011	14760	7.9
Grand Total	109844	51742	161587	100.0	125711	61761	187472	100.0

Source : ABS 1976 and 1981 Censuses.

THE REGIONAL LABOUR MARKET

The Hunter regional workforce exhibits specific characteristics which reflect the heavy industrial and mining basis of the local economy. It has also experienced a certain amount of structural change in recent years. Table 11.1 shows changes in the occupational status of the regional workforce over this period between the 1967 and 1981 censuses. The overall participation rate rose by 1.4 percentage points to 57.5 per cent over this period, due entirely to a substantial increase in the female participation rate, from 35.9 to 39.0 per cent. That for men actually fell slightly from 76.7 to 76.2 per cent. However, participation rates for both men and (particularly) women in the Hunter Region in 1981 remained lower than the Australian averages, which at that time, were 77.3 per cent for men, 45.6 per cent for women and 61.3 per cent overall. This lower female participation rate can be explained by the fact that in the Hunter Region the tertiary sector, which traditionally provides the bulk of female job opportunities, employs a considerably lower percentage of the regional workforce (50.4 per cent) than does the national tertiary sector of the national workforce (58.7 per cent). The proportion of the regional workforce who were wage and salary earners rose slightly, from 82.5 to 83.5 per cent over the 1976-81 period. This is somewhat higher than the national average of 79.6 per cent of the workforce (employed as wage and salary earners) probably reflecting the region's economic reliance on a number of large manufacturing enterprises. Table 11.2 outlines changes in the broad sectoral distribution of the regional workforce between the 1976 and 1981 censuses.

The reliance of the Hunter regional economy on heavy industry and manufacturing in general, is illustrated by the fact that in 1981, 21.4 per cent of the regional workforce was employed in this sector, compared to only 17.7 per cent of the overall Australian workforce. However, there has been a 3.2 percentage point drop in this sector's share of total employment since the 1976 census, even though there has been a slight (0.8 per cent) increase in the actual number of people employed in manufacturing. Most of this relative decline has occurred in the metal products and machinery industries, which in 1981 employed 14.2 per cent of the workforce, compared to 16.2 per cent in 1976. Nevertheless, only 7.3 per cent of the national workforce is employed in this sector. Agricultural employment actually experienced an absolute decline over the period 1976 to 1981, as well as a 26 per cent fall in its contribution to total regional employment, from 4.5 to 3.3 per cent. Since agriculture provides 5.7 per cent of overall Australian employment, this sector has now declined to the point where it is a relatively minor direct employer in the region. On the other hand, there has been a rapid expansion of employment in the mining industry, which has grown from 4.7 per cent to 5.4 per cent of the workforce, and in the construction industry, where employment rose from

212

Table 11.3   Occupational distribution of the regional
workforce, Hunter Region, 1976 and 1981

Industry	1976				1981			
	Males	Females	Persons	Prop %	Males	Females	Persons	Prop %
Professional, Technical -								
Medical, Dentist, Nurse etc	1240	3582	4822	3.0	1529	4070	5599	3.0
Teachers	2536	3248	5784	3.6	3068	4405	7473	4.0
Other, Incl Veterinarians	5787	1123	6910	4.3	7527	1890	9417	5.0
Total	9563	7953	17515	10.8	12124	10365	22489	12.0
Administrative etc	7062	1322	8384	5.2	5865	801	6666	3.6
Clerical Workers	6038	14184	20222	12.5	6885	17115	24000	12.8
Sales Workers	5507	7776	13283	8.2	6546	8695	15241	8.1
Farmers, Fishermen etc -								
Frmrs, frm wor, wool clsr	6407	2333	8740	5.4	5147	1865	7012	3.7
Huntrs, Timb wkrs, Fishmn	323	0	323	0.2	782	47	829	0.4
Total	6730	2333	9063	5.6	5929	1912	7841	4.2
Miners, Quarrymen, etc	4131	2	4133	2.6	5485	8	5493	2.9
Transport, Communication								
Shipping, Air Transport	479	2	481	0.3	421	7	428	0.2
Rail Transport	1765	8	1773	1.1	1660	18	1678	0.9
Road Transport	5262	341	5603	3.5	5611	311	5922	3.2
Other Tpt, Communication	752	663	1414	0.9	733	624	1357	0.7
Total	8257	1014	9271	5.7	8425	960	9385	5.0
Tradesmen etc -								
Textiles	771	1905	2676	1.7	576	928	1504	0.8
Metal Electrical	25353	561	25914	16.0	27052	574	27626	14.7
Wood Technology Building	7509	32	7541	4.7	9216	77	9293	5.0
Other Prodn Process Wrkrs	4041	1344	5385	3.3	6085	2520	8605	4.6
Labourers	7768	254	8022	5.0	10919	420	11339	6.0
Other	6951	306	7257	4.5	7383	407	7790	4.2
Total	52395	4402	56796	35.1	61231	4926	66157	35.3
Service, Sport, Recreation-								
Fire, Police, Other Services	1182	35	1217	0.8	1388	51	1439	0.8
Domestic Service Workers	407	3495	3902	2.4	724	3794	4518	2.4
Other	2788	5549	8338	5.2	3118	6620	9738	5.2
Total	4378	9079	13457	8.3	5230	10465	15695	8.4
Members Armed Services	2276	96	2372	1.5	2451	155	2606	1.4
Inadequately Desc or N/S	3508	3582	7090	4.4	5540	6359	11899	6.3
Grand Total	109844	51742	161587	100.0	125711	61761	187472	100.0

Sources: ABS; 1976 and 1981 Census.

6.6 to 7.8 per cent of total regional employment. Mining employs only 1.4 per cent of the total Australian workforce and the construction industry, 6.3 per cent. Employment in most tertiary sectors, with the exception of wholesaling, retailing and public administration, also grew as a proportion of the total workforce over 1976-1981. Although the electricity and gas industriês employ only a small proportion of the workforce, this expanded by 26 per cent, from 1.9 to 2.4 per cent, during the inter-censoral period and now makes almost twice the contribution to regional employment than it does to national employment; only 1.3 per cent in 1981.

Hence, reasonably rapid structural change is occurring in the regional economy, reflecting in large part the long-term trend decline of agriculture and manufacturing and the growth of tertiary sectors which is evident in most developed countries. However, this restructuring also exhibits specific regional characteristics, which mainly reflect the Hunter Region's improved international and national comparative advantage as a supplier of energy, in the form of steaming and coking coal and thermally generated electricity. As a result of this structural change in the regional economy, there have been some significant shifts in the occupational distribution of the region's workforce. These are outlined in Table 11.3.

It can be seen from Table 11.3 that between 1976 and 1981, the proportion of tradesmen in the regional workforce declined from 22.4 to 20.5 per cent, including a noticeable drop of eight per cent (from 16.0 to 14.7 per cent) in the percentage of metal and electrical tradesmen. On the other hand, the proportion of process workers and labourers rose 28 per cent to 10.6 per cent, possibly reflecting the trend towards the increasing automation of industry in recent years. No doubt due to the industrial bias of the regional economy, the proportion of the workforce who are skilled tradesmen is still considerably higher than of the national average (15.8 per cent). Industrial process workers and labourers also form a larger proportion of the regional than of the national workforce (8.7 per cent).

The percentage of farmers and farm workers dropped dramatically, by 31 per cent from 5.4 to 3.7 per cent of the workforce during the inter-censoral period. As noted above, employment in agriculture now represents a considerably smaller proportion of regional than of national employment (6.1 per cent). The relative importance of both miners and construction tradesmen in the regional workforce increased between 1976 and 1981, by 12 and six per cent (to 2.9 and 5 per cent) of the workforce, respectively. In the case of miners, this represents almost five times the proportion of these workers in the national workforce (0.6 per cent) but in the case of construction tradesmen it is only a slightly higher proportion than in the national workforce (4.7 per cent). Professional, clerical, sales, transport and other service employees formed a reasonably stable proportion of the total workforce and represent a slightly lower percentage of regional than of national employment, reflecting the smaller size of the region's tertiary sector.

Overall, it appears that even in 1976 the region possessed a workforce which was considerably more skilled than the national workforce in trades relevant to the metal and metal products, mining and electricity supply sectors. It was therefore better placed than many development areas to accommodate the rapid expansion of these sectors anticipated by 1979. The 1981 Census data indicates that there has been a considerable growth in the numbers of skilled, semi-skilled and unskilled workers employed in these sectors in the region. Presumably, this growth was achieved by a movement of skilled and experienced workers from other sectors of the regional economy to jobs in the growing sectors, by the recruitment of newly qualified apprentices for jobs in the growth industries and (probably more importantly) to fill jobs vacated by more experienced workers in non-growth sectors, as well as by the migration to the region of skilled workers from other parts of NSW, the rest of Australia and overseas. The relative importance of various potential sources of labour supply in meeting the requirements of these expanding sectors is examined in more detail in the section on Multiplier Effects on Regional Employment, Available Labour Supply and Anticipated Excess Demand (Supply).

A PROFILE OF UNEMPLOYMENT IN THE HUNTER REGION

Numbers, Age and Sex of Persons Unemployed

Since February, 1981 when the Commonwealth Government instructed the Commonwealth Employment Service (CES) and the Department of Employment and Industrial Relations to cease publishing data the total number of people who are registered as unemployed, no satisfactory measure of regional unemployment has been available in Australia. (This series was recommenced in April 1983 by the new Labor Government) The estimates of unemployment levels published by the Australian Bureau of Statistics are based on a very small sample of the population (less than 0.5 per cent, and for N.S.W. are only disaggregated for "Metropolitan Sydney" and the "rest of NSW".

Although data from the five yearly censuses, outlined in Table 1.1 gives a "snap shot" view of the regional labour market situation, it is obviously not a satisfactory method of assessing short term changes in the level of unemployment. However, the census data on unemployment does enable some assessment to be made of the validity of using CES Registrant figures as a proxy for unemployment in the region. This is discussed later.

Hence, accurate data on short-term changes in the level and structure of unemployment in the Hunter region is not currently published. The Department of Social Security (DOSS) does however collect data on the recipients of unemployment benefits in each post code area, including their ages, sex, marital status, length of receipt of benefit, previous occupation and nationality, etc. The main problem associated with using this data as a proxy for total unemployment is that several major groups of unemployed persons are not eligible to receive unemployment benefits, including people under 16 years of age and the spouses of people who are already receiving an income above a means tested level. School levers and those who have become unemployed voluntarily must wait six weeks before they are eligible for unemployment benefits. Consequently, the DOSS figures were consistently lower than Commonwealth Employment Service, CES, figures for corresponding geographical areas during the period up to February 1981 when both were being collected.

Furthermore, even when it was published, CES data on those who were registered as unemployed was only a proxy for total unemployment because for various reasons, some people who are looking for work do not register with the CES. Professional groups traditionally have not used the CES and most importantly, those people who are in any case ineligible to draw unemployment benefits (such as the spouses of employed people) may see little benefit in registering as unemployed. As mentioned above, data on unemployment in the 1981 Census (Table 11.1) provides a useful method of checking how accurately CES registrant figures measure actual unemployment. Unfortunately, CES data ceased to be published in May 1981, the month before the Census. The figure for registered unemployment for June 1981, however, could be expected to be about 200 persons lower than the May 1981 figure of 11,038, or about 10,800 people, on the basis of previous years' experience, and the fact that the calculations in Table 6 indicate there were approximately 10,500 unemployed people in the region in September 1981. Comparing this estimate with the Census figure of 11,316 unemployed indicates that the CES figures do appear to underestimate total unemployment, but only by about 4.6 per cent. However, a comparison of Census and CES data (in Tables 11.3 and 11.5) for men and women produces the interesting result that whereas the CES data is actually extremely close to the Census figure for male unemployment, registered unemployment data is likely to underestimate female unemployment (as revealed in the Census) by as much as 8.9 per cent. This quite large downward bias should be borne in mind when examining the data in the remainder of this section.

It is also quite possible that labour force participation rates in the Hunter are lower in the current situation of high unemployment than they would be if full employment existed, because of the existence of "discouraged workers". Such people may, during periods of high unemployment, become so dejected as a result of long, unsuccessful job searches that they withdraw from the labour force altogether. Alternatively, those who would otherwise enter the workforce will not attempt to do so at times of depressed labour demand. A negative relationship between labour force participation rates and unemployment has been found in many countries (Sapsford, 1981). Hence, if full employment were approached in the region (as a result of the new coal-based projects,

Table 11.4   Unemployment benefit recipients, Hunter Region, February 1980 to May 1982

		FEMALE			MALE			OVERALL
		JUNIOR	ADULT	TOTAL	JUNIOR	ADULT	TOTAL	TOTAL
FEB 80	Newcastle & Lower H	3,017	1,272	4,289	1,951	3,474	5,425	9,714
	Upper Hunter	178	45	223	41	179	220	443
	Eastern Hunter	35	9	44	19	42	61	105
	Total	3,230	1,326	4,556	2,001	3,695	5,706	10,262
MAY 80	Newcastle & Lower H	2,736	1,261	3,997	1,449	3,157	4,606	8,603
	Upper Hunter	169	42	211	91	149	240	451
	Eastern Hunter	38	14	52	22	32	54	106
	Total	2,943	1,317	4,260	1,562	3,338	4,900	9,160
AUG 80	Newcastle & Lower H	2,580	1,265	3,845	1,299	3,153	4,452	8,297
	Upper Hunter	165	45	210	107	178	285	495
	Eastern Hunter	30	8	38	21	27	48	86
	Total	2,775	1,318	4,093	1,427	3,358	4,785	8,878
NOV 80	Newcastle & Lower H	2,169	1,235	3,404	1,135	2,864	3,999	7,403
	Upper Hunter	132	40	172	68	117	185	357
	Eastern Hunter	27	7	34	19	27	46	80
	Total	2,328	1,282	3,610	1,222	3,008	4,230	7,840
FEB 81	Newcastle & Lower H	2,882	1,345	4,227	1,527	3,246	4,773	9,000
	Upper Hunter	170	47	217	85	128	213	430
	Eastern Hunter	40	12	52	13	28	41	93
	Total	3,092	1,404	4,496	1,625	3,402	5,027	9,523
MAY 81	Newcastle & Lower H	2,516	1,337	3,853	1,240	3,043	4,283	8,136
	Upper Hunter	146	44	190	49	107	156	346
	Eastern Hunter	40	10	50	8	26	34	84
	Total	2,702	1,391	4,093	1,297	3,176	4,473	8,566
SEP 81	Newcastle & Lower H	2,176	1,321	3,497	1,161	3,060	4,221	7,718
	Upper Hunter	91	37	128	38	94	132	260
	Eastern Hunter	40	15	55	11	28	39	94
	Total	2,307	1,373	3,680	1,210	3,182	4,392	8,072
NOV 81[2]	Newcastle & Lower H.	560	309	869	304	798	1,102	1,971
	Upper Hunter	71	33	104	34	81	115	219
	Eastern Hunter	31	9	40	12	34	46	86
	Total	662	351	1,013	350	913	1,263	2,276
FEB 82	Newcastle & Lower H	2,562	1,625	4,187	1,493	3,692	5,185	9,372
	Upper Hunter	96	44	140	43	104	147	287
	Eastern Hunter	39	14	53	13	38	51	104
	Total	2,697	1,683	4,380	1,549	3,834	5,383	9,763
MAY 82	Newcastle & Lower H	2,335	1,543	3,878	1,659	4,016	5,675	9553
	Upper Hunter	116	61	177	57	122	179	356
	Eastern Hunter	34	15	49	34	39	73	122
	Total	2,485	1,619	4,104	1,750	4,177	5,927	10,031
AUG 82	Total, Hunter Region[1]	2,527	1,854	4,381	2,171	5,696	7,867	12,248
		(2,498)	(1,832)	(4,330)	(2,146)	(5,630)	(7,776)	(12,106)

1.   Excludes approximately 150 unemployed persons in the Upper Hunter and 700–800 in the Eastern Hunter who are registered at the Armidale and Taree CES Offices, respectively.

2.   Figures affected by DOSS industrial action.

3.   Figures in brackets are deflated by approximately 1.2 per cent to take account of the slight change in the DOSS's method of collecting UB recipient data from August 1982.

Source: Commonwealth Department of Social Security, Canberra.

Table 11.5   Persons registered with the CES as unemployed,
                 Hunter Region, January 1980 to May 1981

		Adult		Junior		Total
		Male	Female	Male	Female	
End	January 1980	4605	2104	3092	4540	14341
	February 1980	4457	1931	2651	4110	13149
	March 1980	4090	1729	2278	3815	11912
	May 1980	4103	· 1888	2107	3545	11643
	June 1980	3971	1775	1979	3521	11246
	July 1980	4061	1819	1866	3333	11079
	August 1980	3997	1815	1808	3300	10920
	September 1980	3957	1763	1773	3022	10515
	October 1980	3724	1791	1570	2959	10044
	November 1980	3707	1810	1847	3057	10421
	December 1980	3997	1900	2320	3987	12204
	January 1981	4390	2056	2461	4235	13142
	February 1981	4235	1931	2150	3794	12110
	March 1981	4122	1992	1904	3595	11613
	May 1981	3810	2034	1783	3411	11038

Data for April, 1980 and April 1981 are unavailable because of CES industrial action during
those months.

1   Aggregate of the five employment districts of Broadmeadow, Cessnock, Charlestown,
    Maitland and Newcastle.

Sources: Department of Employment and Industrial Relations (previously DEYA), Monthly
           Review of the Employment Situation, January, 1980 - March, 1981. Files at the
           DEIR Canberra for May, 1981 data.

for example), this would be likely to stimulate an increase in labour force participation rates, and hence would increase available labour supply beyond the level indicated by the current unemployment level.

A necessarily very approximate picture of the current unemployment situation in the Hunter can be obtained by determining the relationship between DOSS and CES unemployment data between February 1980 and May 1981, for adult and junior males and females. Using this relationship and recent DOSS data on unemployment benefit recipients (for February, May and August, 1982) it is possible to forecast what CES data for registered unemployment would have been in these three months, had it still been collected. In August 1982, the Department of Social Security altered the method of collecting unemployment benefit recipient data. Rather than counting the number of unemployment benefit cheques sent out in a specific fortnight in the sample month it now calculates the actual number of people paid for a particular day in that month – in this case, Friday 27th August. The use of this new method of estimation has apparently resulted in an increase of approximately 5,000 (or 1.17 per cent) in the number of people, Australia wide, who were estimated to be receiving unemployment benefits (426,000), compared to the number who would have been counted as unemployment benefit recipients in August under the old method of collection (421,000 people). Hence, to preserve the comparability of the time series data sets on unemployment benefit recipients and estimated CES registrants, the August 1982 DOSS data for the Hunter region has been deflated by 1.17 per cent. However, the new method of collecting DOSS data is no doubt more accurate, as people may receive two cheques in one fortnight, or one cheque for several fortnights (if arrears payments are made), whereas the new method specifically counts the number of people in receipt of unemployment benefits for the selected day.

Table 11.4 gives DOSS data on unemployment benefit recipients in the five CES employment districts in the Lower, Upper and Eastern Hunter[2] from February 1980 to August 1982, while Table 11.5 shows CES data on the number of people registered as unemployed in the Hunter region from January, 1980 to May, 1981. Using simple regression analysis to determine the relationship between these two sets of data up till May 1981, for each of the four sex and age categories, makes it possible to deduce that from September, 1981 to August 1982, registered unemployment in the Hunter would have been approximately equal to the estimates in Table 11.6. It was not possible to calculate the level of unemployment in November, 1981 because an industrial dispute disrupted the collection of DOSS data during that month. The figures in brackets for August 1982 are deflated by 1.17 per cent to retain approximate comparability of the data series, as discussed earlier.

Table 11.6 indicates that between February and August, 1982, the number of unemployed people in the Hunter Region actually increased in non-seasonally adjusted terms by 2900 to (at least) 15205 people, or by a substantial 23 per cent, to 7.6 per cent of the workforce.

Table 11.6   Estimates of registered unemployed in the Hunter, May 1981 to August 1982

	Adult		Junior		Overall Total	Prop 1981/3 Workforce %	Rate of Increase over Previous Quarter (%)
	Male	Female	Male	Female			
May '81 (CES)	3810	2034	1783	3411	11038	6.4	-
September '81	3881	1948	1701	2939	10469	6.1	- 5.2
February '82	4634	2381	2086	3372	12473	7.1	+ 19.1
May '82	5031	2292	2288	3137	12748	6.4	+ 2.2
August '82	6786	2620	2784	3183	15373	8.8	+ 20.6

September '81 - August '82 data are estimates from DOSS data, May '81 data was provided by CES zonal office, Newcastle.

Table 11.7   Change in registered unemployment in the Hunter Region, February to August, 1977–1982

	Male			Female			Overall Total	Percentage Change
	Adult	Junior	Total	Adult	Junior	Total		
February 1977	N/A	N/A	8956	N/A	N/A	4565	13521	
May 1977	N/A	N/A	8600	N/A	N/A	4163	12763	– 5.6
August 1977	N/A	N/A	7527	N/A	N/A	3473	11000	–13.8
February 1978	N/A	N/A	8890	N/A	N/A	5480	14370	
May 1978	N/A	N/A	8329	N/A	N/A	4734	13063	– 9.1
August 1978	N/A	N/A	8265	N/A	N/A	3941	12206	– 6.6
February 1979	5300	3324	8624	1869	4148	6017	14641	
May 1979	5199	2783	7982	1770	3604	5390	13372	– 8.7
August 1979	4843	2402	7245	1632	3122	4754	11999	–10.3
February 1980	4457	2651	7108	1931	4110	6041	13149	
May 1980	4103	2107	6210	1888	3620	5508	11643	–11.5
August 1980	3997	1808	5805	1815	3300	5115	10920	– 6.2
February 1981	4235	2150	6385	1931	3794	5725	12110	
May 1981	3810	1783	5593	2034	3411	5445	11038	– 8.9
September 1981*	3881	1701	5582	1948	2939	4887	10469	– 5.2
February 1982*	4638	2088	6726	2381	3374	5755	12481	
May 1982*	5031	2288	7319	2292	3137	5429	12748	+ 2.1
August 1982*	6709	2756	9465	2589	3151	5740	15205	+19.3

Estimates from Table 11.3

Source: Australian Department of Employment and Industrial Relations 1977–81 Monthly Review of the Employment Situation. Canberra : DEIR.

This represents an overall increase of 4736 people at 45 per cent over the estimate for September 1981 and is the highest August unemployment since the Depression. Hence after two years of improvement, the employment situation is again deteriorating rapidly in the Hunter region.

Unemployment rose among all four age and sex categories (male and female, adult and juniors) between may and August 1982, but the deterioration in adult male, and to a lesser extent adult female and junior male, employment opportunities was very rapid. Between February and May, the number of adult and junior women who were unemployed actually fell by 324 people to 5429,[3] though both adult and junior male unemployment rose strongly, by 599 to 7319 people. This is most probably due to the fact that in the earlier stages of the economic down-turn, the sectors which were hardest hit were iron and steel, ship-building and related heavy industry which are traditionally areas of male employment. By August, as negative multiplier effects started to be felt in retailing and commerce, where most women are employed, female employment opportunities also started to decline rapidly.

The seriousness of the recent rise in unemployment can be seen from Table 11.7, which indicates that in all years since 1977 (and no doubt in most previous years) there has been a rapid fall in unemployment over the months from February to August as new school leavers found jobs. This is the usual pattern of unemployment in Australia in normal years. The reversal of this pattern evident from the 23 per cent increase in unemployment between February and August of this year indicates that there is an extremely serious underlying deterioration in the employment situation in the Hunter Valley. this no doubt reflects the down-turn currently evident throughout the Australian economy, as well as specific factors apparent in the Hunter Region, such as the recently announced lay-offs in the local steel, steel products and ship building industries and the consequent decline in production at BHP's coal mines.

Occupational Distribution of Unemployed Persons

In order to obtain a profile of the previous occupations of people in the Hunter Region who are currently unemployed, the average percentage occupational distribution of adult and junior males and females over the period January, 1980 to February, 1981 was calculated from CES data. This data series, was also discontinued in February, 1981. If it is assumed that persons (estimated to be) registered as unemployed in the Hunter region in August, 1982 have a similar occupational distribution to the 1980-81 average, the approximate occupational distribution outlined in Table 11.8 can be constructed.

The major inaccuracy which could arise from using this rather simple method is the over-estimation of the number of unemployed skilled construction and electrical tradesmen in August, 1982. However

Table 11.8   Estimated occupational distribution of
unemployed people in the Hunter Region, August
1982

| | | PERCENTAGES | | NUMBERS | |
		Male	Female	Male	Female
Rural	Adult	2.01	0.36	135	9
	Junior	3.01	0.81	83	26
Professional and Semi-professional	Adult	2.15	7.77	144	201
	Junior	1.26	2.19	35	69
Clerical and Admin.	Adult	10.10	47.82	678	1238
	Junior	7.62	70.27	210	2214
Skilled Building and Construction	Adult	3.61	0	242	0
	Junior	5.04	0.06	139	2
Skilled Metal and Electrical	Adult	5.17	0.35	347	9
	Junior	5.71	0.15	157	5
Other Skilled	Adult	1.85	1.53	124	40
	Junior	1.70	1.54	47	49
Semi-skilled	Adult	33.67	14.29	2259	370
	Junior	36.10	11.17	995	352
Unskilled Manual	Adult	29.05	4.79	1949	124
	Junior	32.78	2.04	903	64
Service Corps	Adult	12.38	23.07	831	597
	Junior	6.77	11.75	187	370
	Adult	100	100	6709	2589
	Junior	100	100	2756	3151

Table 11.9   Education level of unemployed juniors in the Hunter

	Year 8	Year 9	Year 10	Year 11	Year 12	Tech	CAE	University
Percentages	7.9	22.6	49.1	3.0	11.0	0.5	1.20	0.5
Numbers (approximate May 1982)	533	1297	2818	172	631	29	69	29

Sources: Community Task Force for Youth Employment: A Profile of Youth Unemployment in Newcastle and an Analysis of Occupational Preferences of the Young Unemployed, Newcastle, September, 1980 and Table 11.3

the retrenchments in the iron and steel and metal fabricating industries in Newcastle in recent months will no doubt have reversed the trend towards improved employment opportunities for skilled metal tradesmen.

If overall, Table 11.8 gives a reasonably accurate picture of the occupational distribution of unemployed persons in August 1982, it would appear that the major problem areas of unemployment in the Hunter are those of females, particularly junior females, seeking clerical and administrative jobs (28 per cent of all job seekers), and males seeking semi-skilled and unskilled manual jobs (36 per cent of job seekers). Juniors represent 43 per cent of unemployed job seekers, considerably higher than their percentage of the total workforce in the Hunter (29 per cent). Junior females alone represent 27 per cent of all job seekers, but only 12 per cent of the workforce.[4]

A sample survey carried out in September, 1980 by the Community Task Force for Youth Employment, which interviewed 920 young unemployed people attending CES offices in the Hunter, found inter alia that 80 per cent of unemployed juniors achieved only year 10 education standard or less. If it is assumed that the survey sample was reasonably representative and that the educational achievement of young unemployed people has remained much as in 1980, Table 11.9 could give an approximate picture of the educational standards of unemployed juniors in the Hunter.

Information obtained from young unemployed people regarding their occupational preferences indicated that relatively few were interested (and by implication skilled) in the types of jobs which are likely to be directly created by resource developments in the region. Only 15.5 per cent of the sample indicated an interest in jobs which could be directly associated with resource developments; 6.5 per cent related to construction activities and nine per cent to the operational phase of developments.

This supports the data outlined in Table 11.8, which indicates that (as a high estimate) only five per cent of unemployed juniors are skilled in building and construction skills and 5.7 per cent have metal and electrical trade skills. Consequently, if it is found in subsequent sections that the majority of job opportunities will arise for people possessing such skills, then unemployed juniors, in particular, but also the overwhelming majority of unemployed people in the Hunter, may receive little direct benefit from the employment created by the new coal-based developments, unless steps are taken to provide additional training schemes for them.

The following sections examine the types of jobs likely to be directly and indirectly created by the new coal-based developments, and inter alia, compare these to the above occupational distributions

Table 11.10   Construction and operational employment on new coal-based projects in the Hunter Region, 1981 to 2000

Construction	'81	'82	'83	'84	'85	'86	'87	'88	'89	'90	'91	'92	'95	2000
Coal Mining	1080	2338	2421	1333	889	710	260	60	10	10	10	10	10	10
Metal pro-cessing etc	2050	2050	270	140	0	0	0	400	800	800	800	0	0	0
Infra-structure	1203	1723	2713	3432	700	400	250	250	250	0	0	0	200	200
TOTAL	4333	6111	5404	4905	1589	1110	510	710	1060	810	810	10	210	210
Operation														
Coal mining	730	1793	3916	5252	6467	7260	7737	8102	8435	9642	9658	9712	9734	9912
Metal pro-cessing etc	0	480	900	930	1192	1192	1192	1192	1192	1192	1342	1442	1442	1442
Infra-structure	20	320	713	856	1199	1463	1508	1533	1566	1566	1566	1566	1566	1566
TOTAL	750	2593	5529	7038	8858	9915	10437	10827	11193	12400	12566	12720	12742	12920
Total Construction & Operational Employment	5083	8704	10933	11943	10447	11025	10947	11537	12253	13210	12152	12730	12952	13130

of unemployed people in the region.

ANTICIPATED LABOUR REQUIREMENTS OF THE NEW PROJECTS

The current international economic recession and resultant fall in real
energy prices and demand, as well as bottlenecks in the provision
of infrastructure, have created uncertainties regarding the timing, and
in some cases the ultimate financial viability of several of the pro—
jects proposed for the Hunter Valley . However, assuming that there
is no radical decline in OPEC crude oil prices, that the world
economic situation gradually improves over the next 18 months or so
and that infrastructure bottlenecks are ultimately overcome, it could
be expected that the great majority of these projects will eventually
proceed. The major exception to this assumption is likely to be the
proposed coal—oil liquefaction plant, which would probably not be
viable unless there is another major real oil price rise, equivalent
to those in the early and late 1970s.

Table 11.10 therefore represents only approximate estimates of the
construction and operational workforces which could be expected to
be employed on the new projects in the hunter, over the period 1981—
2000. Data on coal mine employment was obtained from the most recent
survey carried out by the NSW Coal Association to assess, inter alia,
the size and composition of its members existing and proposed work—
forces. Some adjustments have been made to take account of recent
press statements by several coal mine developers that their develop—
ment and expansion plans have been postponed, as a result of the
(recently removed) coal export quotas and reduced world demand.
Industrial bans which have been placed on the commencement of
new Upper Hunter mines following the closure of some underground
mines on the Southern coalfields, may also have an impact on employ—
ment in some new mines. Data on employment in the processing and
Infrastructure projects was obtained from their respective Environmental
Impact Statements (EIS's) information published by the Commonwealth
Department of Industry and Commerce, the NSW Department of Indust—
rialisation and Decentralisation and the Hunter Valley Research Found—
ation (HVRF), inter alia, on the workforces of these new projects.
Announced delays in the commissioning of some infrastructure and
processing projects (such as Alcan's third potline at Kuri) have also
been taken into account.

Another possible source of information on the labour require—
ments of the new projects would be the 1976 census data on employ—
ment by industry and the 1976/77 direct requirements and occupation
co—efficient matrices produced for the region by the HVRF Garlick,
(1979). These tables would enable an approximate estimate to be made
of the direct labour requirements for producing a million dollar incre—
ment in the output of each sector of the regional economy. However,
these employment coefficients reflect the average productivity of exist—
ing productive capacity rather than that of marginal additions to this
capacity, in the form of new projects. The latter are likely to employ

227

the latest technologies, which may have quite different input coefficients, paticularly in relation to labour useage, than the technologies
employed by existing enterprises in these industries.

There are also problems associated with the level of aggregation
of input-output data. In the case of coal mining, for example, neither
the regional nor the national input-output tables are disaggregated for
open-cut and underground coal mining. (The mining sector in the HVRF
tables also includes a small number of non-coal mines). The HVRF
tables are calculated for mining in the Hunter region as a whole where
only 44 per cent of coal mines are open-cut. As the labour productivity (saleable coal output per man shift) of Upper Hunter open-cut
mines is almost four times that of its underground mines, utilization
of available regional input-output table data based on average employment per dollar of regional coal production is likely to bias upwards
quite significantly estimates of total employment created in the new and
predominantly open-cut, mines in the Upper Hunter. A similar problem
would arise if use were made of the national input-output tables. The
building and construction sector in the HVRF (and ABS) input-output
tables are also likely to encompass a different mix of projects to
those currently under way in the Hunter, where there is an unusually
heavy emphasis on capital intensive civil engineering infrastructure
projects such as road building, dams, railways and power stations.

Given the very fluid investment situation in the region at present,
it is possible that the data summarised in Table 11.10 may rapidly
become outdated. Nevertheless, it is presented to provide an indication of the order of magnitude of the labour requirements of those
projects which appear relatively firm at the time of writing. In any case,
it will be possible to update this information to take account of any
announced changes in projects as it is based on the detailed employment data for individual projects which is outlined in Table 11A.2 in
the Appendix.

Table 11.10 indicates that the total construction workforces on
the new mining, processing and infrastructure projects will rise from
approximately 4,300 in 1981 to 5,400 in 1983 but will (in the event
of no new projects being announced) fall of to around 700 to 1,000
people in the late 1980s. Thereafter, the requirement for construction
workers will decline even further. However, at the peak of construction
in 1983 there will be a 37 per cent increase in the size of the
region's 1981 construction workforce. The operational workforces on
new Hunter projects, on the other hand, will rise steadily from 750
people in 1981 to about 8,900 in 1985 and 12,400 in 1990. This will
represent a 6.6 per cent increase in the Region's 1981 workforce and
a 29 per cent increase in employment in the three major sectors
examined, mining, processing and infrastructure.

Examining the sectoral distribution of the new construction jobs
created in 1982, approximately 38 per cent are associated with the
development of new mines, 34 per cent with new processing projects

228

Table 11.11 Major development projects in NSW 1980/81 to 1985/86 – estimated occupational distribution of on-site average construction in workforce by industry

Skills	Coal Mining	Other Mining	Alum. Smltg.	Iron/Steel	Other Mfg.	Exploration	Infra-struct.	All Industries
	%	%	%	%	%	%	%	%
Prof. & Managerial	14	–	9	5	39	–	13	12
Building Trades	17	–	21	3	9	–	10	11
Metal Trades	17	–	24	25	13	–	17	19
Electrical Trades	9	–	10	8	6	–	9	8
Semi-skilled	41	100	5	58	19	–	25	30
Unskilled	2	–	31	1	14	–	26	29
TOTAL	100	100	100	100	100	–	100	100

Source: Commonwealth Department of Employment and Industrial Relations – Report on the February 1981 Survey of Major Development Projects in NSW.

Table 11.12   Major development projects in NSW 1980/81 to 1985/86 — estimated occupational and distribution of average operational workforce by industry

Skills	Coal Mining %	Other Mining %	Alum. Smltg. %	Iron/ Steel %	Other Mfg. %	Explor- ation %	Infra- struct. %	All Industries %
Prof. & Managerial	15	5	15	N/A	28	69	18	17
Building Trades	-	-	)	N/A	-	-	-	-
Metal Trades	14	32	) 30	N/A	24	-	21	17
Electrical Trades	8	-	)	N/A	14	-	11	9
Semi-skilled	57	62	) 55	N/A	26	25	39	50
Unskilled	6	-	)	N/A	8	6	11	7
TOTAL	100	100	100	N/A	100	100	100	100

Source: As for Table 11.11

(principally Tomago) and 28 per cent with new infrastructure projects. However, by 1983 50 per cent of all construction jobs will be on infrastructure projects and 45 per cent on coal mine development. Approximately 76 per cent of all permanent production jobs will be in coal mining, while the remainder will be shared relatively evenly between capital intensive resource processing and infrastructure projects. Each million dollars of investment in coal mining will create 3.3 permanent jobs but a similar amount of investment in metal processing will create only 0.8 of a permanent operational job and in infrastructure, only 0.3 of an operational job. The indirect and multiplier employment created by these projects is considered in the following section.

In a few cases the occupational structure of the new projects' operational workforces can be determined from the relevant environmental impact statements (as in the case of Glendell, Mount Arthur North and Mount Thorley and Kurri Kurri's third potline). However, in most cases it is not possible to obtain any reasonably comprehensive data on the occupational distribution of the new projects' construction and operational workforces, in part because of the sensitive nature of union-employer negotiations on this issue prior to the commissioning of projects. One of the few sources of this data is therefore a survey of major NSW development projects which was carried out by the Commonwealth Department of Employment and Industrial Relations in February 1981. Tables 11.11 and 11.12 outline the survey's findings regarding the average occupational distribution of the (actual or projected) construction and operational workforces of surveyed projects in seven major industry groups.

Since new investments in the Hunter region represent about 55 to 60 per cent of the value of all major new NSW projects, it is probably reasonable to assume that the occupational distribution of the Hunter projects is similar to that of the NSW averages, outlined in Tables 11.11 and 11.12. If this is so, the overall occupational distribution of the workforces on the new coal-based projects in the Hunter would be as outlined in Table 11.13

During the construction phase, Table 11.13 indicates that there will be a rapid increase in the demand for additional skilled tradesmen, peaking at a requirement for 2,717 additional skilled workers in 1982. The peak demand for skilled building and construction workers, 977 people in 1982, represents just over 10 per cent of the skilled construction trades workforce in the region, while the peak demand for metal and electrical tradesmen, 1,174 and 566 people respectively corresponds to a six per cent increase in the region's existing skilled metal and electrical trades workforce. There will also be a substantial increase in the demand for semi-skilled and unskilled labour, reaching about 2,637 people in 1982, or approximately a 7.8 per cent increase in people in these skill categories in the Hunter region in 1981. Demand for both skilled and unskilled construction workers will, however, be short-lived and while local workers have secured a reasonable proportion of these jobs, contractors also appear to be

Table 11.13   Estimated occupational distribution of construction and operational workforce on coal-based projects in the Hunter Region, 1981–2000

Construction	'81	'82	'83	'84	'85	'86	'87	'88	'89	'90	'91	'92	'95	2000
Prof. & Managerial	512	757	760	702	225	161	69	196	345	345	313	1	27	27
Bldg Trades	712	977	680	598	233	171	69	71	99	99	74	2	22	22
Metal Trades	873	1174	892	848	282	199	87	105	149	149	106	2	36	36
Elec. Trades	406	566	466	446	149	106	45	52	71	71	49	1	19	19
Semi-skilled	895	1541	1684	1473	568	418	170	164	219	219	156	4	54	54
Unskilled	935	1096	782	940	202	120	70	122	177	177	112	–	52	52
TOTAL	4333	6111	5264	5005	1659	1175	510	710	1060	1060	810	10	210	210

Operational	'81	'82	'83	'84	'85	'86	'87	'88	'89	'90	'91	'92	'95	2000
Prof. & Managerial	118	418	890	1146	1392	1525	1612	1672	1728	1898	1942	1977	1978	2016
Bldg Trades	–	–	–	–	–	–	–	–	–	–	–	–	–	–
Metal Trades	110	464	986	1230	1511	1647	1730	1786	1840	1999	2037	2068	2068	2104
Elec. Trades	63	193	419	557	675	750	797	829	858	949	971	990	990	1010
Semi-skilled	441	1196	2633	3541	4217	4648	4964	5181	5385	6031	6079	6136	6136	6280
Unskilled	48	372	771	878	1104	1168	1204	1229	1252	1320	1334	1346	1345	1360
TOTAL	780	2643	5699	7353	8899	9738	10307	10697	11323	12197	12363	12517	12517	12770

extensively recruiting construction gangs from outside the region. These workers are, in the main, part of a highly mobile section of the Australian construction industry which works on major development sites throughout the country.

The operational phases of the new projects and the indirect and induced employment created as a result of the projects should offer better long-term job opportunities for local people. Table 11.13 indicates that a relatively small proportion of the additional demand for operational labour will be for unskilled workers; 14 per cent in 1983 falling to 11 per cent of the plateau employment level in the early 1990s, or about 1,100 people in all. Approximately half of net additional operational labour demand, about 5,400 people, will be for semi-skilled workers. There will also be a significant increase in the demand for skilled metal and electrical tradesmen as the new projects enter their operational phases. Demand for metal tradesmen will rise rapidly initially, approaching about 1,500 people and thereafter should increase more gradually, reaching about 2,000 by the 1990s. Electrical tradesmen will also be in heavy demand, with 750 new operational jobs being created by 1986 and a total of approximately 900 positions being created by the 1990s. By 1986, new direct operational jobs for metal and electrical tradesmen will represent an increase of 8.6 per cent in the region's 1981 workforce of such skilled tradesmen, (27,626 people).

MULTIPLIER EFFECTS ON REGIONAL EMPLOYMENT, AVAILABLE LABOUR SUPPLY AND ANTICIPATED EXCESS DEMAND (SUPPLY)

In order to make a comparison of the anticipated demand for labour and the potential labour supply, it is necessary to calculate the indirect and induced demand for labour which will be created by the new projects, in addition to the direct employment provided. Indirect labour requirements refer to the additional labour needed by firms which supply goods and services to the new projects. Induced employment created is defined as the additional labour required by enterprises which fulfil the increased demand of households for goods and services, as a result of direct and indirect increase in regional income (in the form of wages, salaries and profits) as a result of the projects' construction and operation.

Because of the problems, discussed above, associated with using static input-output tables to assess the impact of major additions to existing productive capacity, the direct employment effects of the new projects were estimated on a survey basis from published material regarding individual developments. However, when assessing the likely indirect and induced impact of the projects on regional employment and income, the shortcomings of using input-output tables are likely to be less serious. This is because in the main, it could be expected that the goods and services demanded by new projects, and the consumer demand generated by their workforces, could be

233

Table 11.14   Total direct, indirect and induced employment
created by the new development projects, 1981
to 2000

Employment Multipliers:

| Type I | Direct & Indirect Employment Generated | | Type II | Direct, Indirect & Induced Employment | |
| | Direct Employment Created | | | Direct Employment Created | |

	HVRF	Adjusted	HVRF	Adjusted
Construction	1.6416	1.6416	2.6904	2.9604
Mining	1.4460	1.3918	2.3617	2.3074
Basic Metal (Processing)	1.3580	1.2973	1.9666	1.9062
Electricity, Gas and Water	1.5331)		)	
	) 1.6005[1]	1.5890	) 2.3352[1]	2.1654
Public Authority and Defence	1.8027)	2.2663	)	

Construction Phases of Coal Mining, Metal Processing, Infrastructure

	'81	'82	'83	'84	'85	'86	'87	'88	'89	'90	'91	'92	'95	2000
Direct Empl.	4333	6111	5404	4905	1589	1110	510	710	1060	1060	810	10	210	210
Direct & Indirect Empl.	7113	10032	8871	8052	2609	1822	837	1166	1740	1740	1330	16	345	345
Direct, Indirect & Induced Empl created	11656	16441	14539	13196	4275	2986	1372	1910	2852	2852	2179	27	565	565

Operational Phases of Coal Mining, Processing and Infrastructure

	'81	'82	'83	'84	'85	'86	'87	'88	'89	'90	'91	'92	'95	2000
Direct Employment														
Coal Mining	730	1793	3916	5252	6467	7260	7737	8102	8435	9642	9658	9712	9734	9912
Processing	0	480	900	930	1192	1192	1192	1192	1192	1192	1342	1442	1442	1442
Infra-structure	20	320	713	856	1199	1463	1508	1533	1566	1566	1566	1566	1566	1566
TOTAL	750	2593	5529	7038	8858	8915	10437	10827	11193	12400	12566	12720	12742	12920

234

Table 11.14 continued

Direct and Indirect Employment

Coal Mining	1016	2496	5451	7309	9000	10105	10769	11276	11740	13419	13442	13518	13547	13796
Processing	0	623	1167	1207	1547	1547	1547	1547	1547	1547	1741	1870	1870	1870
Infra-structure[1]	32	508	1133	1360	1905	2325	2397	2436	2488	2488	2488	2488	2488	2488
TOTAL	1048	3627	7751	9876	12452	13977	14713	15259	15775	17454	17671	17876	17905	18154

Direct, Indirect and Induced Employment

Mining	1684	4137	9036	12118	14922	16752	17852	18695	19463	22248	22284	22409	22460	22871
Processing	0	915	1715	1773	2272	2272	2272	2272	2272	2272	2558	2749	2747	2749
Infra-structure[1]	43	693	1544	1854	2596	3168	3265	3320	3391	3391	3391	3391	3391	3391
TOTAL	1727	5745	12295	15745	19790	22192	23389	24287	25126	27911	28233	28549	28600	29011

Total Construction and Operational Employment

Direct Empl	5083	8704	10933	11943	10447	11025	10947	11537	12253	13460	12152	12730	12952	13130
Direct and Indirect Emp	8161	13655	16622	17928	15061	15799	15550	16425	17575	19194	19001	17892	18250	18499
Direct, Indirect and Induced Emp	13383	22186	26834	28941	24065	28363	26371	28363	27978	30763	30412	28576	29165	29576

Note[1]   Multipliers used for Infrastructure projects are the weighted average of those for the electricity, gas and water sector (75%) and the public authorities sector (25%), where these weights reflect the direct employment created in these two sectors by the new projects.

satisfied by a reasonably limited, incremental expansion of the capacity of industries already operating in the region. Obviously, it could be expected that some firms producing new products will be encouraged to establish in the region (particularly in industries such as fabricated metal products) as new opportunities, associated with economies of scale or savings in input or output transport costs, present themselves. However, in general it may be reasonable to assume that the technical co-efficients of the input-output matrices would remain approximately stable, and that employment (and income) multipliers derived from these should therefore give an indication of the indirect and induced employment effects of the new projects.

Because all of the developments are in some way related to the coal-mining projects in the region, either as suppliers of inputs to coal mining (in the case of infrastructure and electricity generation projects) or as users of coal (metal processing, electricity generation projects, etc.) several of the indirect employment effects of these projects which would be anticipated from the manipulation of input-output tables, are in fact already included in the direct employment effects of the impactor projects. To avoid the double counting of these indirect employment effects in Table 11.14, the employment multipliers calculated by the Hunter Valley Research Foundation were adjusted by subtracting the indirect employment effects which the projects are expected to have on the construction, mining, basic metal and electricity generation sectors from the total indirect employment effects of the projects. The induced employment impacts in these sectors are, however, included in the calculation of the total second round employment effects, as the increased consumer demand for metal products, electricity and infrastructure services, etc. (as a result of income earned directly and indirectly from the projects) will not necessarily be accommodated by the planned impactor projects.

Table 11.14 uses these adjusted Type 1 and Type 2 employment multipliers and data from Table 11.10 regarding total direct construction and operational employment in mining, processing and infrastructure to estimate the total direct, indirect and induced employment which will be created as a result of the new projects.

type I employment multipliers = $\dfrac{\text{direct and indirect employment}}{\text{direct employment created}}$; and

type II employment multiplier = $\dfrac{\text{direct, indirect \& induced employment}}{\text{direct employment created}}$.

The data in Table 11.14 confirms that if all of the developments based on new coal mines currently planned in the Upper Hunter proceed to completion, they will have a substantial impact on the regional employment market. By the end of the decade, approximately 30,000 direct, indirect and induced construction and operational jobs will be created in the region representing a 16.5 per cent increase in its 1981 workforce. The mining industry will be by far the largest employ-

Table 11.15   Industrial distribution of the employment created by new projects in the Hunter Region, 1981 to 2000

Direct and Indirect Employment	1981	1982	1983	1984	1985	1986	1987	1988	1989	1990	1991	1992	1995	2000
Rural	41	64	67	68	44	43	39	42	47	50	49	42	44	45
Mining	789	1910	4123	5515	6764	7589	8084	8466	8816	10077	10092	10144	10168	10354
Food, Beverage, Tobacco	25	40	43	43	30	30	27	29	32	35	34	30	31	31
Textile, Clothing, Footwear	1	3	5	6	7	7	7	8	8	9	9	9	9	9
Basic Metal	56	617	1078	1106	1357	1350	1343	1345	1350	1350	1515	1617	1619	1619
Fabricated metal	183	290	320	329	234	234	220	235	256	279	274	247	255	258
Chemicals, Coal Products, etc	9	15	19	21	18	18	18	19	21	23	23	21	22	22
Glas, Clay Products	206	298	279	263	117	100	75	86	104	110	99	62	72	73
Wood, Wood Products	282	418	423	420	244	233	206	225	254	278	264	216	229	233
Paper, Paper Products	32	50	54	56	39	39	37	40	43	47	46	40	42	42
Other Manufacturers	164	268	322	348	285	297	292	310	331	367	362	340	347	352
Electricity, Gas, Water	25	261	564	674	932	1135	1169	1189	1215	1215	1215	1213	1213	1213
Building, Construction	5127	7230	6394	6803	1880	1313	603	840	1254	1254	958	12	248	248
Wholesale, Retail	296	444	440	427	236	220	187	205	233	247	234	184	197	199
Transport, Storage	254	563	1029	1298	1502	1666	1751	1831	1909	2154	2162	2161	2171	2207
Financial, Professional	589	886	908	906	552	540	484	526	586	632	602	501	528	535
Public Authorities	30	154	300	352	465	563	577	588	602	602	601	597	598	598
Community Services	47	78	96	105	90	95	94	100	106	118	117	110	112	114
TOTAL	8157	13588	16464	17739	14795	15473	15214	16084	17168	18848	18654	17546	17905	18153

237

Table 11.15 continued

Direct, Indirect and Induced Employment

	1981	1982	1983	1984	1985	1986	1987	1988	1989	1990	1991	1992	1995	2000
Rural	289	471	557	597	480	499	488	517	555	611	602	561	574	582
Mining	808	1941	4161	5556	6798	7625	8119	8503	8856	10120	10135	10184	10209	10395
Food, Beverage, Tobacco	269	440	525	564	459	478	469	497	532	586	578	540	552	560
Textile, Clothing, Footwear	2	5	7	8	8	9	9	9	10	10	11	11	11	11
Basic Metal	78	654	1123	1154	1396	1392	1384	1389	1396	1401	1565	1664	1668	1668
Fabricated Metal	215	343	383	397	290	293	278	297	321	352	346	314	323	328
Chemicals, Coal Products, etc	14	23	28	31	26	27	27	29	30	34	33	31	32	32
Glass, Clay Products	277	415	420	415	243	231	204	222	250	271	258	211	224	227
Wood, Wood Products	319	479	496	499	309	301	272	296	330	362	347	294	308	313
Paper, Paper Products	84	135	156	166	130	134	130	138	149	164	161	148	152	154
Other Manufacturers	194	317	381	412	338	352	346	367	393	435	429	402	411	417
Electricity, Gas, Water	63	323	639	754	999	1205	1237	1261	1293	1301	1299	1292	1294	1295
Building, Construction	5601	8009	7331	6816	2715	2186	1462	1749	2227	2327	2017	1004	1262	1277
Wholesale, Retail	3212	5264	6284	6747	5509	5759	5643	5978	6398	7028	6928	6471	6613	6706
Transport, Storage	499	965	1512	1820	1933	2116	2193	2300	2411	2708	2709	2673	2694	2737
Financial, Professional	1088	1705	1895	1971	1431	1459	1388	1483	1610	1761	1716	1546	1595	1617
Public Authorities	305	605	843	938	949	1069	1075	1115	1166	1224	1215	1172	1185	1194
Community Services	498	817	986	1066	882	923	909	963	1029	1136	1121	1052	1074	1090
TOTAL	13816	22911	27727	29911	24895	26058	25632	27114	28955	31831	31469	29572	30180	30604

ment creator, directly employing from 9,000 to almost 10,000 workers in the 1990s and creating a further 11,000 indirect and induced jobs. By comparison, only 1,200 to 1,400 jobs will be directly created by new processing investments and about 1,500 by new infrastructure projects (mainly power stations). Indirect and induced employment created by these two sectors will provide a further 5,000 to 6,000 jobs.

It is, however, necessary to be cautious of taking these regional employment multipliers completely at face value. It has been argued that such multipliers are likely to overstate indirect and induced impacts, not only because of double counting of the jobs created (for which some adjustments have been made) but also because of their tendency to underestimate the possible existence of excess capacity which could be utilized by regional industries without expanding employment and productive capacity. there is also likely to be some under-estimation of the likely employment and income leakages from the region, at least in the short to medium term, as developers are forced to buy more goods (and services) outside the region because of the sudden increase in demand for particular products. (The impacts of external sourcing are explored in more detail later in the section.) For this reason it is sometimes argued that Type 1 multipliers represent a more reliable indication of the magnitude of total expected employment impacts. Mandeville and Jensen (1978) maintain that Type II multipliers should be viewed as measuring the absolute maximum employment impact which could only be achieved after some time lag. The follow-ing analysis will therefore examine both the projects' direct and indirect impact (Type I multiplier) and their direct, indirect and induced impact (Type II multiplier) on the total demand for labour in the region.

In order to make more detailed forecasts of likely future employ-ment trends, it is necessary to determine the industrial and occupat-ional distribution of the total direct and indirect employment which is likely to be created, i.e. in which industries and occupations these workers will be employed. This should make it possible to identify, inter alia, the skill categories in which labour shortages are likely to occur and those in which unemployment is likely to remain a problem.

The industrial distribution of new employment can be determined using regional input-output data (Garlick, 1979), and estimates of the direct employment created by the projects outlined in Table 11.10. Similar adjustments to those in Table 11.14, are made to correct for double counting of the projects' impact on employment. Table 11.15 summarizes the results of this analysis.

As would be expected from the distributon of the direct employ-ment created by the projects, Table 11.15 indicates that the mining sector will have the largest requirement for additional labour, providing over 8,000 jobs or 32 per cent of total direct, indirect and induced employment created in 1987 and over 10,000 jobs or 34 per cent of

239

Table 11.16 Occupational distribution of direct, indirect and induced employment created by the impact of projects in the Hunter Region, 1982 to 1986

Direct Employment	1981	1982	1983	1984	1985	1986	1987	1988	1989	1990	1991	1992	1995	2000	%
Professional) Managerial) Clerical)	630	1175	1650	1848	1617	1686	1681	1868	2073	2243	2255	1978	2005	2043	15
Skilled metal trades	983	1638	1878	2078	1793	1846	1817	1891	1989	2148	2143	2070	2104	2140	17
Skilled elect. trades	469	759	885	1003	824	856	842	881	929	1020	1020	992	1009	1029	8
Skilled bldg. trades	712	977	680	598	233	171	69	71	99	99	74	2	22	22	2
Other skilled trades	-	-	-	-	-	-	-	-	-	-	-	-	-	-	0
Semi-skilled	1336	2737	4317	5014	4785	5066	5134	5345	5604	6250	6235	6140	6190	6334	48
Unskilled	983	1468	1553	1818	1306	1288	1274	1351	1429	1497	1446	1346	1397	1412	12
Rural workers	-	-	-	-	-	-	-	-	-	-	-	-	-	-	0
Total	5113	8754	10963	12359	10558	10913	10817	11335	12123	13257	13173	12528	12727	12980	100

Direct and Indirect Employment	1981	1982	1983	1984	1985	1986	1987	1988	1989	1990	1991	1992	1995	2000	%
Professional	127	235	305	331	304	325	322	336	354	380	381	366	372	376	2
Administrative	601	986	1146	1206	948	980	946	1002	1075	1167	1152	1066	1092	1106	7
Clerical	1238	1992	2250	2336	1756	1807	1725	1831	1976	2133	2089	1900	1955	1978	12
Skilled Metal, Elect.	1558	2683	3394	3716	3275	3450	3432	3616	3837	4224	4205	4014	4082	4139	23
Skilled Building	1648	2364	2165	2008	801	645	430	513	653	676	586	289	365	368	6
Other Skilled	28	45	50	52	38	38	36	39	42	46	45	41	42	43	.3
Semi and Unskilled	2861	5098	6909	7824	7414	7936	8033	8446	8915	9897	9875	9565	9687	9852	49
Rural	86	135	147	151	106	107	100	107	117	127	123	109	113	115	.7
															100

Direct, Indirect and Induced Employment	1981	1982	1983	1984	1985	1986	1987	1988	1989	1990	1991	1992	1995	2000	%
Professional	284	492	615	665	581	614	607	638	677	735	732	695	708	716	2
Administrative	1266	2082	2470	2636	2136	2225	2172	2299	2462	2694	2659	2480	2536	2570	9
Clerical	3459	5656	6682	7128	5741	5987	5840	6187	6629	7255	7146	6647	6800	6892	24
Skilled Metal, Elect.	2077	3538	4428	4834	4203	4423	4389	4629	4921	5417	5383	5119	5210	5283	17
Skilled Building	1874	2735	2612	2492	1201	1064	842	949	1119	1190	1094	765	850	861	5
Other Skilled	209	343	411	441	362	378	371	393	420	462	456	426	436	442	1
Semi and Unskilled	4178	7265	9524	10648	9753	10386	10443	10999	11644	12904	12842	12349	12529	12715	40
Rural	371	602	710	758	607	631	616	654	701	771	759	706	722	732	2
															100

the total by the year 2000. A further 6,000 to 7,000 jobs will be created in the wholesaling and retailing sector as new employees spend their incomes. Transport, storage and communication will provide about 2,500 jobs or nine per cent of those created, and on average the construction industry will create approximately 3,000 jobs per annum over the next two decades. Despite the large direct investments in these industries, electricity, gas and water will create only 1,300 jobs, four per cent of the total and basic metal approximately 1,500 jobs or five per cent of all new jobs. The public authorities and defence sector will account for about 1,100 new jobs, four per cent of the total and finance and business services approximately 1,500 jobs, or five per cent of the 30,000 new direct, indirect and induced jobs created as a result of the projects examined. The remainder of manufacturing industry will receive little output or employment stimulus from the new developments.

Table 11.16 gives details of the occupational distribution of the total new direct, indirect and induced employment among major skill categories. These categories are based on the occupational grouping system devised by the IMPACT group, but because this system does not correspond exactly with the skill categories used in Tables 11.11, 11.12 and 11.13, it has beeen necessary to make some modifications. In calculating the information in Table 11.16 use was made of data from Table 11.15 on the direct, indirect and induced employment created in the 18 sectors of the regional economy, as well as a direct occupational coefficient matrix for the region calculated by Garlick (1979), at the HVRF, from 1976 census data on occupational distribution by industry.

Table 11.16 indicates that the bulk of all jobs created directly, and to a lesser extent indirect and by induced employment created, will be for semi–skilled and unskilled workers. Approximately 60 per cent of all jobs created directly are expected to be workers in these skill categories, 49 per cent of those created directly and indirectly and 40 per cent of total direct, indirect and Induced employment created. About 25 per cent of all new direct employment will be for skilled metal and electrical tradesmen, but only 17 per cent of total direct, indirect and induced employment. It is interesting to note that while directly created professional, management and clerical jobs are only 15 per cent of the total, together they represent 35 per cent of new direct, indirect and induced employment, with clerical employment alone representing 24 per cent of the total new jobs.

It is now possible to put together data regarding unemployment and that calculated above to make a necessarily very approximate estimate of the total regional demand for and supply of labour in various skill categories over the next few years. For each skill category, the total labour requirements of impactor projects, as well as the indirect and induced labour demand they will generate is compared with the total number of people with these skills who are either currently unemployed, or are expected to be laid off directly by major

Table 11.17 Net labour demand in the Hunter Region by skill categories, 1982 to 1986 (pessimistic scenario)

(Man Years)

1982	Professional	Managerial	Clerical	Metal Trades	Electrical Trades	Building Trades	Other Trades	Semi-Skilled[1]	Unskilled	Rural
Additional Demand										
- direct		418		1638	759	977	-	2737	1468	-
- direct, indirect	235	986	1992	2683		2364	45	5098		135
- direct, indirect, induced	492	2082	5656	3538		2735	343	7265		602
Available Supply										
- unemployed	449	4340		518		383	260	5961	3040	253
- announced redundancies[2]	81	157	184	369	217	48	3	784	247	3
- negative multipliers[3]	51	199	612	259		72	46	590		77
- new apprentices	-	-	-	110	124	81	162	-	-	-
Excess demand (- supply)	-89	2646		1941		2151	-128	-3357		269
1983										
Additional Demand										
- direct		1906		1878	885	680	-	4317	1553	-
- direct and indirect	305	1146	2250	3394		2165	50	6909		147
- direct, indirect, induced	615	2470	6682	4428		2612	411	9524		710
Available supply										
- unemployed	449	4340		518		383	260	5961	3040	253
- announced redundancies[2]	159	307	360	722	424	93	5	1532	484	7
- negative multipliers[3]	102	398	1215	525		145	92	1191		151
- new apprentices	-	-	-	234	250	164	327	-	-	-
Excess demand (supply)	-95	2532		1755		1827	-273	-2684		299

Table 11.17 continued

(Man Years)

1984	Professional	Managerial	Clerical	Metal Trades	Electrical Trades	Building Trades	Other Trades	Semi–Skilled[2]	Unskilled	Rural
Additional demand										
- direct	1848 (})			2078	1003	598	-	5014	1818	-
- direct, Induced	331	1206	2336	3716 (})		2008	52	7824 (})		151
- direct, Indirect, Induced	665	2636	7128	4834		2492	441	10648		758
Available Supply										
- unemployed	449	4340 (})		518 (})		383	260	5961	3040	253
- announced redundancies[1]	217	420	491	987	580	35	2	526	177	3
- negative multipliers[2]	141	546	1668	348	724	200	126	1642 (})		179
- new apprentices	-	-	-	-	379	248	496	-	-	-
Excess demand										
- (supply)	-142	2299 (})		1298 (})		1534	-448	-2750 (})		315

1985	Professional	Managerial	Clerical	Metal Trades	Electrical Trades	Building Trades	Other Trades	Semi–Skilled[2]	Unskilled	Rural
Additional demand										
- direct	1617 (})			1793	824	233	-	4785	1306	-
- direct and Indirect	304	948	1756	3275 (})		801	38	7414 (})		106
- direct, Indirect, Induced	581	2136	5741	4203		1201	362	9753		607
Available supply										
- unemployed	449	4340 (})		518 (})		383	260	5961	3040	253
- announced redundancies[1]	256	495	580	1163	683	150	8	2468	780	11
- negative multipliers[2]	167	645	1967	457	857	236	149	1940 (})		216
- new apprentices	-	-	-	-	512	328	661	-	-	-
Excess demand (supply	-291	-150 (})		3 (})		104	-761	-4436 (})		127

243

Table 11.17 continued

1986 (Man Years)

	Professional	Managerial	Clerical	Metal Trades	Electrical Trades	Building Trades	Other Trades	Semi-Skilled[2]	Unskilled	Rural
Additional demand										
- direct		1686		1846	856	171	-	5066	1288	-
- direct, Indirect	325	980	1807	3450		645	38	7936		107
- direct, Indirect, Induced	614	2225	5987	4423		1064	378	10386		631
Available Supply										
- unemployed	449	4340		518		383	260	5961	3040	253
- announced redundancies[1]	256	495	580	1846		150	8	2468	780	11
- negative multipliers[2]	167	645	1967	857		236	149	1940		216
- new apprentices	-	-	-	647		416	837	-	-	-
Excess demand (- supply)	-255	185		-31		-121	-876	-3804		151

Summary of Excess Demand (Supply) Situation,
(Man Years)

	Professional	Managerial & Clerical	Metal Trades & Electrical Trades	Building Trades	Other Trades	Semi-Skilled & Unskilled	Rural	Total
1982	-89	2246	1941	2151	-128	-3357	269	3033
1983	-95	2532	1755	1827	-273	-2684	299	3361
1984	-142	2299	1298	1534	-448	-2750	315	2104
1985	-291	-150	3	104	-761	-4436	127	-5404
1986	-255	185	-31	-121	-876	-3804	151	-4751

Notes:

1   Includes unemployed service occupation workers.

2   Figures reflect the worst scenario regarding BHP's future operations.

3   Indirect and Induced unemployment as a result of the lay-offs of BHP, the State dockyards, etc.

industries like BHP, Comsteel and the State dockyards, or because of the negative multiplier effects of these lay—offs. Apprentices who have recently completed their training, or are expected to do so in future years, are also included (Hunter Development Board, 1980, para 7.6.4).

Due to the impossibility of forecasting underlying levels of un—employment in the region in future years, it will be assumed that the pool of unemployed people, who are unable to find jobs other than those associated with the new investment projects in the region, will remain approximately constant at the August 1982 level over the next five years. Anticipated new school—leavers entering the workforce are not included among the potential sources of labour supply because those who do not find jobs as a result of the on—going underlying growth of the local economy or the need to replace retiring workers, could be expected to be incorporated in the data on unemployed people included in Table 11.17. However, the disturbing trends towards increased unemployment in the region evident from the August 1982 data and recent retrenchments indicate that (at least in the short—term) unemployment is likely to continue to rise.

In Table 11.17, projected unemployment due to the redundancies announced and anticipated by several major firms in the region are also added to this underlying level of unemployment. Initially, the most pessimistic of the scenarios mooted for BHP Newcastle's future operat—ions is considered. This envisages and end to primary steel product—ion at the plant and entails the dismissal of 1,593 workers in 1982 (already announced), 2,000 more workers in 1983, 1,500 in 1984 and 1,000 in 1986, reducing the total workforce to 3,500. Five hundred state dockyard retrenchments are also included in the 1982 redundancy estimates. Negative employment multipliers, by occupation group, were calculated in the same way as the positive multipliers in Table 11.16. Since Table 11.17 is in terms of man years and inclueds, for each year, total new jobs offered (not just new jobs created in that year), the data relating to redundancies at major industries and the negative employment multiplier effects of these, is cumulative year by year.

Obviously not all of the region's annual output of new apprentices will be available to join the new projects, or replace workers in other industries who take these jobs, as some will be required to replace the (approximately) 1,500 skilled tradesmen who are currently aged 60—64 and will retire over the next five years, and to meet the demand generated by the underlying growth of the regional economy. Furthermore "wastage rates" for tradesmen who recently have completed apprentice—ships have been as high as 20 to 40 per cent in NSW in recent years. Hence, total apprenticeship completions represent the absolute upper bond on newly trained skilled workers available from this source, and in Table 11.17 it is assumed that only 50 per cent of these young tradesmen will actually be available to meet the additional demand for skilled workers generated by the impactor projects.

Table 11.18   Net labour demand in the Hunter Region by skill categories 1982 to 1986 (optimistic scenario)[1]

(Man Years)

Excess demand (supply -), summary

	Professional	Managerial & Clerical	Metal & Electrical Trades	Building Trades	Other Trades	Semi & Unskilled	Rural	Total
1982	-89	2246	1941	2151	-128	-3357	269	3331
1983	34	3560	2840	1945	-225	-1098	377	7533
1984	84	4272	2744	1741	-364	26	425	8928
1985	0	2385	1861	370	-608	-869	274	3413
1986	33	2720	1827	145	-768	-236	298	4019

Note[1]   The Table embodies the most optimistic scenario regarding BHP's future operations (1593 redundancies in 1982 but no additional retrenchments).

It should also be borne in mind that while the impacts of projects being considered encompass most of the major developments planned for the region, they do not include new coal-mining investments in the Lower Hunter or non-coal (or non-electricity) based manufacturing and infrastructure projects. These projects will generate additional labour demands within the region. Furthermore, because of the simplifying assumptions made regarding some of the data in Table 11.17 (such as that relating to unemployment and apprentices available), and the possibility discussed above the total direct, indirect and induced employment data may overestimate actual employment impacts, it is appropriate to view the estimates of excess labour demand (or supply) as being merely indicative of the approximate order of magnitude of these variables.

Hence, Table 11.17 indicates that while labour shortages are likely to occur in several skilled trades as well as in the clerical and managerial categories over the next five years as a result of the construction and operation of the impactor developments, unemployment among semi-skilled and unskilled workers, tradesmen in the "other trades" category and professionals is likely to continue throughout this period. Overall, excess demand for various types of labour could be expected to exceed excess supply in the Hunter by about 2,000-3,000 man years up till 1985. Thereafter, as a result of the direct, indirect and induced effects of retrenchments by BHP and other major firms, even if all planned projects proceed, there will be an overall excess supply of labour in the region of between 4,500 and 5,500 people, with only a few key categories of skilled tradesmen and managerial personnel being in short supply in most years. If, as now seems increasingly likely, many coal projects are post-phoned till 1985-6, excess labour demand is unlikely to be evident even in the 1983-5 period.

As the future of BHP Newcastle has not yet been decided, the more pessimistic assumptions incorporated in Table 11.17 may not be justified. The most optimistic option being (tentatively) floated is that BHP could upgrade its Number Four blast furnace and construct a bloom-casting plant. This may mean that only those redundancies already announced would be necessary. The improvements to blast furnace four are expected to be labour saving, but labour made surplus in this area could conceivably be absorbed in the bloomcasting plant, if this were to be installed. Table 11.18 therefore incorporates these more optimistic assumptions regarding BHP Newcastle's future to determine the likely situation regarding the net demand for labour in the region in the next five years.

If this more optimistic scenario eventuates, labour shortages could be expected to arise in most skill categories over the next five years, with the notable exception of the "other trades" (non-metal, electrical or building trades) category. By 1984 the total excess demand for labour in the region could peak at almost 9,000 people, and thereafter decline to about 4,000 people by 1986. The most serious

Table 11.19   Occupational distribution of direct, indirect and induced employment created in non-tradeable goods industries in the Hunter Region, 1981 to 2000

Direct and Indirect Employment

	1981	1982	1983	1984	1985	1986	1987	1988	1989	1990	1991	1992	1995	2000
Professional	116	218	287	312	292	312	310	324	340	365	366	353	358	362
Administrative	526	871	1024	1081	866	898	871	921	986	1070	1057	983	1007	1012
Clerical	1115	1804	2048	2132	1619	1672	1599	1696	1827	1970	1932	1762	1812	1833
Skilled Metal, Electrical	1361	2372	3048	3358	3014	3188	3182	3349	3548	3907	3894	3733	3792	3845
Skilled Building	1564	2238	2036	1879	724	570	363	440	571	587	501	217	289	292
Other Skilled	16	26	29	30	23	23	22	23	25	28	27	25	26	26
Semi and Unskilled	2451	4475	6258	7168	6998	7530	7664	8046	8472	9414	9408	9165	9268	9407
Rural	36	59	67	71	55	57	55	58	63	68	66	61	62	63
TOTAL	7185	12063	14797	16031	13591	14250	14065	14857	15832	17409	17251	16298	16614	16847

Direct, Indirect and Induced Employment

	1981	1982	1983	1984	1985	1986	1987	1988	1989	1990	1991	1992	1995	2000
Professional	249	437	552	599	531	563	558	586	621	674	671	640	651	659
Administrative	1078	1782	2129	2279	1865	1945	1903	2014	2153	2358	2330	2179	2227	2257
Clerical	3006	4920	5829	6228	5035	5253	5130	5434	5821	6377	6284	5853	5986	6068
Skilled Metal, Electrical	1771	3048	3868	4246	3755	3964	3948	4160	4414	4862	4838	4620	4697	4763
Skilled Building	1745	2536	2397	2271	1050	913	700	798	953	1008	917	609	689	697
Other Skilled	135	222	267	289	238	249	245	259	277	305	302	283	289	293
Semi and Unskilled	3413	6060	8181	9252	8735	9351	9459	9947	10503	11655	11621	11245	11391	11561
Rural	74	120	142	151	122	128	125	132	142	155	152	141	145	147
TOTAL	11471	19125	23365	25315	30066	22615	22068	23330	24884	27394	27115	25570	25930	26445

Note: [1] Tradeable goods industries which encompass the development projects are included.

248

shortages would be likely to arise in the clerical and managerial, metal, electrical and building trades categories, and to a lesser extent in the rural labour category. It should, however, be born in mind that participation rates are likely to increase as job opportunities expand. Although this is unlikely to bring forth many more tradesmen whom studies have shown have relatively high participation rates, availability of clerical personnel could well increase as a result of increased participation by females.

There are several possible ways that major developers and other industries in the region may attempt to overcome these labour shortages. Firstly, those tradeable inputs required by the new projects which are currently purchased from local firms could be purchased outside the region, either from the rest of Australia or from overseas. In order to assess the likely direct, indirect and induced employment impact of the new projects on regional employment, if developers (as well as input suppliers and consumers) followed a policy of sourcing all tradeable inputs and purchases outside the region, modifications were made to the Hunter Valley Research Foundation's 20 by 20 direct requirements matrix for the region. Six tradeable goods industries were deleted from the table completely (textiles, clothing and footwear; fabricated metal products; chemicals, petroleum and coal products; wood and wood products; paper and paper products; and other manufacturing) and the value of the output purchased from and supplied by three other industries was reduced by 70 per cent (rural and food, beverage and tobacco) and 50 per cent (glass, clay and other non—metallic mineral products). A proportion of semi—tradeable industries such as clay and glass products, rural and food and beverages, was included because high transport costs (bricks, cement products) and the demand for fresh food (bread, milk, vegetables) are likely to make these goods into semi or non—tradeables. These tradeable goods sectors which include the development projects (mining, basic metal processing and electricity generation) were of course also included.

The resulting 13 by 13 direct requirements matrix (excluding house-holds) was inverted to obtain a modified input—output matrix of the direct and indirect requirements of producing a $1 change in final demand. The 14 by 14 direct requirements matrix (including households) was also inverted, giving the input—ouput table of the direct, indirect and induced requirements of producing a $1 charge in final demand. Using these modified tables, data on direct employment created from Table 11.10 and the labour coefficients matrix for the 13 industries, the same procedure was followed as in Tables 11.15 and 11.16, to determine the industrial and occupational distribution by total direct, indirect and induced employment which would be created by the new projects if tradeables used by the new developments were purchased outside the region. The occupational distribution of the labour requirements which would be created in (mainly) non—tradeables industries is summarised in Table 11.19.

249

Table 11.20   Net additional demand for labour, by occupation groups, assuming external sourcing of tradeable inputs, Hunter Region, 1982—1986

	1982	1983	1984	1985	1986
Professional	- 144	- 29	18	- 50	- 18
Administrative and Clerical	1210	2465	3015	1408	1706
Skilled Metal and Electrical	1451	2280	1778	1413	1368
Skilled Building	1952	1730	1520	217	- 6
Other Skilled	- 243	- 369	- 516	- 732	- 897
Semi and Unskilled	-4562	-2441	-1370	-1887	-1271
Rural	- 213	- 191	- 182	- 211	- 205
TOTAL	- 549	2896	4263	4421	677

If developers, their supplies and consumers deriving income from their activities source all purchases of tradeables (except those produced by the projects) outside the region, the decline in direct and indirect employment created would only be of the order of seven to nine per cent, while the fall in total direct, indirect and induced employment created would be by approximately 13 to 14 per cent. However, while demand for most skill categories would decline by about 10 to 12 per cent in these circumstances, requirements for the "other trades" category, which in any case will be in excess supply in the region, would fall by about 35 per cent. This is because the bulk of such tradesmen are employed in manufacturing industry which would receive little indirect stimulus from the new projects if they sourced their tradeable goods inputs outside the region. The level of rural employment created would also drop very substantially, by about 80 per cent.

If it is assumed that developers, their suppliers and retailers will respond to labour shortages (which, inter alia, will cause delays in receiving supplies from local firms) by purchasing their requirements of tradeables outside the region, the situation regarding the net demand for labour in the region (assuming no further BHP lay- offs beyond those announced for 1982) would be as outlined in Table 11.20.

This shows that while the overall impact of external sourcing on labour demand is only of the order of seven to 14 per cent, the effect on the excess demand for various categories of labour (after labour supply from unemployed people and new apprentices are netted out), is quite substantial. In 1982, for example, this policy could result in a 115 per cent decline in the overall excess demand for the various labour categories and in fact result in an overall excess supply of labour. In the following years, the decline in excess labour demand would be approximately 50 to 60 per cent. However, this reduction in overall excess demand would be achieved mainly by an increase in the excess supply (unemployment) of semi-skilled, unskilled and rural workers and tradesmen in the "other skills" category, as well as some decline in excess demand for managerial and clerical workers, rather than by a significant drop in the excess demand for skilled metal, electrical and building tradesmen. It is, however, the shortage of these skilled tradespeople within the region which is expected to be one of the most serious labour problems confronting the new developments.

The excess demand for skilled tradesmen could be met either by training local unskilled or semi-skilled unemployed workers or school leavers, by attracting skilled tradesmen back to their trades, or by encouraging the immigration of workers with the required skills from other parts of Australia or overseas. Data on the evel of migration within and into the region provided by the 1976 and 1981 Censuses indicates that the rate at which people have been migrating to the Hunter has in fact increased since 1976. In that year, 6.8 per cent of the regional population had moved into their local government area

251

since 1975, from other New South Wales local government areas, the rest of of Australia or overseas. A substantial 18.8 per cent had moved into their current LGA since 1971. In 1981, however, the proportion of the population who had taken up residence in their present LGA since 1980 had increased to 8.7 per cent and the percentage who had moved there since 1976 had risen to 21.2 per cent.

One important question is whether there are already sufficient skilled tradesmen available in the economy to meet any increase in demand from new resource projects, but are either unemployed or working outside their trades because of the relatively low remuneration received by skilled tradesmen or the non-availability of trades jobs in their area. These issues have been raised by several authors, particularly those from the trade union movement (Cook, 1981). This and other problems associated with meeting the likely demand for skilled tradesmen are discussed in the final section, which details with the policy implications of the observed and anticipated impact of the new developments on the regional labour market.

THE MARKET AND SOCIAL OPPORTUNITY COST OF LABOUR REQUIREMENTS OF THE NEW PROJECTS

The impactor projects could be expected to make a significant direct, indirect and induced contribution to regional income over the next two decades. The direct wages, salaries and supplements paid annually by these projects, as well as the multiplier income which they will generate, is estimated below, to determine its importance in relation to total regional (wage and salary) income. This estimation of the value of the labour resources used by the new projects will also make a contribution to the broader project, of which this labour market analysis forms part; the assessment of the overall costs (resources utilised) and benefits (goods and services produced) of the new projects (Perkins, 1982).[5] The question of whether the market cost of the labour employed diverges from its social opportunity cost is discussed later in the section.

It is possible to make an approximate estimate of the market cost of the labour demanded by the new projects from data on average weekly earnings, by the industry and occupation, published by the ABS. However, given the boom town nature of the labour market in parts of the Hunter and the very high wages common in sectors such coal mining, and to a lesser extent, electricity generation, it is essential to augment this average, Australia-wide data by more project specific information. Two other potential sources of information on the wage and salary component of the projects' operational costs would be the regional input-output tables which have been compiled by the Hunter Valley Research Foundation (Garlick, 1979) and the national input-output tables compiled by the ABS. However, similar problems arise when using static input-output table coefficients to determine the direct income effects of the new projects as were encountered when considering their use to determine direct employment effects. These

Table 11.21 The total market wage bill of the major coal—based development projects

Construction	'81	'82	'83	'84	'85	'86	'87	'88	'89	'90	'92	'95	2000
Coal Mines (Upper Hunter)	17.4	37.7	36.8	25.1	15.5	12.5	4.2	1.0	.2	.2	.2	.2	.2
Processing	32.7	32.7	4.5	2.3	0	0	0	6.2	12.4	12.4	0	0	0
Infra-structure	19.1	27.4	43.1	54.5	11.1	6.3	4.0	4.0	4.0	0	0	3.2	3.2
SUB TOTAL	69.2	70.4	84.4	79.9	26.6	18.8	8.2	11.2	16.6	12.6	.2	3.4	3.4
Operation													
Coal Mines (Upper Hunter)	24.1	58.4	129.5	176.4	206.2	224.5	241.1	252.6	263.2	299.1	301.3	301.3	309.4
Processing	0	7.6	8.0	18.6	19.0	19.0	19.0	19.0	19.0	19.0	19.0	19.0	19.0
Infra-structure	.3	5.2	11.6	13.9	19.5	23.8	24.5	24.9	25.4	25.4	25.4	25.4	25.4
SUB TOTAL	24.4	71.2	149.1	208.9	244.7	267.3	284.6	296.5	307.6	343.5	345.7	345.7	345.7
OVERALL TOTAL	93.6	165.7	233.5	288.8	271.3	286.1	292.8	307.7	324.2	358.1	345.9	349.1	357.2

Sources: Australian Bureau of Statistics: Series 6306.0, May 1981 Table 21; 6312.0, May 1982, Table 2 6310.0, August 1981, Table 3, EIS's from coal mines at Glendell, Mount Thorley and Alcan Refinery at Kurri Kurri and Joint Coal Board, Black Coal In Australia, 1981/82.

253

income coefficients reflect the average productivity of existing capacity rather than that of marginal additions to capacity, which the new projects represent.

Consequently, in Table 11.21, ABS data on average weekly earnings for various skill categories is in the main used to calculate the total annual cost of employing the operational and construction workforces directly required by the new coal-mining, processing and infrastructure projects.

The average annual wage bill for the construction workforces in the various sectors was estimated by constructing an average annual earnings "index", weighted by the proportion of professionals, clerical workers, building, electrical and metal tradesmen and semi-skilled and unskilled workers employed on the construction workforces of the various projects (as shown in Table 11.11) Similar weighted "indices" of average annual earnings were constructed to obtain the annual wage bills for the operational workforces in the major coal mining, processing and infrastructure projects. However, in the case of coal mining, weight was also given to estimates of the projected wage bills of the Mount Thorley and Glendell coal mines, contained in their respective EIS's, and to Joint Coal Board data on the average weekly earnings of coal miners in the Upper Hunter. This was because, as mentioned above, the boom industry nature of coal mining in the Hunter and the strength of the mining unions have kept wage rates above average mining industry earnings. Nevertheless, the estimates of 1982 average weekly earnings used to calculate the annual wage bill of the coal mining sector in Table 11.21 were only 12 per cent higher than the published ABS data for the average weekly earnings of miners and quarrymen.

Table 11.21 indicates that wages and salaries paid to construction workforces on the new projects will peak at about $84 million (in 1982 dollars) within the next year or so and, in the absence of new projects being announced, will fall rapidly away thereafter. This may be at least partially due to the so-called bow-wave affect caused by the fact that new projects are not usually announced until a few years before their commencement. However, the current serious downturn in world coal demand and rising Australian production costs could be expected to cause a slackening in investment in future years and the postponement or cancellation of tentative plans for a number of new mines. Real wages and salaries paid to the projects' operational workforces, on the other hand, are expected to rise rapidly to $200 million (in 1982 dollars) over the next three to four years, and then to grow more steadily to over $300 million in the early 1990s in constant 1982 dollars. These wages and salaries will, of course, represent a permanent increment in regional income.

As could be expected from the data on the distribution of total direct employment outlined in Table 11.10, the construction and operation of new coal mines in the Upper Hunter will provide approximately 82 per cent, or $220 million (1982 dollars) of the impactor projects'

Table 11.22   Direct, indirect and induced income generated
by the new developments, 1981 to 2000

TYPE I Multiplier (HVRF)
Direct and Indirect Income Generated

TYPE II Multiplier (HVRF)
Direct, Indirect and Induced Income Generated

	TYPE I	TYPE II
Construction	1.4323	2.0523
Mining	1.3017	1.8650
Basic Metal	1.3897	1.9911
Electricity)		
Gas & Water)Infrastructure	1.7299	2.8787
Public Authority)		
and Defence)		

Direct Income Generated ($ millions, 1982 dollars)

	'81	'82	'83	'84	'85	'86	'87	'88	'89	'90	'91	'95	2000
Construction Phase	69.2	70.4	84.4	79.9	26.6	18.8	8.2	5.0	4.2	0.2	0.2	3.4	3.4
Operational Phase													
Coal Mining	24.1	58.4	129.5	176.4	206.2	224.5	241.1	252.6	263.2	299.1	301.3	301.3	309.4
Processing	0	7.6	8.0	18.6	19.0	19.0	19.0	19.0	19.0	19.0	19.0	19.0	19.0
Infrastructure	0.3	5.2	11.6	13.9	19.5	23.8	24.5	24.9	25.4	25.4	25.4	25.4	25.4
TOTAL	93.6	141.6	233.5	288.8	271.3	286.1	292.8	301.5	311.8	343.7	345.9	349.1	357.2

Indirect and Direct Income ($ millions, 1982 dollars)

	'81	'82	'83	'84	'85	'86	'87	'88	'89	'90	'91	'95	2000
Construction Phase	99.1	100.8	120.9	114.5	38.1	26.9	11.7	7.2	6.0	0.3	0.3	4.9	4.9
Operational Phase													
Coal Mining	31.4	76.0	168.6	229.6	268.4	292.2	313.8	328.8	342.6	389.3	392.2	392.2	402.7
Processing	0	10.6	11.1	25.8	26.4	26.4	26.4	26.4	26.4	26.4	26.4	26.4	26.4
Infrastructure	0.5	9.0	20.1	24.0	33.7	41.2	42.3	43.1	43.9	43.9	43.9	43.9	43.9
TOTAL	131.0	196.4	320.7	393.9	366.6	386.7	394.2	405.5	418.9	459.9	462.5	462.5	473.0

Total Direct, Indirect and Induced Income ($ millions, 1982 dollars)

	'81	'82	'83	'84	'85	'86	'87	'88	'89	'90	'91	'95	2000
Construction Phase	142.0	144.5	173.2	164.2	54.6	38.6	16.8	10.3	8.6	0.4	0.4	7.0	7.0
Operational Phase													
Coal Mining	45.0	108.9	241.5	329.0	384.6	418.7	449.7	471.1	490.9	557.8	561.9	561.9	577.0
Processing	0	15.1	15.9	37.0	37.8	37.8	37.8	37.8	37.8	37.8	37.8	37.8	37.8
Infrastructure	0.7	12.9	28.8	34.5	48.3	59.0	60.7	61.7	63.0	63.0	63.0	63.0	63.0
TOTAL	187.7	281.4	459.4	564.7	525.3	554.1	565.0	580.9	600.3	659.0	663.1	669.7	684.8

Source: Type I and Type II multipliers from Garlick, 1979.
Direct Income data from Table 11.21

total contribution to regional income by the mid 1980s. In the same year, 1985, processing industries will generate $19 million or seven per cent of this additional income while infrastructure projects, including the new power stations, will contribute 11 per cent of the new income generated in the Hunter. The total direct wage and salary income, generated by the new projects will reach about $300 million in 1988 and $350 million by the year 2000. As data from the 1981 census indicates that total income accruing to individuals in the Hunter Region in that year was $2,727.3 million, this implies that the impactor projects will stimulate an 11 and 13 per cent real increase in 1981 regional income by 1988 and 2000, respectively. However, as the projects are also expected to encourage the production of goods and services, and hence the generation of income, indirectly, it is necessary to assess the scale of these effects in order to gauge the total impact of the new coal-based developments on regional income.

In order to estimate comprehensively the indirect and induced effects of the new projects on regional income, it would be necessary to supplement the information in Table 11.21, regarding the wages and salaries which will be paid by these developments, with data on non-wage income (profits, dividends and interest) which directly accrues to households in the region as a result of the operation of the new projects. This data could be derived at a national level from the national input-output tables produced by the ABS, as these show the relationship between wages and salaries and non-wage income in various industries. However, the HVRF input-output data does not differentiate between the various types of income accruing to households in the region from various productive activities. Consequently, the indirect and induced income effects given in Table 11.22 measure only the multiplier effects of wage and salary income earned directly by the workforces of the new projects, and not those of any profits accruing to local shareholders or debt holders. However, non-wage income earned indirectly from the supply of inputs to the projects and from the induced suply of consumer and investment goods is included. Furthermore, it could be expected that the wages and salaries paid by projects will represent the bulk of the income received in the region directly from the new projects, as most of the mines and all of the processing and infrastructure projects are national, multi-national or Government owned enterprises, with shareholders and debt holders spread throughout Australia and overseas. Nevertheless, the data in Table 11.22 on the direct, indirect and induced income effects of direct wages and salaries earned will be somewhat lower than the total anticipated direct, indirect and induced income effects.

The type I and type II multipliers calculated by the HVRF (Garlick, 1979) have not been corrected for double counting of direct and indirect effects in the way that the employment multipliers were adjusted. This adjustment had only a small impact on the employment multipliers and in any case, the indirect and induced income impact of the projects on the region will be slightly underestimated because of the lack of data on direct profit, dividend and interest earnings mentioned above. Hence these two sources of bias will possibly tend to off—set each other.

Table 11.22 indicates that total direct, indirect and induced income generated by the construction and operation of the impactor projects will rise from under $300 million in 1982 to $525 million by 1985 and over $680 million by 2000, (all in 1982 dollars). By 1985 this will represent a very substantial real increase of 19 per cent in the 1982 regional income and a 25 per cent real increase by the year 2000. Once again, the great bulk (over 80 per cent) of indirect and induced income will be generated by the operational phase of the coal mining projects. Processing industries will provide only about six per cent and infrastructure projects less than 10 per cent of the total direct, indirect and induced increase in regional income.

In the presence of widespread structural or regional employment, the social opportunity cost (that is, the value in its best alternative use) of the labour employed on any new project would be zero. This is because there would be no off—setting decline in production as a result of the employment of previously unemployed worker. Even if the workers actually recruited to a new project are drawn from other jobs in the region, so long as they are ultimately replaced (directly or indirectly) by a previously unemployed worker, then the social opport-unity cost of the labour resources employed would be zero. However, Table 11.18 demonstrates that if all (or even most) of the planned impactor projects proceed, there could well be an excess demand for labour in the region. Hence, the social opportunity cost of the labour requirements of these projects cannot be zero, as (in the absence of immigration) an off—setting decline in the output of other regional industries will be necessary to accommodate the new projects' demand for the labour.

Other labour market imperfections will also cause the wages and salaries paid to people in various skill categories (calculated in Table 11.21) to diverge from the social opportunity cost of these man-power resources to the community. The imposition of a closed shop by strong unions, in conjunction with the closing of union books to new members at various times has (for example) enabled the unions representing coal miners in the Hunter to force up mining wages well above the level necessary to attract sufficiently skilled and experienc-ed workers to the mines. On the other hand, in some circumstances, employers with monopsony (buyer monopoly) power may be able to hold wages below the social opportunity cost of the labour they employ.

In the Hunter, the existence of long queues of workers wishing to join the two miners' unions and secure mining jobs is an indication that miners wages are higher than would obtain in a freely operating labour market. To a lesser extent, militant unions in the electricity industry have also achieved real wage levels which are considerably above those which would prevail if there were a freer interplay of market forces in this industry. It will therefore be necessary to correct

Table 11.23 Social opportunity costs of the labour requirements of the Impactor projects, 1981 to 2000

	'81	'82	'83	'84	'85	'86	'87	'88	'89	'90	'92	'95	2000
Construction													
- Total	69.2	70.4	84.4	79.9	26.6	18.8	8.2	11.2	16.6	12.6	0.2	3.4	3.4
Operation													
- coal miners	18.1	44.5	97.1	130.3	160.4	180.1	191.9	200.9	209.2	239.1	240.9	241.1	245.8
- processing	0	7.6	8.0	18.6	19.0	19.0	19.0	19.0	19.0	19.0	23.2	23.2	23.2
- infrastructure	.3	5.2	11.6	13.9	19.5	23.8	24.5	24.9	25.4	25.4	25.4	25.4	25.4
TOTAL	87.6	127.7	201.1	373.8	225.5	241.7	243.6	249.8	257.8	296.1	289.7	293.2	297.9

for the apparent divergence of market wages from the social opportunity cost of this labour by adjusting these wages down to the average earnings of people performing comparable work elsewhere; that is, to average mining, and electricity industry earnings.

In all sectors except mining, ABS data on the average Australian weekly earnings of each skill category employed was used to calculate the projects' wages bills. Hence, it is only necessary to modify the mining sectors' labour cost (estimated in Table 11.21) to calculate the approximate social opportunity cost of the labour employed on the new projects. When these adjustments are made, in Table 11.23, it appears that the social opportunity cost of the labour requirements of the new projects was approximately 15 to 17 per cent lower than the market cost of this labour in 1982. When determining the net benefits of the development projects to the Australian community, it is appropriate to use the social opportunity cost rather than the market cost of their labour requirements when assessing their total costs (value of resources used). This will be more closely equivalent to marginal productivity of these labour resources in their best alternative uses, and hence, to the value of the production which has been lost as a result of the employment of this labour on the new projects.

CONCLUSIONS AND POLICY IMPLICATIONS

The Hunter region's labour market reflects the strong orientation of the local economy towards heavy industry, and in particular metal processing, coal mining and to a lesser extent, electricity generation. Compared with the rest of Australia, the region has traditionally had a small tertiary sector and a low female participation rate. In recent years, quite a substantial amount of structural change has occurred, reflecting the relative increase in importance of coal mining, electricity generation and some tertiary activities.

The underlying level of unemployment in the region is increasing rapidly and had by August 1982 reached 7.6 per cent of the 1981 workforce. This is due both to the general economic down-turn and to the specific difficulties being faced by several major Newcastle enterprises — most importantly, BHP, its subsidiary Comsteel, and the State dockyard. The most serious unemployment problems are those of male, semi and unskilled workers, and junior females with clerical skills.

The $9 billion of new coal—based investments planned for the Hunter will, if they proceed to completion, create a substantial growth in total labour demand in the region. The direct labour needs of the projects could be expected to rise from about 6,000 people in 1982 to 11,000 people in 1983 and over 12,000 by the end of the decade. However, recent downward revisions in Japanese coal demand over the next few years may well postpone this period of rapid employment growth till 1985-1986 or later. If announced plans are more or less adhered to, then there will also be a substantial growth in the indirect and induced labour requirements in the region as a result of the local purchasing of inputs by the new developments and increased consumer spending from incomes earned directly and indirectly from the projects. Once adjustments have been made to avoid double counting of the impacts of new projects, it could be anticipated that approximately 5,000 new jobs would be created indirectly and a further 10,000 induced jobs would be created by the mid 1980s. Over a third of these 30,000 new jobs will be in the mining sector, (as will over 80 per cent of all direct employment created), more than 20 per cent will be in retailing and five per cent in transport. In the early years of this decade, about 20 per cent of total new jobs will be in the building and construction industry, but this will decline to about only four per cent by the end of the decade. Together, the metal processing and electricity generation industries will provide less than 10 per cent of the total new jobs.

Of the labour directly required by the new projects, 27 per cent will be skilled metal, electrical and building tradesmen, 60 per cent semi and unskilled workers and 15 per cent professional, clerical and administrative personnel. However, once all the employment multiplier effects work through the economy only 17 per cent of the total new workers required will be metal, electrical and building tradesmen, 40 per cent will be semi and unskilled workers and 35 per cent clerical, professional and administrative workers. The occupational distribution of the total new labour requirements was compared to the skill distribution of the labour supply likely to be available in the region to meet this demand: people who are currently unemployed; those being retrenched by major industries like BHP; and newly qualified tradesmen. Under the worst scenario regarding BHP's future (an end to primary steel production by 1985) a relatively modest excess demand for labour of 3,400 people in 1983 (as a result of demand by the impactor projects), would become an excess supply of 4,500 to 5,500 people by 1986. There would continue to be unemployment among semi and unskilled workers, professionals and tradesmen in the "other trades" category throughout the period 1982-1986 and excess demand for metal, electrical and building tradesmen as well as clerical and managerial personnel would fall to low levels or disappear by 1985-86. Hence, if BHP does decide to reduce drastically its Newcastle operations, the policy of recruiting labour from outside the region (particularly from overseas) to fill positions in the coal mines and other new projects, will ultimately contribute to a growth in the substantial numbers of the region's existing workforce who will be unable to find work in the post 1984 period. If many proposed coal projects are postponed till 1985-86, labour surplus conditions will not occur, even in the short-term.

If more optimistic assumptions are made regarding BHP's future, however, excess demand for labour in the region could be expected to be as high as 9,000 people by 1984, with the most severe shortages being for skilled metal, electrical and building tradesmen (4,500) and clerical and managerial personnel (4,300). One (partial) solution available to developers and their suppliers would be to source all

260

traded good inputs outside the region. This would have the effect of reducing total additional labour demand in the region by up to 14 per cent and would bring down total excess demand for labour (after available supply is subtracted) to a peak of about 4,200 in 1984. However, this reduction would be achieved mainly by increasing un-employment among the semi and unskilled labour and "other trades" categories, rather than by eliminating excess demand for crucial metal, electrical and building tradesmen or for managerial and clerical personnel.

Hence, developers may need to seek more specific solutions to the problem of skilled labour shortages, including recruiting workers outside the region, training local unemployed workers and school leavers and increasing skilled tradesmen's wages. If jobs are only expected to be available for a short period, as in the case of most of the construction jobs, recruitment from outside the region would appear to be a reasonable means of overcoming labour shortages. As mentioned previously, this appears to have been the policy followed by many of the major construction contractors in the region, (though at Bayswater the Electricity Commission and its contractors are employ-ing 150 or so apprentices). On the other hand, if this labour will be required on a long term basis, and cannot be recruited from the exist-ing national pool of unemployed people or from among those who have recently been retrenched (or expect to be in the near future) the training of local school leavers or unemployed people would be one of the most desirable options.

Alternatively, it may be possible to induce some of the estimated 300,000 Australian working age males with tradesmen qualifications, who are currently working in non—tradesman jobs, to return to job opportunities in their trades which have been directly and indirectly created by resource developments. Only 500,000 or so of the 813,000 people in the workforce with trades qualifications were employed as skilled tradesmen in Australia in 1980. [6] About seven per cent of these people have left jobs as skilled tradesmen to become employees or managers, 10 per cent to do manual jobs and a further 24 per cent have taken jobs as bus, truck and taxi drivers, policemen or other semi—skilled and service sector workers, either because of the relatively low remuneration received by skilled tradesmen, particularly in manufacturing industry or the non—availability of trades jobs at the time and place tradesmen were searching.

Data from the 1976 census for example indicates that the 26 per cent of males reporting trades qualifications who were working in managerial and other non—manual jobs had a mean income which was 12 per cent higher than tradesmen working in their trade. However, the 12 per cent of qualified tradesmen who were working in manual jobs had a reported income which was six per cent lower than that of tradesmen generally. Hence, while some tradesmen appear to have left their trades voluntarily for higher paid jobs (with better working conditions, etc.) others have probably been forced out because of lack of work. The

261

substantial decline in the number of trades jobs since 1971 (nine per cent between 1971 and 1976) would explain this phenomenon.

Some observers argue that the perceived "shortages" of skilled labour, which have been given publicity in Australia in most years since World War II, may be the result of our uncompetitive manufacturing sector's inability to pay sufficiently high wages to retain skilled workers and of the narrowing of wage differentials between skilled and unskilled workers, which has been apparent in Australia and most other developed countries over this period. Evidence of the narrowing of wage differentials for Australian skilled metal workers, for example, is given in Wallace (1978) and similar data from Britain for all skilled workers is outlined in Sapsford, (1981). Possible reasons for the narrowing of differentials include the growth of mass unions, in which unskilled and semi-skilled workers dominate policy-making regarding wage objectives, the erosion of wage differentials during boom times of high labour demand (such as during World War II and in the 25 years thereafter) and the increased supply of skilled tradesmen available since the spread of mass education.

Assuming, initially that claims regarding skilled labour shortages are valid, Australia's rather antiquated apprenticeship system cannot be blamed for shortages if more than sufficient tradesmen have been trained (which would appear to be the case if the 300,000 workers mentioned above are included), but sufficient incentives (including remuneration) has not been offered to persuade these tradesmen to remain in their trades. The Williams Report on Education, Training and Employment (1979), found that 40 per cent of apprentices plan to leave their trade after completion of indentures (Williams et al, 1979). A similar survey carried out in 1977 by the New South Wales Department of Technical and Further Education (TAFE) of 1,400 Stage III apprentices found that 45 per cent planned to leave their trade within a few years. Lack of financial return and promotion opportunities were the reasons most frequently given for this decision (Wallace, 1980, p.38). However, the high mobility of young tradesmen is apparently not a recent phenomenon, and is common among many education and skill groups. If most follow through with this intention, and Census data on the number of people holding trades certificates who are working outside their trade is an indication that many do, the training of additional skilled workers from among school leavers and the young unemployed will be necessary to compensate for this high wastage.

If, because of inappropriate wage differentials, the wastage rate is very high, increased training will be a costly short-term solution to skilled labour shortages, as many could be expected to move on to other, more highly paid employment at an early date. Such training may nevertheless be a valuable means of overcoming deficiencies in academically biased schools' curriculae, which frequently fail to provide sufficiently vocationally orientated courses. Consequently, until wage relativities between skilled and semi-skilled occupations move in favour of skilled tradesmen, it seems unlikely that so called "skilled labour shortages" will be overcome. Much of manufacturing industry which is the major employer of skilled tradesmen is probably unable to afford such age increases, however, because it has been allowed to grow up behind high tariff barriers and is now basically uncompetitive. Increases in skilled workers' real wages should therefore be offset by a reduction in the real wages of administrative personnel, unskilled and semi-skilled workers and in real profits (if these are super-normal). Alternatively, such real wage increases should be facilitated by a depreciation of the Australian dollar (to offset any loss in competitiveness of Australian tradeables).

Similarly, if it is believed that skilled labour is in short supply, recruiting skilled migrants from overseas will be only a short-term solution to skilled labour shortages as skilled migrants are also likely to gravitate to more lucrative jobs outside their trade as such opportunities arise. If on the other hand, there is a surplus of tradesmen in Australia at present, and it is assumed that an historically high level of unemployment will continue in the foreseeable future, the policy of encouraging the immigration of tradesmen will also have the more serious long term consequence of increasing the number of existing residents who will become unemployed. This is because, if this policy is pursued, less young school leavers will secure the benefits of trade training and work experience, which would have enabled them to obtain some employment (in their trade or out of it). Instead, migrant tradesmen will hold these jobs.

An increasing number of recent studies have in fact challenged the popular wisdom that there have been skilled labour shortages in Australia in recent years, including throughout the down-turn in the mid and late 1970s (Kinnaird, 1979; Scheer, 1981, 1983). These studies document the steadily rising ratios of unemployed tradesmen registered with the CES to unfilled tradesmen vacancies during the period. ABS data throughout the 1970s also shows a steady decline, to historically low levels, in the ratio of unfilled vacancies to total job stock (vacancies plus those jobs already filled), from 4.9 per cent for all manufacturing in March 1974 to 1.3 per cent for selected trades occupations in September 1977. Hence the rhetoric of governments and employers claiming that there are overall skilled trades shortages does not match the data published by the CES and ABS. Studies by the Department of Employment and Industrial Relations (Kinnaird, 1979), which sought to explain this apparent paradox, found that a geographic and occupational mismatch of skills (categorised at the four digit International Standard Classification of Occupations, ISCO, level) may have accounted for between 11 and 39 per cent of the apparent unsatisfied demand for skilled labour in 1978. Also it was found that about 24 per cent of registered unemployed skilled tradesmen did not have formal trades qualifications but had merely been doing tradesmen's jobs in their previous employment. Furthermore, in a proportion of cases difficulty in filling skilled trades vacancies, which could have been interpreted as skilled labour shortages, appears to have been due to the failure of CES offices to advise registered tradesmen of notified vacancies and to the increasing selectivity of employers regarding

263

previous experience of applicants, as they used slack labour demand conditions to upgrade their workforce. However, the majority of registered skilled tradesmen were qualified and in the opinion of CES officers motivated and capable of taking employment but unable to get a job because none was available.

The implication of these findings for the Hunter region, and other development areas is that even if skilled labour shortages do appear in the region as major developments get underway, it will be possible to recruit workers with the necessary skills from outside the region (for example from Western suburbs of Sydney and the Woolongong area where unemployment is high), so long as sufficient incentive is provided to these workers to relocate. Scherer (1981) makes the point, however, that skilled workers will find non-skilled work reasonably easily and may be unwilling to return to skilled jobs, and risk future unemployment (with its high attendant costs), given that the wage differentials between skilled and semi-skilled workers are so small. Hence a significant movement in skilled wage differentials may be necessary in the development areas to recruit the workforces necessary and (as discussed above) government should make every effort to ensure that wage determination systems remain flexible, in recognition of this factor.

If there is an overall excess supply of skilled labour (which objective evidence appears to support has been the case in the 1970s), policies should be directed towards increasing the mobility of this labour and reducing frictional unemployment by increasing human and capital resources at the disposal of the employment services like the CES (e.g. Job Bank). Because of the high risks involved in selling homes and moving to a new area (where housing may be scarce and expensive), particularly if there is no guarantee of long-term employment, it will be necessary to allow some award loadings for jobs on the new development projects (or alternatively, increased public and developer involvement in housing provision in development areas to increase housing availability and reduce its cost). If on the other hand, there really are "skilled labour shortages" in Australia, these are not absolute, due to a lack of trained tradesmen, but market induced, due to imperfections in the wage determination system. Increased apprenticeship training will be necessary to meet these shortages if the current wastage rate remains unchanged. More importantly, it will be necessary to increase skilled wage differentials to induce sufficient tradesmen to stay in their trade if resource development investments, and their multipliers impacts on production increase overall labour demand and skilled labour requirements in particular. Under neither of the two (conflicting) conditions which different observers argue exist in the skilled labour market (excess supply or excess demand) can there be any justification for existing or increased levels of skilled labour in-migration from overseas, while overall unemployment levels are at current levels.

NOTES

1. These include, _inter alia_, Athansou, J.A. (1982); Central Planning
   and Research Unit, Department of Industrial Relations, NSW (1980)
   Hunter Development Board (1980); Coal Resources Development
   Board (1981); DOLAC Working Party (1980); Department of Industrial
   Relations, TAFE and Advisory Committee on Employment (1981);
   Hunter Development Board and Community Task Force for Youth
   Employment (1982); Commonwealth Department of Employment and
   Industrial Relations (1981).

2. Data for the Eastern Hunter is substantially deflated because it
   includes only those people living in the Forster, Dungog and
   Gloucester LGA's who are not registered at the Taree CES office.
   Similarly, the Upper Hunter data is deflated because it only
   includes people in the Murrurundi, Scone, Muswellbrook, Merriwa
   and Singleton Shires who are registered at the Maitland, rather
   than the Armidale, CES office.

3. Bearing in mind that CES female registration data could underestimate
   female unemployment by about 9 per cent, the actual number of
   women looking for work in the Hunter could be as high as 5900
   people, or 8.8 per cent of female workforce.

4. Australian Bureau of Statistics, 1981 Census

5. As the total investment cost of the new projects listed in Table
   11A.1 of the Appendix includes the cost of construction labour,
   it will only be necessary to add the cost of the operational
   labour employed by these developments when making the overall
   assessment of the project's costs.

6. Unpublished data from ABS 1980 Population Survey, Feb, 1980, in
   Scheer (1983). Also, Blandy, (1981). The 1981 Census in fact
   showed that 1,030,000 Australians held trade certificates. If it
   could be assumed that about 10 per cent of these are retired,
   this would leave almost 500,000 people holding trade certificates
   working outside their trades.

NOTES ON CONTRIBUTORS

E.M. Anderson, Department of Home Affairs and Environment, Canberra

E. Brookbanks, Department of Immigration and Ethnic Affairs, Canberra

G.J. Butler, Queensland Department of Education, Brisbane

N.J. Daly, Centre for Resource and Environmental Studies, Australian National University, Canberra

D. Day, Centre for Resouce and Environmental Studies, Australian National University, Canberra

R.A. Day, Department of Geography, University of New England, Armidale

A.K. Dragun, Centre for Resource and Environmental Studies, Australian National University, Canberra

J.A. Gillett, Kinhill Stearns, Melbourne

L.G. Harris, Queensland Department of Education, Brisbane

R. Jackson, Institute of Applied Social and Economic Research, Boroko, Papua New Guinea

A.J. Jakeman, Centre for Resource and Environmental Studies, Australian National University, Canberra

B.L. Johns, Bureau of Industry Economics, Canberra

F. Perkins, Centre for Resource and Environmental Studies, Australian National University, Canberra

A.D. Robertson, Kinhill Stearns, Melbourne

I. Wallace, Department of Geography, Carleton University, Ottawa, Canada

REFERENCES

Alcoa of Australia Limited and Kinhill Planners Pty Ltd (1980), Alcoa Portland Aluminium Smelter Environment Effects Statement, Alcoa, Melbourne.

Anderson, T.W. (1958) An Introduction to Multivariate Statistical Analysis, Wiley, New York.

Athansou, J.A. (1982) Manpower for Major Development Projects in NSW: 1981–86, Central Planning and Research Unit, NSW Department of Industrial Relations, Sydney.

Australian Bureau of Statistics, 1981 Census.

Australian Environment Council (1982) 'Public willingness to pay for Clean Air', AEC Report No. 7, AGPS, Canberra.

Ballard, J.A. (ed.) (1981) Policy Making in a New State 1972–77, Queensland University Press, St. Lucia, Queensland.

Bell, D.M. (1978) 'Gear Reduction/buy–back Programs in British Colombia and Washington State', paper to Conference on Limitation to Entry into Fisheries, University of Washington, Seattle.

Bell, D.P. (1982) 'Transient Families, Caravan–park Kids and Education', Education, 31(2), 23.

Berry, R. and Jackson, R. (1981) 'Inter–Provincial Inequalities and Decentralisation in PNG', Third World Planning Review, 3(1), 57–76.

Blandy, R. (1981) 'Labour problems of the minerals boom', Economic Papers, No. 67, 17–??.

Blandy, R. and Richardson, S. (1982a) 'How Labour Markets Adjust'. Seminar on Understanding Labour Markets in Australia, Flinders University, South Australia, 17–19 May.

Blandy, R. and Richardson, S. (1982b) How Labour Markets Work: Case Studies in Adjustment, Longman Cheshire, Melbourne.

Boiteux, M. (1960) 'Le Clarification des Demands en Point: Application de la Theorie de la Vente en Cout Marginal', – Reprinted in the Journal of Business, 33, 157–79.

Bosson, R. and Varion, B. (1977) The Mining Industry and the Developing Countries, OUP for the World Bank, New York.

Bourke, S.F. and Naylor, D.R. (1971) The Effects of School Change on Army Dependent Children, Army School of Education Cell Project, 4–70.

269

references

Bradley, R.A., Dole, M., Schink, W., and Sotrelli, S. (1977) 'Benefit Effective Oxidant Control', International Conference on Photochemical Oxidant Pollution and Its Control, EPA 600/3-77-001b, Environment Protection Agency, North Carolina.

Brealey, T.B. and Newton, P.W. (1980) 'Migration and New Mining Towns', in I.G. Burnley, R.J. Pryor and D.T. Rowland (eds.) Mobility and Community Change in Australia, University of Queensland Press, St. Lucia.

Brealey, T.B. and Newton, P.W. (1981a) 'Remote Communities in Tropical and Arid Australia', in G. Golany, T.B. Brealey and P.W. Newton (eds.) Urban and Regional Planning in the Arid Zones: the International Experience.

Brealey, T.B. and Newton, P.W. (1981b) 'Mining and New Towns', in J. Holmes and R. Lonsdale (eds.) Rural Australia: Problems and Prospects.

Bureau of Industry Economics (1981) Mining Developments and Australian Industry: Input Demands during the 1980s, AGPS, Canberra.

Burness, H.S. and Quirk, J.P. (1980) 'Water Law, Water Transfers and Economic Efficiency : the Colorado River', Journal of Law and Economics, 23, 111–34.

Butt, J.A., Daly, N.J., and Jakeman, A.J. (1982) 'Dust in the Hunter Valley: Assessing the Effects of Open Cut Coal Mines'. CRES Paper 6, Centre for Resource and Environmental Studies, Australian National University, Canberra, (a shortened version appears in Proc. Half-Day Symposium on Dust Suppression: Problems and Solutions, University of Newcastle, Newcastle Chemical Engineering Group, August 10, 1982, 3–11).

Butt, J.A., Daly, A.M., Daly, N.J., and Jakeman, A.J. (1982) 'The Perception of Environmental Problems in Small Communities in the Hunter Valley (in preparation).

Butt, J.A., Daly, A.M., Daly, N.J., and Jakeman, A.J. (1983) 'Hunter Valley Environmental Survey Data'. CRES Paper 11, Centre for Resource and Environmental Studies, Australian National University, Canberra.

Campbell, D., Cleland, E.A., Goldsworthy, A.J. and Stimson, R.J. (nd) 'Management of the Southern Zone Fishery: Vessel Buy-back', Centre for Applied Social Science Research, Flinders University, Adelaide.

Canadian Transport Commission (1980) Report of the Inquiry into the White Pass and Yukon Railway and Other Surface Transportation Services Into and Out of the Yukon, Government of Canada, Ottawa.

270

Carter, R.A. (1982) 'Resource Related Developments and the Regional Labour Markets: the Effects of the Alcoa Aluminium Smelter on Portland', paper presented to the 52nd ANZAAS Congress, Macquarie University, Sydney NSW, May 10–14.

Chadwick, G. (1971) A Systems View of Planning, Pergamon, Oxford.

Cicchetti, C.J. and Jurewitz, J.L. (eds). The Marginal Cost and Pricing of Electricity, Ballinger, Cambridge, Mass.

Coal Resources Development Board (1981) NSW Coal Strategy, 1981, Department of Mineral Resources (NSW), Sydney.

Coase, R.H. (1946) 'The Marginal Cost Controversy', Economica, 13, 169–83.

Cobbe, J.H. (1979) Governments and Mining Companies in Developing Countries, Westview, Boulder, Colorado.

Collins, J.E. (ed.) (1980) 'Muswellbrook: Preparing for Change', papers delivered at a public discussion of the Impacts of Mining and Industrial Development on the Shire of Muswellbrook, N.S.W., Muswellbrook Shire Council and Department of Community Programmes, University of Newcastle, N.S.W.

Commonwealth Scientific and Industrial Research Organisation, Division of Building Research, Remote Community Surveys 1971–1976, CSIRO, Highett, Victoria.

Community Task Force for Youth Employment (1980) A Profile of Youth Unemployment in Newcastle and an Analysis of Occupational Preferences of the Young Unemployed, Department of Industrial Relations (NSW), Newcastle.

Conway, R.S. (1977) 'The Stability of Regional Input-Output Multipliers', Environment and Planning A, 9, 197–214.

Cook, L.H. and Trengrove, C.D. (1982), The Economic Impact of the Olympic Dam Development, Centre of Policy Studies, Monash University, Melbourne.

Cook, P. (1981) 'Labour Market Implications of Australian Resource Development', Economic Papers No. 67, 23–30.

Copes, P. (1978) Resource Management for the Rock Lobster Fisher of South Australia, a Report to the Steering Committee for the Review of Fisheries of South Australia, March, Adelaide.

Court, J.D., Ross, I.B., and Dean, M. (1981) 'Air Quality Management in the Hunter Valley', Proceedings of the Seventh International Clean Air Conference, Adelaide, Ann Arbor Science Publishers Inc., Ann Arbor, Michigan.

271

references

DOLAC Working Party (1980) <u>Prospective Demand and Supply of Skilled Labour, 1980-83; with Particular Reference to Major Development Projects</u>, Report of the DOLAC Working Party, AGPS, Canberra.

Daly, N.J. (1978) 'Frequency Distributions of Oxidant Forming Potentials in Australia as an Aid to Policy', <u>International Clean Air Conference, Brisbane</u>, Ann Arbor Science Publishers Inc., Ann Arbor, Michigan.

Daly, N.J. (1979) 'The Use of Frequency Distributions of Potential Ozone in Evaluating Policy Options', <u>Environmental Science and Technology</u>, 13, 13-73.

Daly, N.J. (1981) <u>A Guide to the Control of Photochemical Pollution</u>, AGPS, Canberra.

Daly, N.J., and Jakeman, A.J. (1982) 'A Simple Statistical Model for Predicting Distributions of Environmental Events' (in preparation).

Daly, N.J. and Steele, L.P. (1976) <u>Air Quality in Canberra</u>, Report to the Department of the Capital Territory, AGPS, Canberra.

Davidson, B. (1969) <u>Australia Wet or Dry?</u>, University of Melbourne Press, Melbourne.

Davis, P. (1968) 'Australian and American Water Allocation Systems Compared', <u>Boston College Industrial and Commercial Law Review</u>, 9, 647-710.

Day, D.G. (1982a) 'Resources Development and the Non-Built Physical Environment of the Upper Hunter Valley N.S.W.', <u>CRES Working Paper 5</u>, Centre for Resource and Environmental Studies, Australian National University, Canberra.

Day, D.G. (1982b) 'Hydrogeomorphic effects of coal mining, Hunter Valley, N.S.W.', <u>CRES Paper 4</u>, Centre for Resource and Environmental Studies, Australian National University, Canberra.

Day, D.G. and Dragun, A.K. (1983) <u>Water in the Hunter Valley: Demand Supply and Perspectives of Management</u>, CRES Report (forthcoming).

Department of Employment and Industrial Relations (1981) <u>Survey of Major Development Projects in N.S.W.</u>, DEIR, Canberra.

Department of Employment and Industrial Relations (1982) <u>Occupational Demand Schedule</u>, AGPS, Canberra.

Department of Environment and Planning, N.S.W. (1982a) <u>Hunter Region. Regional Environmental Plan No. 1</u>, Department of Environment and Planning (NSW), Sydney.

272

Department of Environment and Planning, N.S.W (1982b) Hunter Region. Background Information, Department of Environment and Planning (NSW), Sydney.

Department of Housing and Construction (1980) Construction Industry Requirements in the Hunter and Fitzroy Statistical Divisions. Second Report to the Major Projects Advisory Group of the Construction Industry Council, Department of Housing and Construction, Canberra.

Department of Immigration and Ethnic Affairs (1981) Community Refugee Settlement Scheme (CRSS): Evaluation.

Department of Immigration and Ethnic Affairs (1982) Please Listen to What I'm Not Saying – A report on the Survey of Settlement Experiences of Indochinese Refugees 1978-80, AGPS, Canberra.

Department of Immigration and Ethnic Affairs, 'General Eligibility Migrants: Settlement Experience and the Utilisation of Services', forthcoming.

Department of Industrial Relations, N.S.W. (1980) Additional Manpower Needs in the Hunter 1980-85, Central Planning and Research Unit, Department of Industrial Relations (NSW), Sydney.

Department of Industrial Relations, TAFE and Advisory Committee on Employment (1981) Progress Report on the Supply of Skilled Labour for Development Projects in the Hunter Valley, Department of Industrial Relations (NSW), Sydney.

Department of Industry and Commerce (1982) Major Manufacturing and Mining Investment Projects, AGPS, Canberra.

Department of National Development and Energy (1981) Submission to the Senate Standing Committee on National Resources, Inquiry into the Development of the Bauxite, Alumina and Aluminium Industries, Canberra.

Department of National Development (1969) Atlas of Australian Resources Second Series: (1) Mineral Industry, (2) Mineral Deposits.

Dick, H.W. (1981) 'The Hunter Valley. Development or Indigestion', Current Affairs Bulletin, 58(1), 4-17.

Dragun, A.K. (1982) Surface Coal Mine Rehabilitation: Social Costs and Policy Options, paper presented to the Eleventh Conference of Economists, Flinders University, Adelaide, 23-27 August.

ERT, Inc. (1979) A Comparison of Alternative Approaches for Estimation of Particulate Concentrations Resulting from Coal Strip-mining

273

references

Activities in Northeast Wyoming, Document No. DOE/PR/50171-T1, Department of Energy, Washington D.C.

Eastwood, R.K. and Venables, A.J. (1982) 'The Macroeconomic Implications of a Resource Discovery in an Open Economy', Economic Journal, 92, 285-99.

Ehrlich, R., Findlay, J.C., Fenters, J.D. and Gardner, D.E. (1977) 'Health Effects of Short-term Exposures to NO2 - 03 Mixtures', International Conference on Photochemical Oxidant Pollution and Its Control, EPA 600/3-77-001a, Environment Protection Agency, North Carolina.

Electricity Commission of NSW (1979) 'Bayswater Power Station', Environmental Impact Statement, Electricity Commission of NSW, Sydney.

Emerson, C. (1980) 'Taxing National Resource Projects', Natural Resources Forum, IV (2), 123-46.

Energy Mines and Resources Canada (1980) Regional Profiles 1979, Mineral Policy Sector Internal Report MRI 80/2, Ottawa.

Energy Mines and Resources Canada (1981) Mineral Policy Alternatives: A Background Essay, Mineral Policy Sector Internal Report MRI 81/4, Ottawa.

Energy Mines and Resources Canada (1982) Mineral Policy: A Discussion Paper, Ottawa.

Feldman, S.L., Breese, J. and Obeiter, R. (1981) 'The Search for Equity and Efficiency in the Pricing of a Public Service: Urban Water', Economic Geography 57(1), 78-93.

Feldstein, M. (1976) 'A New Modelling Technique for Air Pollution Control', Journal of Environmental Management, 1, 147-57.

Fink, E. (1977) Hunter Regional Estate Project: A Study of Land Resources in the Shire of Singleton, The Hunter Valley Research Foundation, Newcastle.

Fish, R. (1979) 'Nanisivik Mines in Canada's High Arctic', Canadian Mining Journal, September 34-45.

Fisher, N. (1982) 'Australian Labour Markets' in Stuart Harris and Geoff Taylor (eds.) Resource Development and the Future of Australian Society, CRES Monograph 7, Australian National University, Canberra, 146-71.

Fitzgerald, R. (1982) From the Dreaming to 1915. A History of Queensland, University of Queensland Press, Brisbane.

274

Fowler, R.J. (1982) EIS Planning and Pollution Measures in Australia, Department of Home Affairs and Environment, AGPS, Canberra.

Further, I. (1981) The Development of the Water Resources in the Hunter Region, The Hunter Valley Research Foundation, Working Paper 12, Newcastle.

Garlick, S. (1979) 'New Input-Output Tables for the Hunter Region, NSW', Hunter Valley Research Foundation, WP No. 5/79, Newcastle.

Garnaut, R. (1981) 'The Framework of Economic-Policy Making', in Ballard, J.A. (ed.) Policy Making in a New State 1972-77, Queensland University Press, St. Lucia, Queensland, 193-?

Garnaut, R. and Clunies-Ross, A. (1974) Taxing National Resource Projects, Australia-Japan Economic Relations Research Project Research Paper No. 7, Australian National University, Canberra.

Gibson, R.B. (1978) The Strathcona Sound Mining Project: A Case Study of Decision Making, Science Council of Canada, Background Study No. 42, Ottawa.

Gordon, M.T. and Gordon, B.L.J., (eds.) (1980) The Shortage of Skilled People, Proceedings of Conference No. 8 in the Conference Series of the Institute of Industrial Economics, University of Newcastle, Institute of Industrial Economics, Newcastle.

Government of British Columbia (1982) Select Standing Committee on Crown Corporations: Report on the Inquiry into the British Columbia, Railway, Government of British Columbia, Victoria, B.C.

Government of Canada (1981) Revised Guide to the Federal Environmental Assessment and Review Process, EN 105-4/1979 Minister of Supply and Services, Government of Canada, Canada.

Greenaway, M.A. (1982) Pollutant Interactions (in preparation).

Gunther, P.E. and Winter, J.R. (1978) 'Fisheries Rationalisation, Employment and Regional Economic Policy', paper to Symposium on Economic Rationalisation of Fisheries, Powell River B.C.

Hanke, S.H. (1981) 'On the Marginal Cost of Water Supply', Water Engineering and Management, Feb, 60-3.

Hanke, S.H. and Wentworth, R.W. (1981) 'On the Marginal Cost of Waste Water Services', Land Economics, 57, 558-67.

Harris, K., Struik, A. and Brookbanks, E. (1982) 'The New Migrant Entry Policy and Australia's Development', paper presented at the 11th Conference of Economists, Flinders University, South Australia, 23-27 August.

275

references

Hartman, L.M. and Seastone, D.A. (1965a) 'Welfare Goals and Organisation of Decision Making for the Allocation of Water Resources',
Land Economics, 42, 21-30.

Hartman, L.M. and Seastone, D.A. (1965b) 'Efficiency Criteria for Market
Transfers of Water', Water Resources Research, 1, 165-71.

Hartman, L.M. and Seastone, D.A. (1970) Water Transfers: Economic
Efficiency and Alternative Institutions, John Hopkins University
Press, Baltimore.

Heuss, J.M., Nobel, G.J. and Colucci, J.M. (1971) Journal Air Pollution
Control Association, 21, 535.

Hinchcliffe, A.K. (1979) 'Conflicts between National Aims in PNG',
Development Studies Discussion Paper No. 46, University of East
Anglia, Norwich.

Hirshleifer, J., De Haven, J.C. and Milliman, J.W. (1960) Water Supply:
Economics, Technology and Policy, University of Chicago Press,
Chicago.

Hornberger, G.M., and Spear, R.C. (1980) 'Entrophication in Peel Inlet
– I. The Problem–Defining Behaviour and a Mathematical Model
for the Phosphorous Scenario', Water Research, 14, 29-42.

Houthakker, H.S. (1951) 'Electricity Tariffs in Theory and Practice', The
Economic Journal, 71, 1-25.

Howard, J. (1982) ABC Radio, December 1, 1982.

Hunt, J. (1977) Hunter Regional Plan, Working Paper No.8: Coal
Resources, NSW Planning and Environment Commission, Sydney.

Hunt, J. (1978) The Impact of Coal Mining on the Upper Hunter.
Commissioned by the Hunter Regional Advisory Council, Newcastle.

Hunter Development Board and Community Task Force for Youth Employment (1982) 'Report on the Labour Requirements Survey, Hunter
Region', Department of Industrial Relations (NSW), Newcastle.

Hunter Development Board (1980) 'Submission to NSW Government on
Labour Requirements for Proposed Industries to Commence
Operations in the Hunter Region 1980-86', HDB, Newcastle.

Hyndman, D. (1979) 'Wopkaimin', unpublished Ph.D. Thesis, University
of Queensland, Queensland.

Ilunkamba, I. (1980) Copper, Technology and Dependence in Zaire,
Natural Resources Forum, IV (2), 147-56.

276

Industries Assistance Commission (1981) 'The Regional Implications of Economic Change' Discussion Paper No 3 Approaches to General Reductions in Protection, AGPS, Canberra.

Iron Triangle Study Group (1982), An Enquiry into the Current Status and Future Development of the Central Part of South Australia, South Australian Government Printer, Adelaide.

Jackson, R. and Tapari, B. (1977) Kiunga Development Study PNG, Department of Finance, Port Moresby.

Jackson, R. (1979) 'The Awin: Free Resettlement on the Upper Fly River', in C.A. Valentine and B.L. Valentine (eds.), Going Through Changes, Institute of Papua New Guinea Studies, Port Moresby, 3–14.

Jackson, R. (1981) 'Secondary Industry in Papua New Guinea: a Social or Economic Investment, in F.E.I. Hamilton and G.J.R. Linge (eds.) Spatial Analysis, Industry and Industrial Environment Vol. II, Wiley, 549–80.

Jackson, R. (1982) Ok Tedi: Pot of Gold, University of Papua New Guinea, Port Moresby.

Jacobsen, M., Rae, S., Walton, W.H., and Rogan, J.M. (1970) 'New Dust Standards for British Coal Mines', Nature, 227, 445–7.

Jacobsen, M., Rae, S., Walton, W.H., and Rogan, J.M. (1971) 'The Relation between Pneumoconiosis and Dust Exposure in British Coal Mines', in W.H. Walton (ed.) Inhaled Particles III, Unwin, Old Woking, Surrey, 903–17.

Jakeman, A.J. (1982) The Role of Recursive Time Series Analysis in Resource Management. Proceedings of a Workshop on Resource Management, Department Civil and System Engineering, James Cook University, Townsville, Queensland (in press) (see also CRES Report AS/R51, Australian National University).

Jakeman, A.J. and Sheridan, S.M. (1982) 'Data Smoothing with Application to the Analysis of Rainfall Trends in the Hunter Valley', Proceedings of the Fifth Biennial Conference, Simulation Society of Australia, University of New England, Armidale, May 10–11, 32–6.

Jakeman, A.J., Steele, L.P., and Young, P.C. (1980) 'Instrumental Variable Algorithms for Multiple Input Systems Described by Multiple Transfer Functions', IEEE Transactions on Systems, Man and Cybernetics, SMC-10, 593–602.

Jakeman, A.J., and Young, P.C. (1979) 'Refined Instrumental Variable Methods of Recursive Time Series Analysis, Part II: Multivariable Systems', International Journal of Control, 29, 621–44.

277

references

Jakeman, A.J., and Young, P.C. (1980) 'Towards Optimal Modelling of Translocation Data from Tracer Studies', Proceedings of the 4th Biennial Conference, Simulation Society of Australia, University of Queensland, Brisbane, August 27-29, 248-53.

Jakeman, A.J., and Young, P.C. (1983) 'Advanced Methods of Recursive Time Series Analysis', International Journal of Control (forthcoming).

Jensen, R.C. and West, G.R. (1980) 'The Effect of Relative Co-efficient Size on Input-Output Multipliers', Environment and Planning A, 12, 659-70.

Jensen, R.C., Mandeville, T.D., and Karunaratne, N.D. (1977) Generation of Regional Input-Output Tables for Queensland, report to the Co-ordinator General's Department and the Department of Commercial and Industrial Development, Queensland.

Jensen, R.C., Mandeville, T.D., and Karunaratne, N.D. (1979) Regional Economic Planning: Generation of Regional Input-Output Analysis, Croom Helm, London.

Johnson, C.J. (1981) 'Mineral Objectives, Policies and Strategies in Botswana', Natural Resources Forum, 5, 347-362.

Johnson, K.N., Gisser, M. and Weiner, M. (1981) 'The Definition of a Surface Water Right and Transferability', Journal of Law and Economics, 24, 273-88.

Johns, B.L. (1982) 'The Effects on Manufacturing Industry', in Stuart Harris and Geoff Taylor (eds.) Resource Development and the future of Australian Society, CRES Monograph 7, Australian National University, Canberra, 61-98.

Joint Coal Board (1982) Black Coal in Australia 1980-81: a Statistical Year Book, Joint Coal Board, Sydney.

Joskow, P. (1976) 'Contributions to the Theory of Marginal Cost Pricing', Bell Journal of Economics, 7, 197-206.

Kahn, A.W. (1970) The Economics of Regulation: Principles and Institutions, Vol 1, Wiley, New York.

Kay, J.A. (1971) 'Recent Contribution to the Theory of Marginal Cost Pricing: Some Comments', The Economic Journal, 81, 367-71.

Kolsen, H.M. (1966) 'The Economics of Electricity Pricing in NSW', The Economic Record, 42, 555-71.

Latrobe Valley Ministerial Council (1981) Towards a Strategic Development Plan for the Gippsland Energy Resources Area, Progress Report No. 2, December.

278

Lazarovich, J. et. al. (1983) 'Mineral Development: Infrastructure and the Role of Government', in Proceedings of the Second Arctic Transportation Conference, Whitehorse, Yukon, Ottawa.

Leontief, W. (1966) Input–Output Analysis, Oxford University Press, New York.

Leung, S., Goldstein, E., and Dalkey, N. (1975) Human Health Damages from Mobile Source Air Pollution, California Air Resources Board, Sacramento, California, 1975.

Littlechild, S.C. (1970) 'Marginal Cost Pricings with Joint Costs', The Economic Journal, 80, 323–35.

Mackay, L.D. and Spicer, B.J. (1975) Educational Turbulence Among Australian Servicemen's Children, 1, Department of Education, AGPS, Canberra.

Macpherson, J.E. (1978) 'The Pine Point Mine', in E.B. Peterson and J.B. Wright (eds.), Northern Transitions: Vol. 1 Northen Resource and Land Use Policy Study, Ottawa, 65–110.

Mahendrarajah, S., Young, P.C. and Jakeman, A.J. (1982) 'Stochastic Time Series Analysis and the Village Dam Management Problem in Sri Lanka', Proceedings of the First Scientific Assembly of the International Association of Hydrological Sciences, Exeter, 19–30 July, IAHS Publication No 135, 251–264.

Maloney, F. and Ausness, R. (1974) 'Administering State Water Resources: The Need for Long Range Planning', West Virginia Law Review, 73, 209.

Mamak, A. and Bedford, R. (1977) Compensating for Development: the Bougain- ville Case, Bougainville Special Publications No. 2, Christchurch.

Mandeville, T.D. (1979) 'The Impact of the Weipa Bauxite Mine on the Queensland Economy', Report to Comalco Limited, Queensland.

Mandeville, T.D. (1980) The Impact of the Boyne Island Aluminium Smelter on the Economy, Department of Economics, University of Queensland, St Lucia.

Mandeville, T.D. and Jensen, R.C. (1978) The Impact of Major Development Projects on the Gladstone/Calliope, Fitzroy, Queensland and Australian Economies: An Application of Input–Output Analysis, Report to the Department of Commercial and Industrial Development and Comalco Ltd, September, Queensland.

references

Mandeville, T.D. and Jensen, R.C. (1978) The Economic Impact of Industrial Developments in the Gladstone Area of Central Queensland, Report to the Department of Commercial and Industrial Development and The Co-odinator General's Department, Department of Economics, University of Queensland, St Lucia.

Mandeville, T.D. and Jenson, R.C. (1979) Economic Impact of Industrial Developments at Gladstone, Department of Economics, University of Queensland, for Department of Commercial and Industrial Development and Comalco Limited, St. Lucia.

Mandeville, T.D., Jensen, R.C. (1978) 'The Impact of Major Development Projects on the Gladstone/Calliope, Fitzroy, Queensland and Australian Economies: an Application of Input-Output Analysis, Department of Economics, University of Queensland, St. Lucia.

McLoughlin, J.B. (1969) Urban and Regional Planning: A Systems Approach, Faber and Faber, London.

Meyers, C.J. and Posner, R.A. (1971) Market Transfers of Water Rights: Towards an Improved Market for Water Resources, Legal study no.4 National Water Commission, Springfield, NTIS.

Mikesell, R.F. (1975) Foreign Investment in Copper Mining, Johns Hopkins University Press, Baltimore.

Miller, C.G. (1980) Public Affairs and the Minerals Industry, Kingston, Ontario.

Mizoguchi, I., Makino, K., Kuduo, S., and Mikami, R. (1977) 'On the Relationship of Subjective Symptoms to Photochemical Oxidant', International Conference on Photochemical Oxidant Pollution and Its Control, EPA 600/3-77-001a, Environment Protection Agency, Raleigh, N.C.

Ng, T.K. and Weisser, M. (1974) 'Optimal Pricing with a Budget Constraint: the Case of a Two Part Tariff', Review of Economic Studies, 41, 337-45.

PNG National Planning Office (1981) National Public Expenditure Plan 1982- 1985, Port Moresby.

Parker, L. (1978) 'Children of the Road', Education News, 16(15), 8-15.

Parker, P. and Hirst, R. (1981) Hunter Region Resources: The Infrastructure Boom, A.I.U.S. Proceedings.

Pearce, D.W. and Nash, C.A. (1981) The Social Appraisal of Projects: a Text in Cost-Benefit Analysis, Macmillan, London.

Pedco Environmental, Inc. (1978) Survey of Fugitive Dust from Coal-mines, prepared for Environmental Protection Agency, Region VIII, Denver, Co., Contract No. 18-01-4489 Document No. EPA-908/1-78-003, February.

Perkins, F. (1982) 'An Economic Overview of Coal-based Developments in the Upper Hunter', CRES Paper 1, Centre for Resource and Environmental Studies, Australian National University, Canberra.

Planning and Environment Commission, NSW (1977) The Hunter Regional Plan: Working Paper No.5, Primary Industry, August, Sydney.

Planning and Environment Commission, NSW (1978) Hunter Regional Plan. Discussion Paper No. 3 Planning Proposals.

Powell, R.A., Jensen, R.C., West, G.R., Conon, M.B. and Wilkinson, J.T. (1981) 'The Impact of the Tobacco Industry on Regional, State and Australian Economies', Department of Agricultural Economics and Business Management, Miscellaneous Publication No. 7, University of New England, Armidale.

Radetzki, M. and Zorn, S. (1979) Financing Mining Projects in Developing Countries: A United Nations' Study, Mining Journal, London.

Randall, A. (1982) 'Resource Allocation in a Maturing Water Economy' in Irrigation Water: Policies for its Allocation in Australia, Australian Rural Adjustment Unit, University of New England, Armidale, NSW, 15-54.

Reid, S. (1981) 'The Politics of Resource Negotiation' Natural Resources Forum, 2, April, 115-28.

Richardson, S. (1981) 'Skilled Metal Tradesmen: Shortages on Surplus?', Australian Bulletin of Labour, 7, 195-204.

Riley, J.G. and Scherer, C.R. (1979) 'Optimal Water Pricing and Storage with Cyclical Supply and Demand', Water Resources Research, 15, 233-39.

Robertson Research (1981) Coal Resources of the Upper Hunter Valley, Vol. 1, June, Sydney.

Roxby Management Services Pty Ltd and Kinhill-Stearns Roger Joint Venture (1982) Olympic Dam Project Draft Environmental Impact Statement, Roxby Management Services, Parkside, South Australia.

Saddler, H. (1970) New Scientist, August 20, 373.

Sapsford, D. (1981) Labour Market Economics, Allen and Unwin, London.

references

Saunders, R.J., Warford, J.J. and Mann, P.C. (1977) 'Alternative Con-
cepts of Marginal Cost for Public Utility Pricing: Problems and
Application in the Water Supply Sector', World Bank Staff Working
Paper No.259, Washington D.C.

Scherer, P.A. (1981) 'Apprenticeship Training and its Effects on the
Labour Market', in C.E. Bavid, R.G. Gregory and F.H. Gruen (eds.),
Youth Employment, Education and Training, Australian National
University Press, Canberra, 5.1–5.32.

Scherer, P.A. (1983) The Supply of and Demand for Scheffield Tradesmen
in Australia, 1971–80, Centre for Economic Policy Research
Discussion Paper No. 64, CEPR, Australian National University,
Canberra.

Sorensen, A.D. and Weinand, H. (1982), 'Recent Changes in Employment
Structures of Non–Metropolitan Queensland', Papers, Australia
and New Zealand Regional Science Association.

Sorensen, A.D. and Weinand, H. (1982) 'Structure of the Workforce in
Towns of N.S.W., Victoria and Queensland 1981', Economic
Papers. No. 67.

Spear, R.C., and Hornberger, G.M. (1980) 'Eutrophication in Peel Inlet
– II. Identification of Critical Uncertainties via Generalised
Sensitivity Analysis', Water Research, 14, 43–9.

Spooner, D. (1981) Mining and Regional Development, Oxford University
Press, Oxford.

State Electricity Commission of Victoria Annual Reports 1979, 1980,
1981, SECV, Melbourne

State Electricity Commission of Victoria and Kinhill Pty Ltd (1981)
Proposed Driffield Project – Environmental Effects Statement,
SECV, Melbourne.

State Planning Authority of NSW (1972) Hunter Region: Growth and
Change: Prelude to a Plan, S.P.A., Sydney.

State Pollution Control Commission (1980) Pollution Control in the
Hunter Valley with Particular Reference to Aluminium Smelting,
SPCC, Sydney.

Tafler, S. (1981) 'How Japan Outmanoevered Canada on the BC Coal
Deal', Energy, Toronto, June, 29–34.

Trebing, H. (ed.) (1976) New Dimensions in Public Utility Pricing,
Michigan State University Press, East Lansing.

Turvey, R. (1969) 'Marginal cost', The Economic Journal, 79, 282–99.

Turvey, R. (1971) Economic Analysis and Public Enterprises, Allen and Unwin, London.

Turvey, R. (1976) 'Analysing the Marginal Cost of Water Supply', Land Economics, 52, 158–68.

Turvey, R. and Anderson, D. Electricity Economics – Essays and Case Studies, John Hopkins University Press, Baltimore.

Twohill, B.A. and Sheehan, W.J. (ed.) (1981) Input–Output Analysis and Regional Multipliers, Proceedings of a colloquium published as Conference No. 10 in the , conference series of the Institute of Industrial Economics, University of Newcastle, Institute of Industrial Economics, Newcastle.

Tyndall, D.G. (1951) 'The Relative Merits of Average Cost Pricing, Marginal Cost Pricing and Price Discrimination', The Quarterly Journal of Economics, 65, 342–72.

US Federal Register (1971) 36, 8187.

US Federal Register (1979) 'National Primary and Secondary Ambient Air Quality Standards: Revisions to the National Air Quality Standards for Photochemical Oxidants', 44, 28, 8202–36.

US Library of Congress, Environmental Policy Division (1974) A Legislative History of the Clean Air Act Amendments of 1970, Congressional Research Service, Library of Congress, Washington, D.C. (Vol. 1 and 2.).

University of Newcastle (1981) The Restless Region. The Challenges to Planning Posed by Development in the Hunter. Proceedings of a Symposium in Honour of K.W. Robinson, Newcastle, NSW.

Urquhart, E. (1980) The Canadian Nonferous Metals Industry: An Industrial Organisation Study, Kingston, Ontario.

Valentine C.A. and Valentine B.L. (eds.), (1979) Going Through Changes, Institute of Papua New Guinea Studies, Port Moresby.

Waddell, J. (1974) Opinion Surveys of Air pollution sufferers, EPA-600/5–74–012, US Environment Protection Agency, Raleigh, NC.

Wallace, I. (1977) The Transportation Impact of the Canadian Mining Industry, Kingston, Ontario.

Wallace, J.P. (1981) 'Shortages of Skilled Tradesmen: a Union View', in M.T. Gordon, B.L.J. Gordon (eds.) The Shortage of Skilled People, Institute of Industrial Economics, Newcastle, 11–48.

references

Water Resources Commission of NSW (1981) Glenbawn Dam Enlargement Proposal Environmental Impact Statement, Sydney, December.

Water Resources Commission of N.S.W. (1982) Hunter Region Water Requirements and Storage Proposals. 1982 Review, Sydney, May.

Wedgwood-Oppenheim, F., Hart, D. and Cobley, B. (1975) 'An Exploratory Study in Strategic Monitoring', Progress in Planning, 5, 1–58.

West, G.R. (1981) 'An Efficient Approach to the Estimation of Regional Input-Output Multipliers', Environment and Planning A, 13, 857–67.

Whitehead, P.G. and Young, P.C. (1979) 'Water Quality in River Systems: Monte Carlo Analysis', Water Resources Research, 15, 451–9.

Whitelaw, E. (1974) A History of Singleton, The Singleton Historical Society, Newcastle.

Whyte, A.V., and Burton, I. (1980) Environmental Risk Assesment, Wiley, New York.

Williams, B.R., et al. (1979) Education, Training and Employment, Report of the Committee of Inquiry into Education and Training, AGPS, Canberra.

Wilson, R.K. (1975) 'Socio-Economic Indicators Applied to Sub-Districts of PNG', Yagl Ambu, 2, 71–87.

Wise, R. (1981) 'How Wran faced up to Australia's Ruhr', Financial Review, September 1, 2, 3, 12–3.

Young, P.C. (1974) 'Recursive Approaches to Time Series Analysis', Bulletin, Institute of Mathematics and its Applications, 10, 209–24.

Young, P.C. (1978) 'A General Theory of Modelling for Badly Defined Systems', in G.C. Vansteenkiste (ed.), Modelling, Identification and Control in Environmental Systems, Amsterdam, North Holland, 103–35.

Young, P.C. (1983a) 'The Validity and Credibility of Models for Badly Defined Systems', in M.B. Beck and G. van Straten (eds.) Uncertainty and Forecasting of Water Quality, IIASA/Pergamon, Oxford (to appear).

Young, P.C. (1983b) 'Systems Methods in the Evaluation of Environmental Pollution Problems', in R.M. Harrison (ed.) Pollution: Causes, Effects and Control, Royal Society of Chemistry, London (to appear).

284

Young, P.C. and Jakeman, A.J. (1979) 'Refined Instrumental Variable Methods of Recursive Time Series Analysis. Part I: Single Input Single Output Systems', International Journal of Control, 29, 1–30.

Young, P.C. and Jakeman, A.J. (1980) 'Refined Instrumental Methods of Recursive Time Series Analysis, Part III: Extensions', International Journal of Control, 31, 741–64.

Young, P.C., Jakeman, A.J. and McMurtrie, R.E. (1980) 'An Instrumental Variable Method for Model Order Identification', Automatica, 16, 281–94.

Printed in the United States
by Baker & Taylor Publisher Services